Images of America
Eastern Iowa's Aviation Heritage

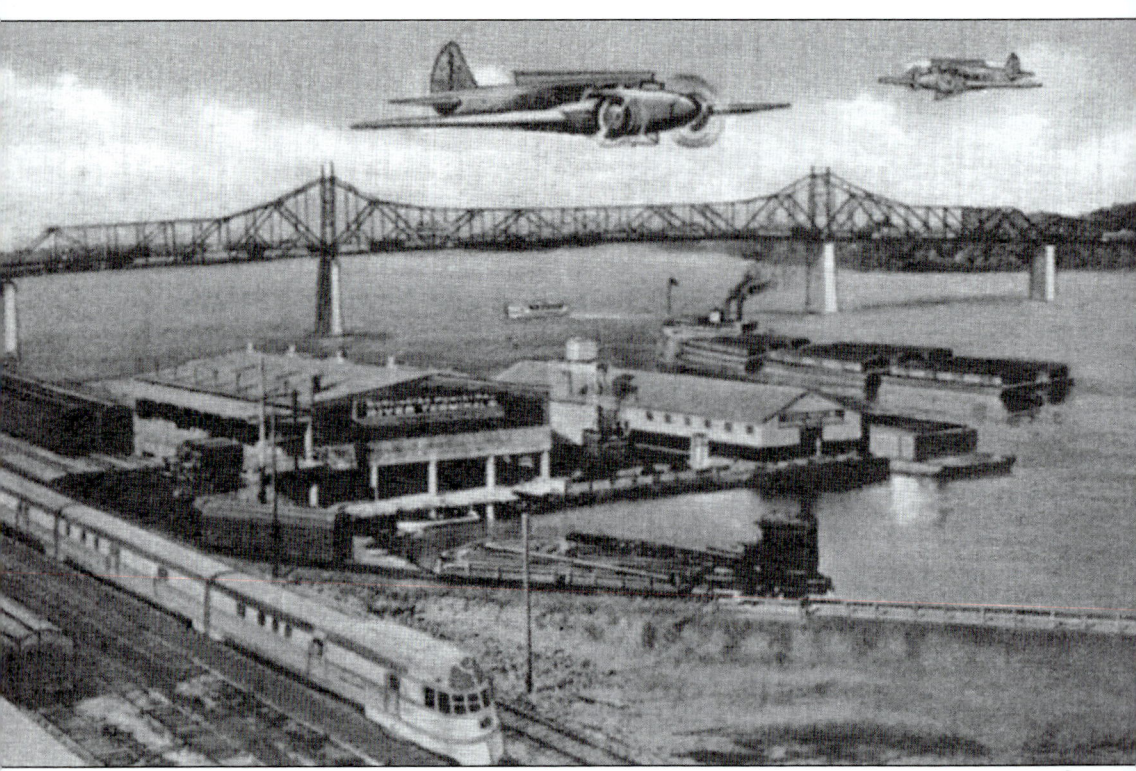

This Great Depression–era Iowa artist's conception depicts a futuristic Burlington "Transportation Center" where rail, river, highway, and air services converge to provide freight and passenger services for regional citizens. (Courtesy of the Des Moines County Historical Society at Burlington.)

ON THE COVER: Two unidentified northeastern Iowans represent a partnership between the aviation and manufacturing industries as the pilot hands a machine part, delivered by air freight, to a company representative. The aircraft is a Canuck, the Canadian version of the Curtiss JN-4 "Jenny." (Courtesy of the Cedar Falls Historical Society.)

IMAGES
of Aviation

Eastern Iowa's Aviation Heritage

Scott M. Fisher

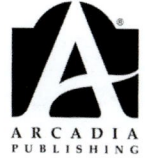

Copyright © 2011 by Scott M. Fisher
ISBN 978-0-7385-8330-3

Published by Arcadia Publishing
Charleston, South Carolina

Printed in the United States of America

Library of Congress Control Number: 2010939907

For all general information, please contact Arcadia Publishing:
Telephone 843-853-2070
Fax 843-853-0044
E-mail sales@arcadiapublishing.com
For customer service and orders:
Toll-Free 1-888-313-2665

Visit us on the Internet at www.arcadiapublishing.com

To my friends Ann Holtgren Pellegreno and Jack Richard Cline

Contents

Acknowledgments 6

Introduction 7

1. Before Powered Flight: 1800s to 1910   9

2. Iowa's Pioneer Aviators: 1910 to 1920   15

3. Barnstormers and Visionaries: 1920 to 1930   33

4. Aviation's Golden Age: 1930 to 1940   53

5. World War II and the Postwar Years: 1940 to 1950   73

6. Into the Jet Age: 1950 to the Present   91

Acknowledgments

The best part of any research project is making new acquaintances and renewing old ones. Special collections archivists, librarians, and curators, many of them volunteers, are the unsung heroes of all historians. My heroes during this endeavor included Jeff Kurtz, Josh McDonnell, and Susan Strohecker of the Cedar Falls Historical Society; Mary Krohlow of the Des Moines County Historical Society at Burlington; Melanie Alexander and Dan Hunter of the Carl & Mary Koehler History Center, Linn County Historical Society; Mary Bennett and Charles Scott of the State Historical Society of Iowa at Iowa City; Eunice Schlicting of the Putnum Museum of Davenport; Tonya Boltz and Ed Kiedaisch of the Keokuk Public Library; Marvin Wicks of the Winneshiek County Historical Society; Valda Johnson of the Jackson County Historical Society; Leigh Ann Randak of the Johnson County Historical Society; Amy Groskopf of the Davenport Public Library; Lynn Smith of the Herbert Hoover Library; Amy Sturm and Trooper Michael Horihan of the Iowa State Patrol; Mary Beaird and Marcie Gaylord of the Southeast Iowa Regional Airport, and Jan Neudeck.

To all the individuals who graciously gave their time to visit with me about eastern Iowa aviation from their perspectives and experiences and to those who offered leads to source materials, I am most grateful. They include Glen Phelps, Richard Phelps, Robert L. Taylor, Brent L. Taylor, Irv Lindner, Sid Yahn, Remby Reminger, Steve Smith, Don and Pat Fisher, Larry and Robert Sharar, and Jackie Warren. Thanks also to Arcadia editor Ted Gerstle for his positive comments throughout the process.

Finally, special thanks to Ann Holtgren Pellegreno, who encouraged me to take on this project and whose three-volume *Iowa Takes to the Air* is the most comprehensive record of the state of Iowa's aviation history.

INTRODUCTION

Aviation in Iowa, like the rest of America, began with the dreamers. They watched the Midwestern birds, from swallows and owls around the farm to hawks and eagles in the hills and woods. The dreamers wondered how they too could climb into the air currents and navigate among clouds. They built kites, experimented with balloons, and flew gliders from barn roofs, windy meadows, and river bluffs, learning a little more with each failure and occasional success. Some of their neighbors called them crazy, but they kept on dreaming and building.

By the late 1800s, county fairs and Chautauquas had become the most popular ways for rural communities to connect with trends, culture, and inventions from each coast and beyond. It was at these annual events that most Iowans got their first exposure to aviation with "death-defying" balloon ascensions, parachute leaps, and, finally, motorized flying machines in the early part of the 20th century. The dreamers realized they were on the right track. They sought out those who had been taught by the Wright Brothers, Glenn Curtiss, and others who had pushed ahead with their aircraft designs and were spreading the word across the country about powered flight.

Keokuk, Fort Madison, and Burlington were the sites of some of the first Iowa "crowds of thousands" that witnessed balloons brave the weather and watched aeronauts be carried many miles into Illinois or fished out of a wet river landing. The Mississippi River was a natural runway for hydroplanes, and citizens of Dubuque, Bellevue, and Clinton cheered from the river bluffs as pilots, both men and women, put on shows at these communities to raise money and awareness in their attempts to traverse the "Big Muddy," from Minneapolis to the Gulf of Mexico, by air. Davenport became the site of the first Iowa flying and mechanic schools and the first of which to include women into their intensive course curriculum.

By 1910, there were several flights of powered aircraft throughout Iowa, with some designed, built, and piloted by Iowans themselves. From Keokuk to Decorah, Iowa's aviation dreamers were moving ahead, happily performing their own flying feats for their neighbors at local festivals, county fairs, or just whenever they wanted to show off a new design.

As the aircraft (as well as the pilots' skills) improved, the demonstrations became more impressive. The dreamers who had pioneered those first frail airplanes now joined other pilots and planes to put on massive air shows, called barnstorming, and were usually well paid for their aerial circuses. They offered rides to convince common citizens how safe flying was, all while inspiring a new generation of dreamers. Along with the barnstormers came another group: the visionaries who dreamed of ways that air travel could become as common and essential in moving people and material as the tugboat, steamship, locomotive, and automobile. This included flying the mail by air from coast to coast—an airborne Pony Express—and a navigation system linking every airfield, as well as lights to keep the air lanes open 24 hours a day. Iowa City was a primary US Airmail stop, one which proved pivotal one snowy night when the future of the entire airmail service rested in the hands of a young pilot named Jack Knight, who needed gas for his DH-4 mail plane and directions during his famous west-to-east flight.

While business-minded entrepreneurs planned their new passenger and freight facilities, others concentrated on improving airframe and engine performance. Aircraft manufacturing companies formed all over the state, especially near industrial and commercial centers like Waterloo, Ottumwa, Davenport, and Fort Madison. Many of them started out as little more than a couple of friends working in a rented building or farmer's barn. Most developed only a few airplanes, but others, with names like Luscombe, Adams, Farwell, and Speer, manufactured airplanes in Iowa that competed successfully with bigger names like Beech, Taylor, and Piper, located a few hundred miles to the west. Other dreamers gained national recognition for their piloting skills by winning air races, setting endurance records, and performing stunts that pushed the envelope of aircraft (and pilot) limits further and further to the edge.

By the 1930s—aviation's "Golden Age"—there were airports, both public and private, located throughout eastern Iowa that were used in hauling freight and carrying passengers and where the newest generation of dreamers was learning how to fly, build, and repair airplanes. Small regional airlines served larger cities, while independent charter services provided connecting flights for rural areas. Businesses such as Morrell Meat Packing Co., John Deere, and other manufacturers bought their own airplanes and hired local pilots to fly them. Airmail became a common occurrence, and air shows, bigger and better than ever, continued to draw huge crowds. The Great Depression, which was devastating to Iowa families and businesses, didn't stop the dreamers.

World War II ended that Golden Age, and many local airports were turned into training sites for the Civilian Pilot Training Program and, later, in places like Iowa City and Ottumwa, they became actual military bases for Navy flight training. Hundreds of military pilots got their initial hours of flight instruction after completion of Navy pre-flight training at the University of Iowa and other college campuses that had partnered with the military to provide coursework in navigation, weather, communication, and aircraft-design concepts. Much of the support work done at the flight-training sites was done by women, some of whom would later join the WASP program, ferrying all types of combat aircraft from factories to training fields and staging areas, allowing more men to fly the combat missions. With the war's end, aircraft manufacturers expected a boom in the sales of small aircraft, assuming that many of the returning airmen would want to continue flying and want to purchase "family-sized" airplanes. While that postwar boom never materialized, the 1950s did see a great resurgence in civilian and corporate aviation. The planes were larger, more powerful, and safer, while airports, thanks to wartime improvements, became modern facilities ready to be part of the jet age. Even the homebuilt aircraft industry surged with more kits and plans being sold than ever before.

Today, modern air travel has become as commonplace as the interstate highway system. Regional airlines share each airport with fleets of corporate jets and rentals for flight instruction. The dreamers (many of them fourth- and fifth-generation men and women descended from those first pioneers) are still experimenting, improving, and spreading the word to anyone who is interested about aviation. Museums all over eastern Iowa have displays and archives that remind us of what the "old dreamers" accomplished and amaze us with their courage and exploits.

Here, in these pages, you will see just a few of the men, women, aircraft, and events that were influential in establishing eastern Iowa's aviation heritage. These few images and bits of information represent only a small taste of the bigger picture. Local museums and libraries are treasure chests full of photographs, diaries, letters, and taped interviews that have preserved each community's aviation history. Each collection is preserved and added to regularly by aviators, historians, curators, and librarians who welcome individuals and groups of all ages to share in the delight of reliving Iowa's rich aviation heritage. Local airports have organizations that also preserve the heritage by linking anyone interested in flying and airplanes with pilots, technicians, and others who are happy to share their time in order to spread the word and inspire that next generation of dreamers.

One
BEFORE POWERED FLIGHT
1800s TO 1910

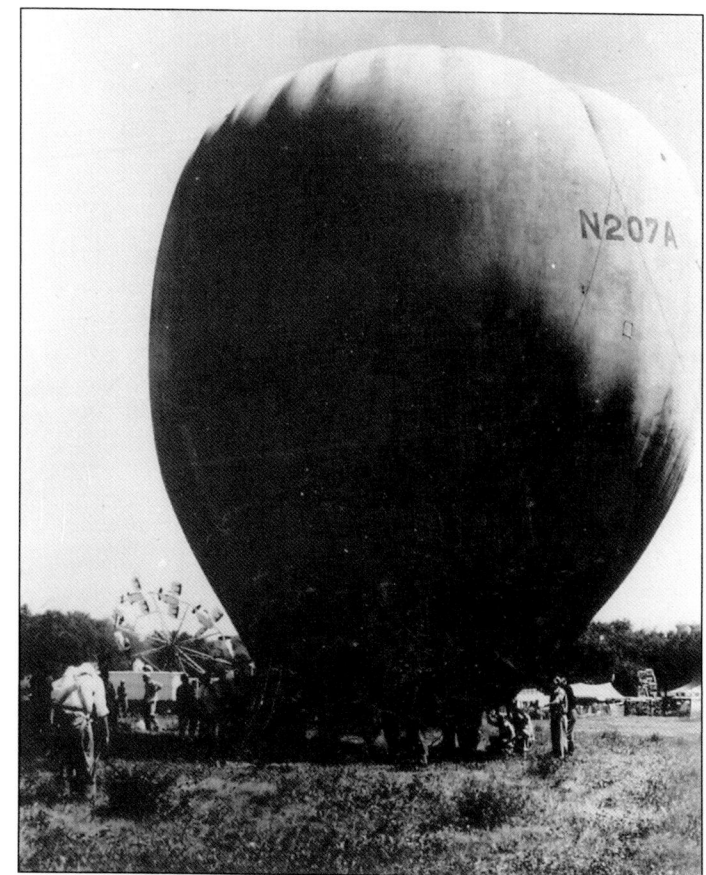

"Come one, come all! See the daring aeronaut attempt a death-defying ascent in his magnificent balloon!" That was how most Iowans were first introduced to aviation. It was during a local fair or annual Chautauqua celebration in the late 1800s that balloonists were hired to entertain large audiences of people who had traveled for miles around to hear speakers like Helen Keller or William Jennings Bryan. The aerial demonstrations added adventure and risk to the event. (Courtesy of the Des Moines County Historical Society at Burlington.)

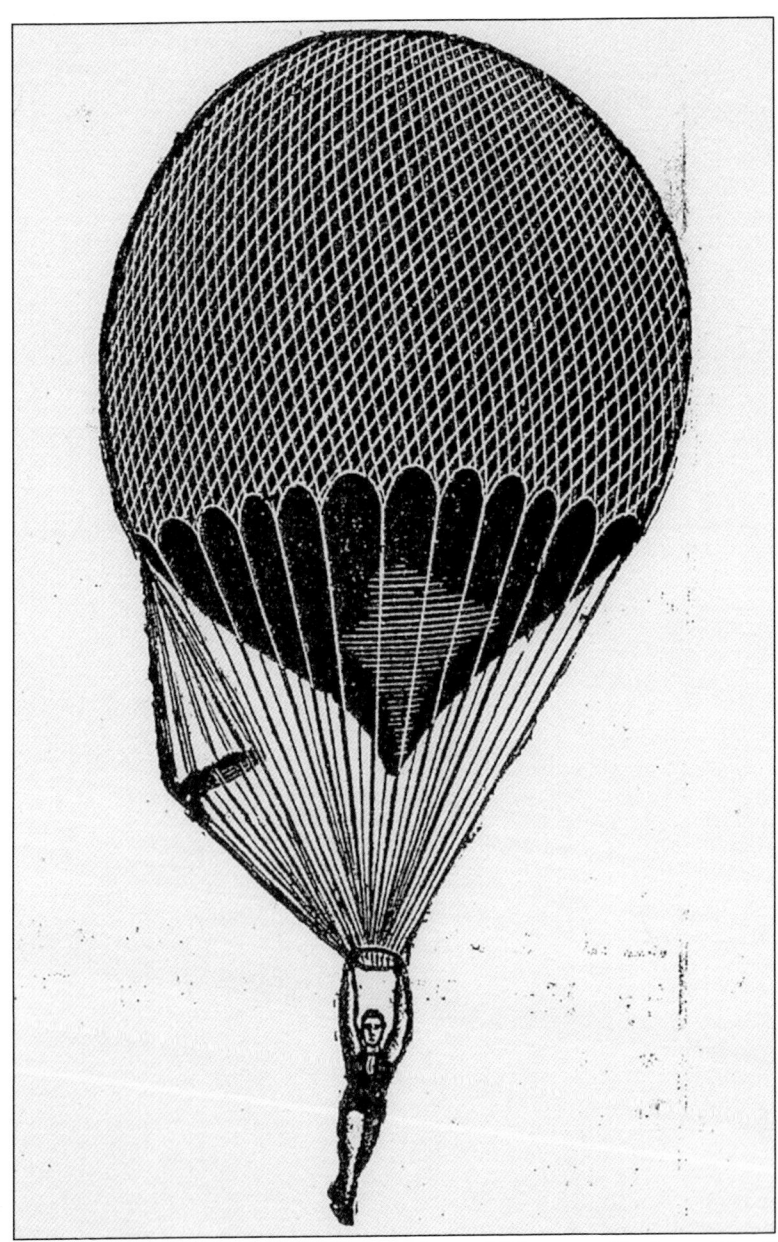

It seems that most of the early balloonists were "professors." There was Professor Silas Brooks, who treated southeast Iowa crowds in the 1850s; a Professor Wilbur, who flew in Ottumwa, among other cities, in the 1860s; Professors Samuel Archer King, who traveled with P.T. Barnum's Hippodrome and performed in Keokuk in the 1870s; and Professors Streif and Thompson in Dubuque in the 1890s, to name but a few. Some used ascension baskets, while others, sporting bathing suits (which came in handy) simply hung from the balloon's ring as the crowd chanted, "Go, go, go!" Occasionally, a balloonist feared that the weather might be prohibitive, but the event's promoter, hearing the crowd's chants and holding a pocketful of gate receipts, insisted that the show go on, sometimes ending in the balloon being carried miles downwind or dragging the unfortunate showman directly into the river. The more risky the challenge, the bigger the crowd—and payoff. (Courtesy of the Keokuk Public Library.)

In the 1880s, the Baldwin brothers, Samuel and Thomas, of Quincy, Illinois, were well-known favorites on the eastern Iowa Chautauqua and county fair circuits. They began each show either in early morning or late afternoon as the balloon's envelope was filled with more than 20,000 cubic feet of gas from the local gas works. It was the Baldwin brothers who popularized the stunt of jumping from an ascending balloon with a parachute. (Courtesy of the Keokuk Public Library.)

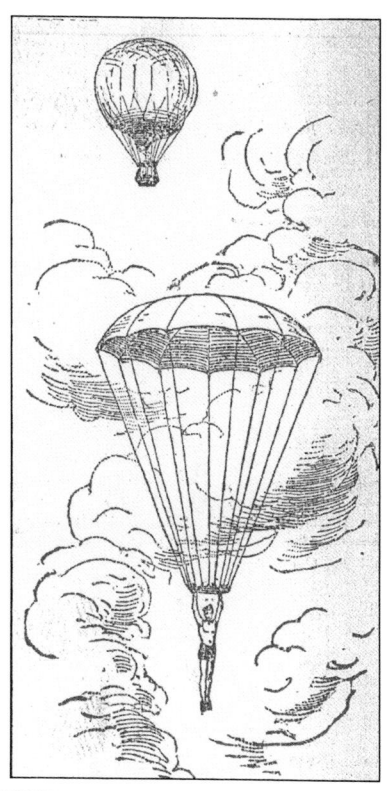

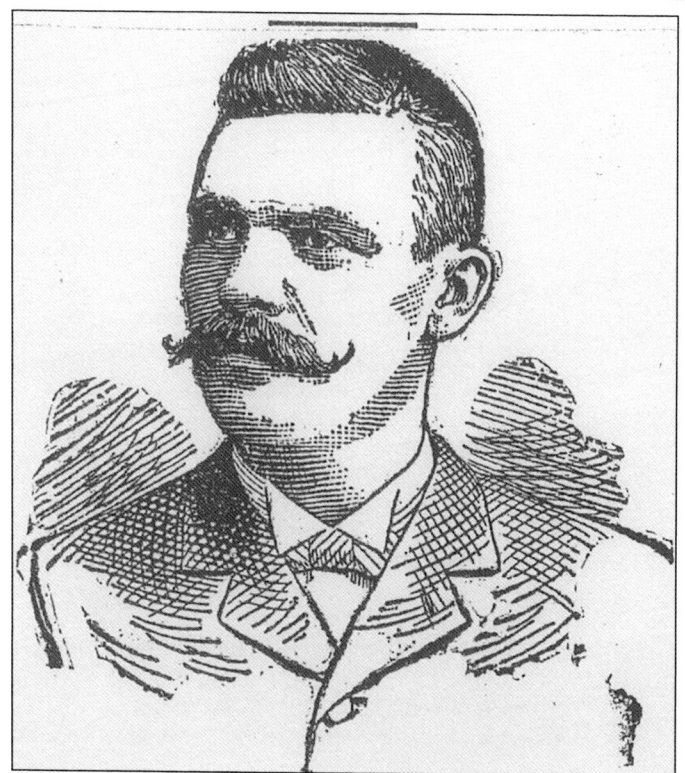

In August of 1888 at Keokuk, 8,000 spectators watched Samuel Baldwin perform a balloon ascension and parachute drop. Four minutes after leaving the ground, Baldwin pulled the rope releasing the balloon's gas and jumped overboard, clinging to the ring attached to the parachute canopy. The crowd applauded, which Baldwin said he could hear right up to the second he splashed into the Mississippi River near the Illinois shore. (Courtesy of the Keokuk Public Library.)

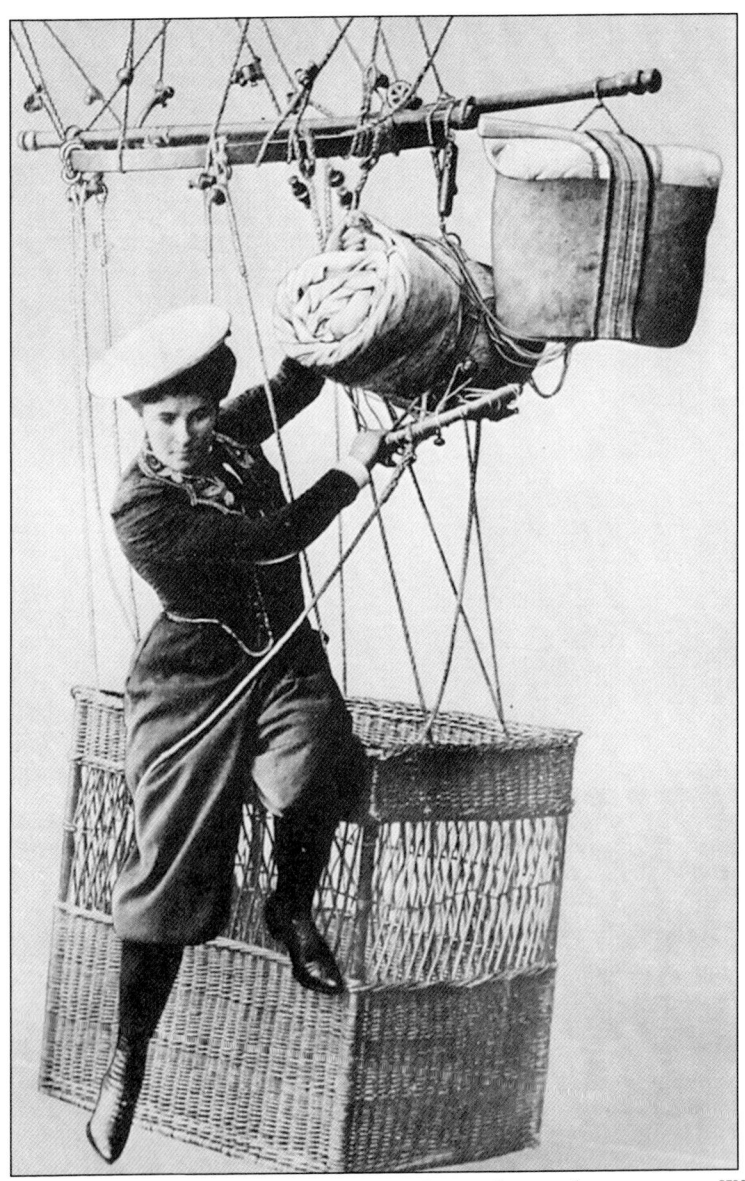

Balloon ascensions and parachute drops were not limited to male aeronauts. Women made headlines and drew huge crowds, matching the men in every aspect of aeronautical feats of bravery. As this late-1800s photograph shows, women aeronauts preferred full costumes, including stylish hats, in contrast to the men's bathing suits. They landed in the Mississippi River just as often, so the costumes made their performances even more risky once they hit the water. In 1888, Louisa Bates performed at the Burlington Fair, while several years later Dubuque native Elsie Lavare, who performed under the name "Daisy Lukens," became one of the foremost female parachutists in the country, jumping until the late 1920s. Another Dubuque female performer, Mrs. Elew Dockstader, was a crowd favorite with her colorful designer suits and banter with onlookers, both during her ascent in the balloon and her drift back to earth in her parachute. In Buchanan County, Dorothy De Vonda, billed as "the one reliable lady balloonist," charmed fairgoers with daily ascensions during which she performed on a trapeze before parachuting back to the fairgrounds. (Courtesy of the Antique Airplane Association.)

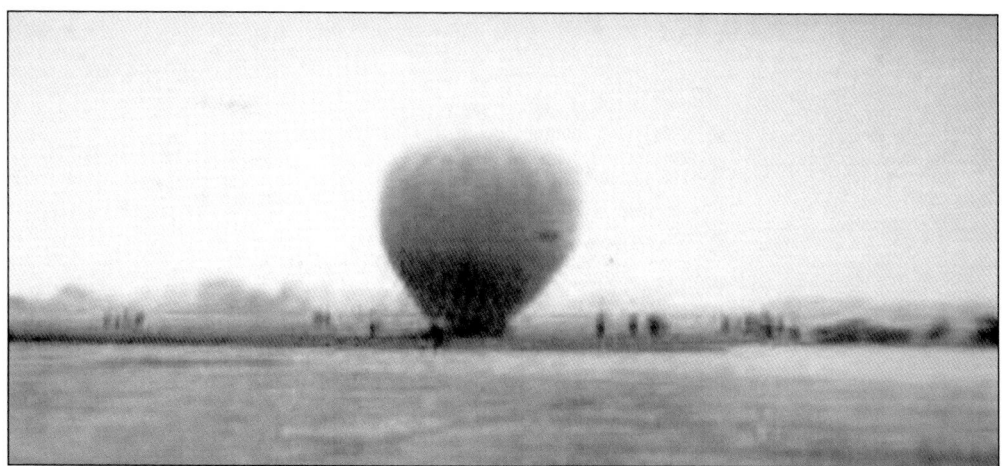

Burlington's own Art J. Hartman was born in 1888 and left home at age 15 to work as a boilermaker in Chicago. Passing the Goddard Balloon Company every day on his way to work, he was so intrigued by the idea of flight that he asked for a volunteer part-time job with the company. It was not long before the young Hartman, performing under the names "A.J. Hart" and "Professor Hart" (so his parents wouldn't worry about his dangerous activities), was touring the Midwest performing balloon ascensions. These photographs show Hartman recreating his 1903 balloon ascensions at the Burlington Airport. (Courtesy of the Burlington Regional Airport.)

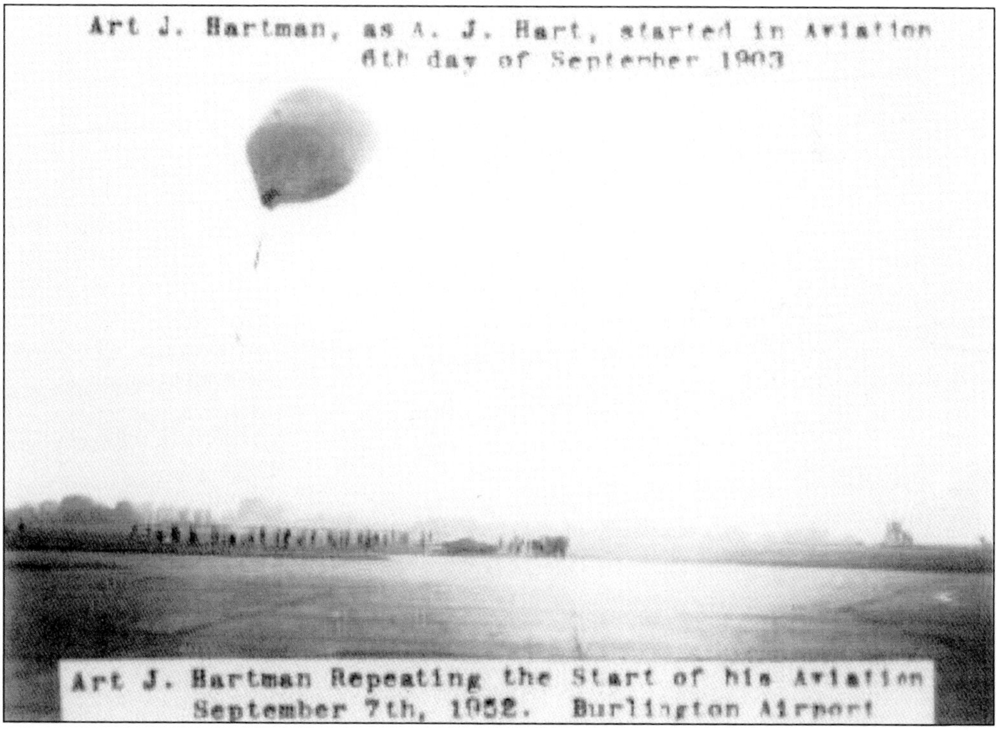

In 1909, Art J. Hartman married Esther Anderson, a girl he had met during one of his balloon ascensions in Moline, Illinois. She worked with her husband sewing balloon envelopes and encouraging his work. For the next several years, he continued to travel the carnival and Chautauqua circuits across the Midwest performing ascensions for huge crowds, often promoting local businesses. (Courtesy of the Des Moines County Historical Society at Burlington.)

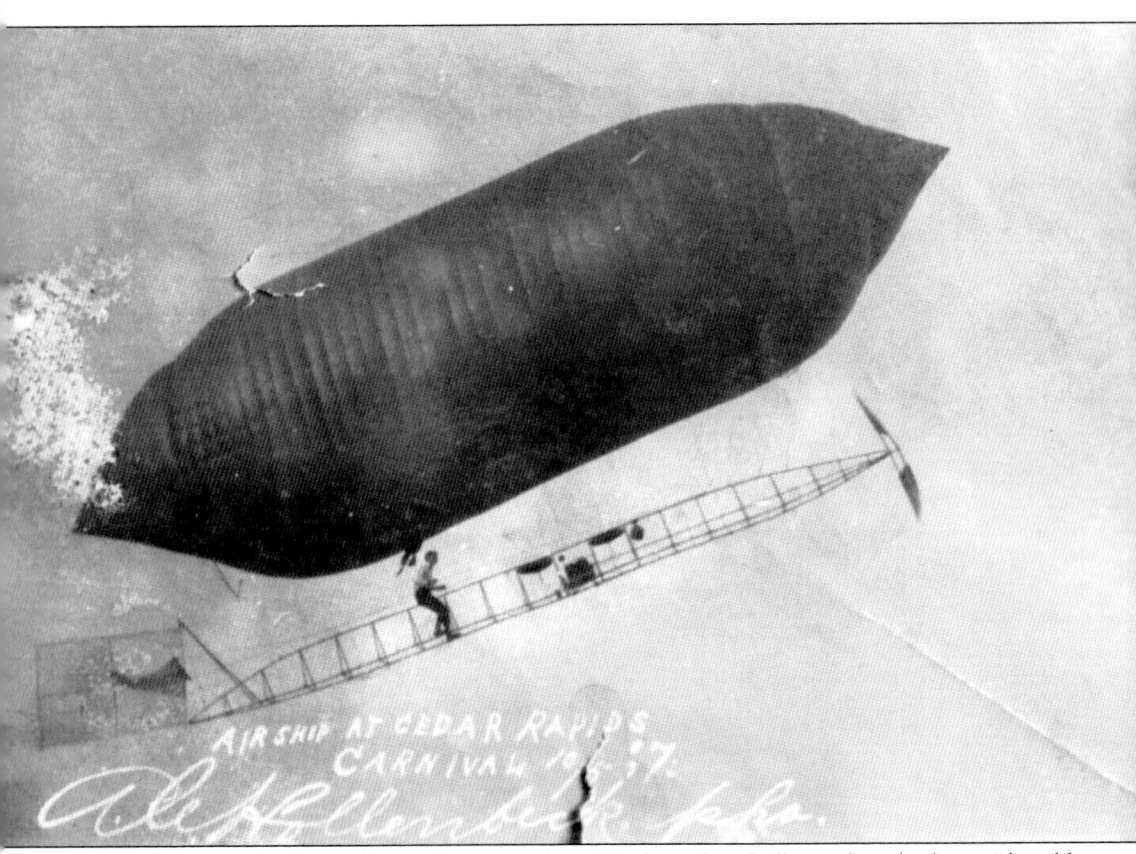

Hartman not only flew traditional hot-air and gas-filled envelope balloons, but also larger "dirigible style" powered balloons like the one shown here with Hartman at the controls during a carnival in 1907 at Cedar Rapids. Hartman recalled, "A favorite advertising gimmick of the early 1900s was the use of a balloonist by real estate men. They'd hire an aerialist to go up in a balloon and throw down a batch of cards. I'd drop the cards and then watch folks on the ground scramble for them." Hartman gave up ballooning several years after he was married, returning to Burlington to work as a boilermaker. However, before long he began experimenting with heavier-than-air aircraft designs and engines in the large garage he had built on Doemland Street in Burlington. (Courtesy of the Carl and Mary Koehler History Center, Linn County Historical Society.)

Two
Iowa's Pioneer Aviators
1910 to 1920

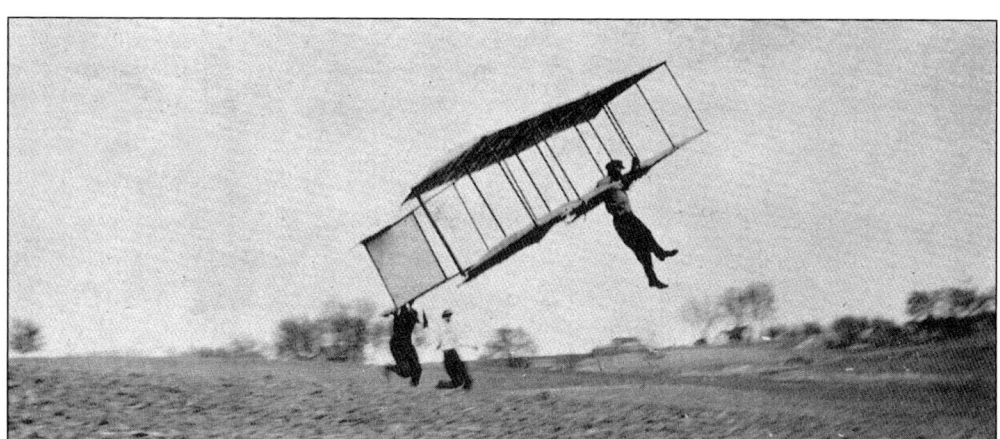

By the early 1900s, gliders had become popular. Here, Arthur Sigafoose from North English flies in his biplane hang glider constructed from spruce, covered with muslin fabric sealed with shellac. With helpers supporting the wingtips, the pilot ran downhill or into the wind, controlling the aircraft by shifting his weight. Crashes were frequent, but with each one, something new was learned. (Courtesy of the Antique Airplane Association.)

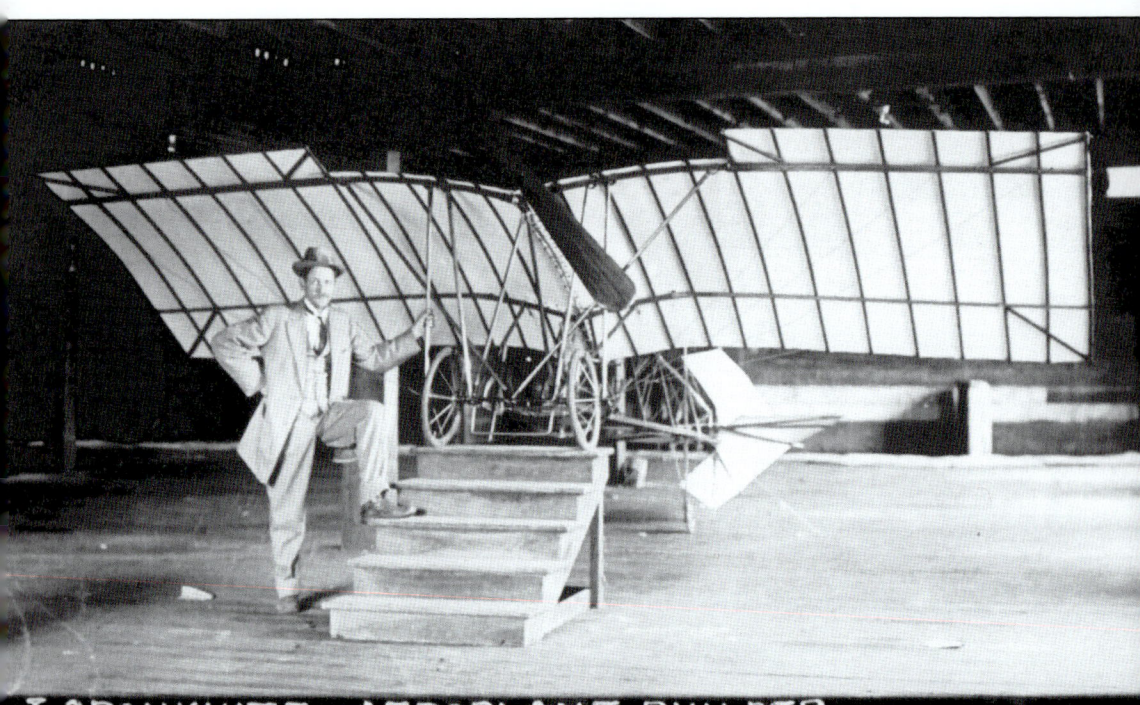

With the passage of the 19th century into the 20th, there were successful powered flights on America's East Coast by aviation pioneers like Orville and Wilbur Wright and Glenn Curtiss. Their designs were little more than gliders fitted with small gasoline-powered engines. As news of their success spread, others who had been experimenting with gliders developed their own powered aircraft designs. F. Oscar Farwell, working with the Adams Company of Dubuque, developed a series of rotary-style aircraft engines called the Adams-Farwell that were advertised in early aeronautical magazines. The engines were tried out on many designs by aircraft builders attempting to equip their gliders with lightweight engines. One experimenter, A.J. Cronkhite, is shown here demonstrating his powered fixed-wing design at an early Cedar Rapids automobile show. (Courtesy of the Carl and Mary Koehler History Center, Linn County Historical Society.)

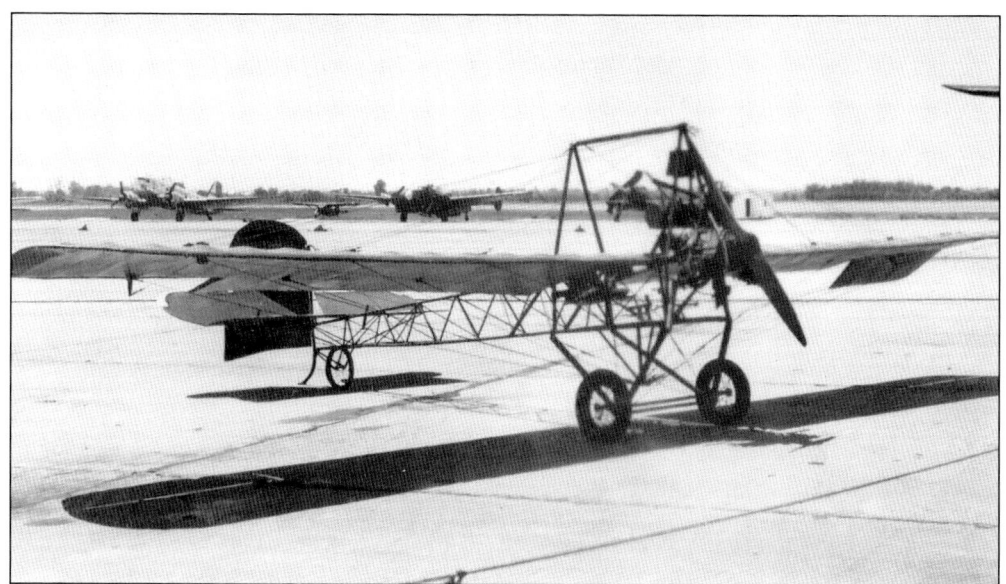

By 1910, Art J. Hartman, convinced that the future of aviation rested in fixed-wing, powered flight, set to work constructing his own aircraft in Burlington. His monoplane had a 28-foot wingspan with cloth-covered wings and tail surfaces and was powered by an 18-horsepower, two-cylinder Detroit Aero engine. This photograph shows Hartman's rebuilt rendition of that original airplane that he flew in air shows from 1939 to 1956. (Courtesy of the Des Moines County Historical Society at Burlington.)

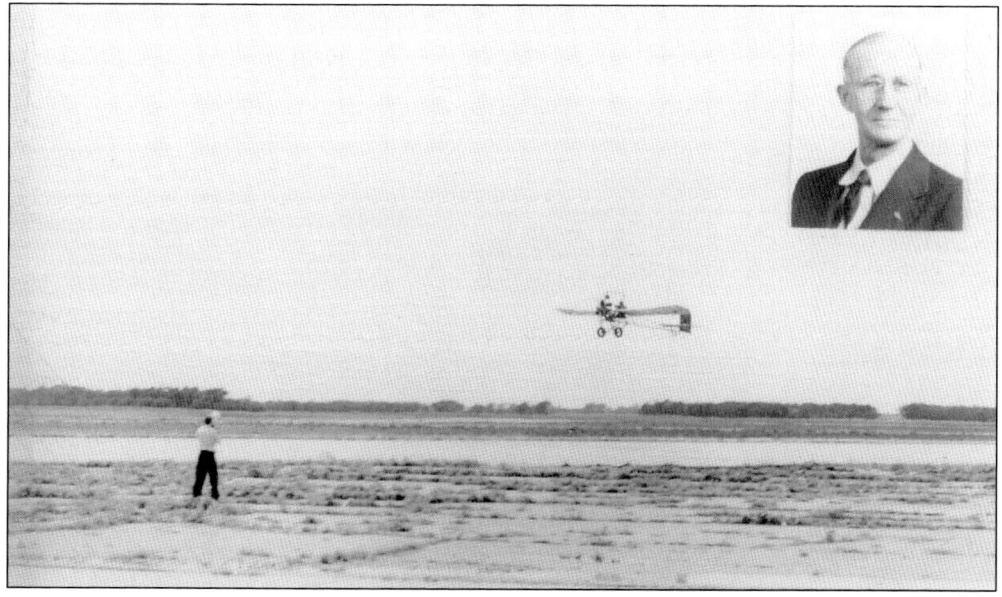

According to newspaper accounts of his first powered flight, "Hartman's little plane took off from the ground, rose to nearly 10 feet into the air and then landed so hard that the undercarriage was damaged." Hartman wrote, "I flew this, the first flying machine ever to leave the ground in the state of Iowa, at the golf course, 1 1/2 miles west of Burlington, Iowa, 5:00 A.M. on May 10, 1910. Five persons witnessed the flight." (Courtesy of the Des Moines County Historical Society at Burlington.)

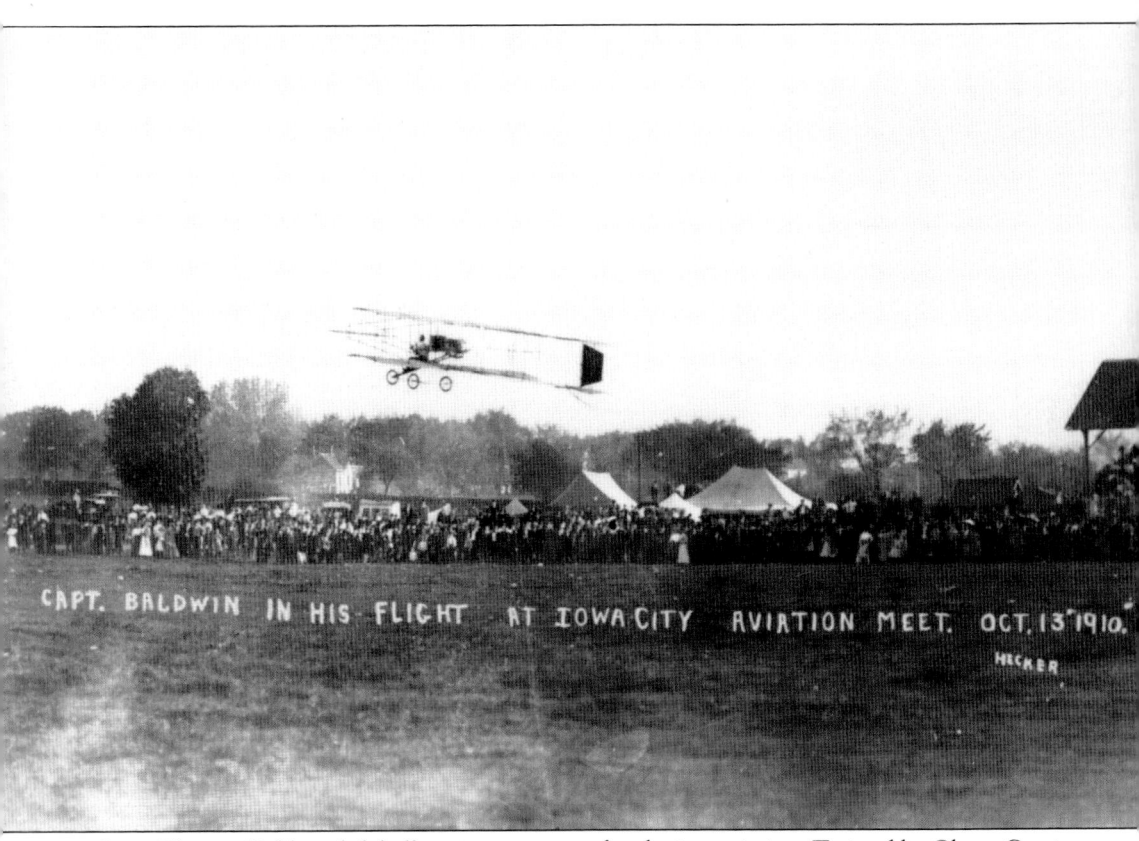

Capt. Thomas Baldwin left ballooning to pursue fixed-wing aviation. Trained by Glenn Curtiss, Baldwin built his own version of a Curtiss pusher biplane that he named Red Devil. Promoters of the 1910 Iowa City Fair contracted with Baldwin to perform. On October 13, he took off from the half-mile racetrack, climbed to just above 100 feet, and turned to fly over the grandstand. After circling the field, he landed in the center of the fairgrounds. On the second takeoff, the Red Devil brushed some treetops, then fought for altitude to clear two barns directly in its path. The tail caught the top of one of the barns just 30 feet off the ground. The impact threw Baldwin to the ground, where he luckily avoided serious injury. Later he said, "I'd have escaped okay if the bad air pocket between the two barns had not caught the biplane." His first flight of the day is now referred to as "Iowa's first 'perfect flight' in an aeroplane." (Courtesy of the State of Iowa Historical Society at Iowa City.)

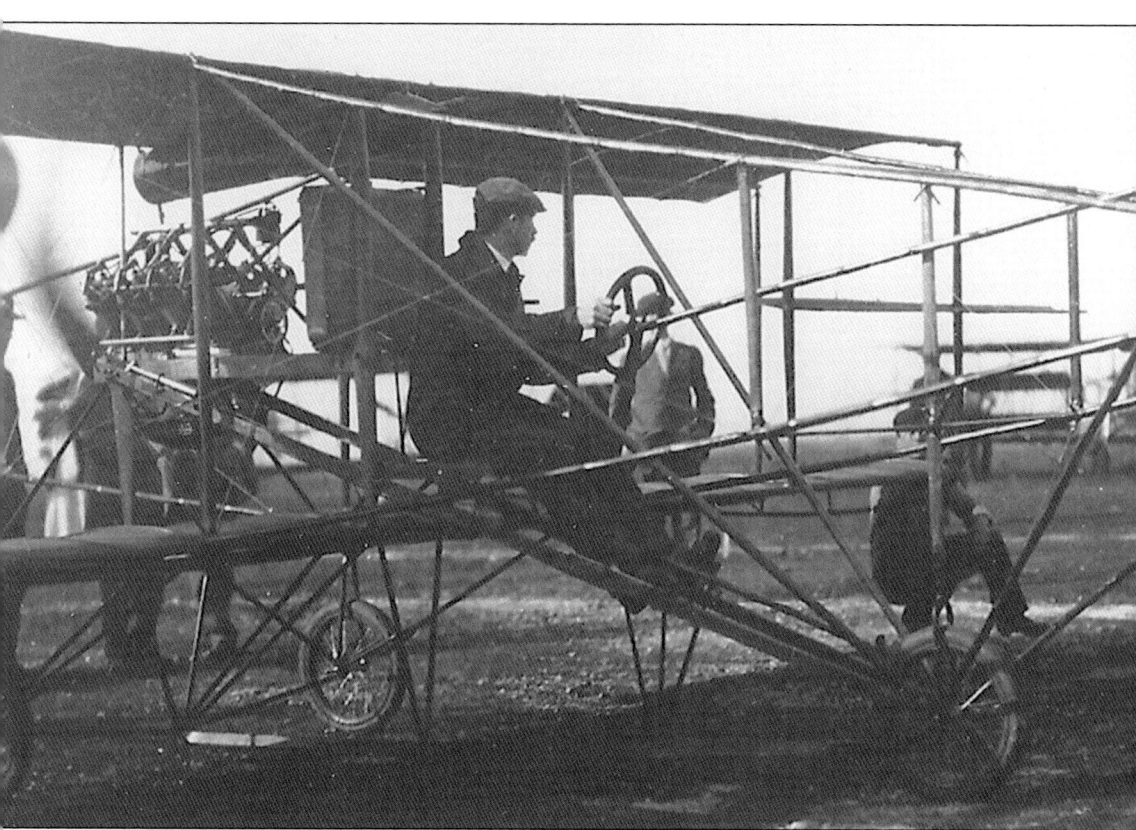

The Curtiss pusher biplane design was the most common type used by the early powered-flight pilots for their community aerobatic demonstrations. Baldwin's Red Devil design, though similar to the Curtiss, was different except for being powered by a 50-horsepower Curtiss V-8 engine. Its 30-foot wingspan was covered by rubberized linen. Only the main wheels actually touched the ground; the nose wheel was used during landing for directional control. A skid supported the tail area during takeoff. Cautious about his flights during his ballooning days with his brother, Baldwin was equally aware of the limitations of his airplane. "I do not make long flights," he said, "or fly to extreme heights because I weigh 200 pounds and cannot carry in my machine a sufficient supply of gasoline for such work." (Courtesy of the *Iowa City Press Citizen*.)

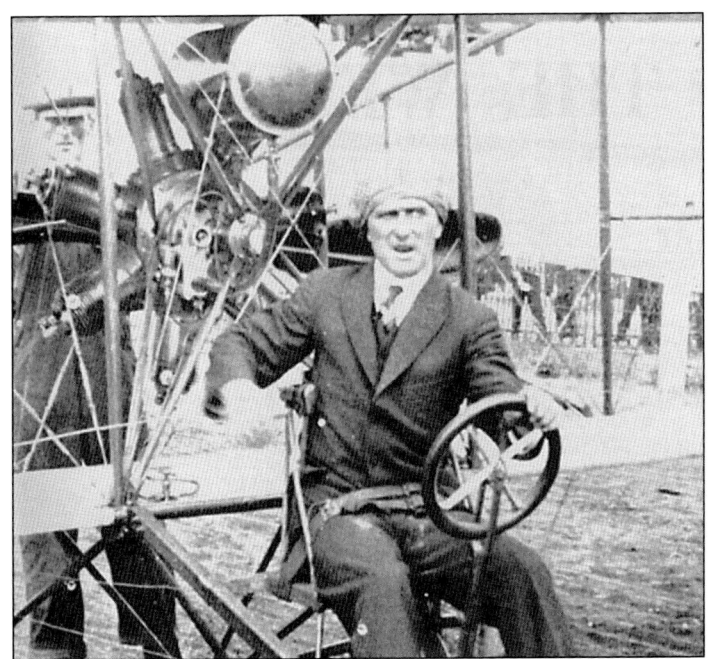

Another former balloonist who had turned to powered flight was Lincoln Beachey. Trained as a member of the internationally renowned Glenn Curtiss Exhibition Company, Beachey took the biggest risks, often leaving wrecked airplanes in his wake, sometimes annoying the Curtiss factory managers. Gruff, flamboyant, and self-confident, Beachey once said, "If you can find somebody to fit an engine on a barn door, I'll fly *that!*" (Courtesy of the Antique Airplane Association.)

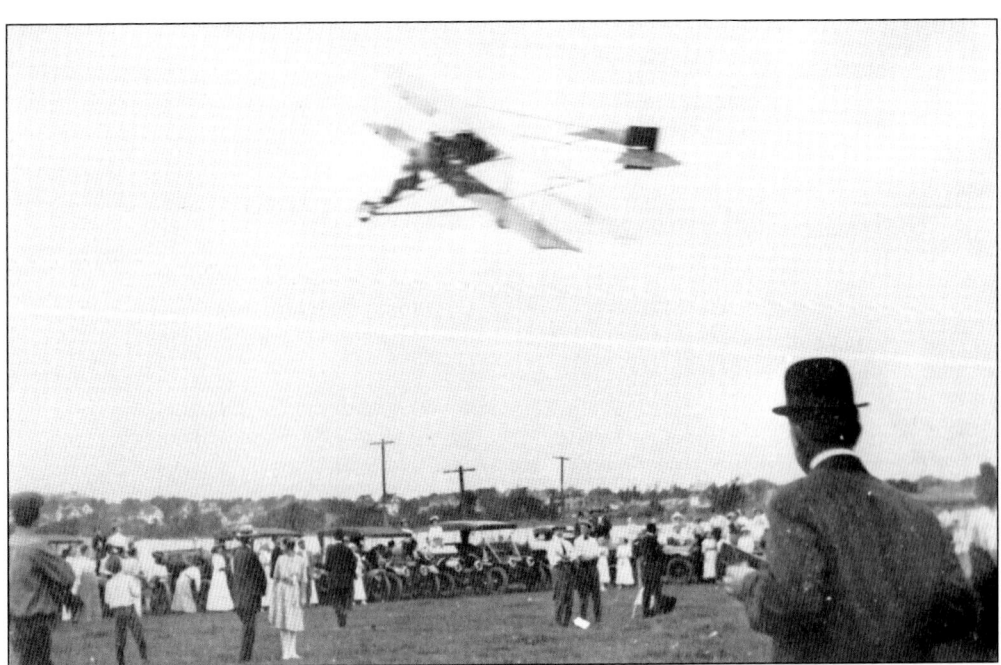

Beachey's Curtiss pusher biplane was fitted with new features, which allowed the pilot to make steep turns by shifting his shoulders in a harness that was attached to airfoil control slats on the wings, called "ailerons." Every event in which he flew became its own unique, death-defying extravaganza drawing crowds like no other, with everyone certain he would crash at any moment. (Courtesy of the Cedar Falls Historical Society.)

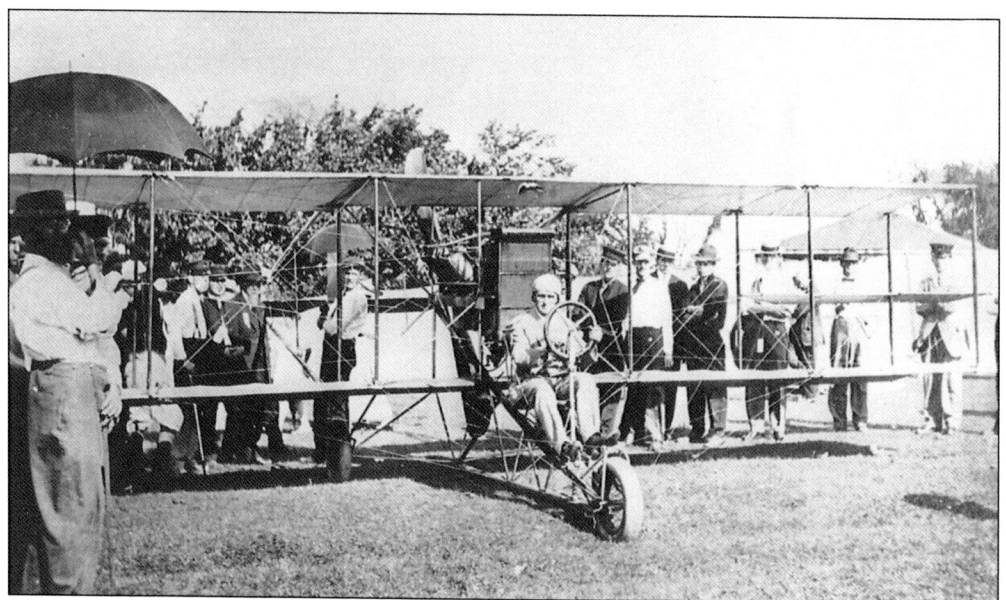

Throughout 1910 and 1911, Beachey thrilled crowds in Muscatine, Dubuque, and this one in Cedar Falls. He made his frail-looking, fabric-covered airplane do things for which it had never been designed, such as climbing and diving and turning so abruptly that onlookers thought surely the wings would tear off. Every time the crowd was certain he would crash into its midst, he regained control and landed smoothly, right where he had taken off. (Courtesy of the Cedar Falls Historical Society.)

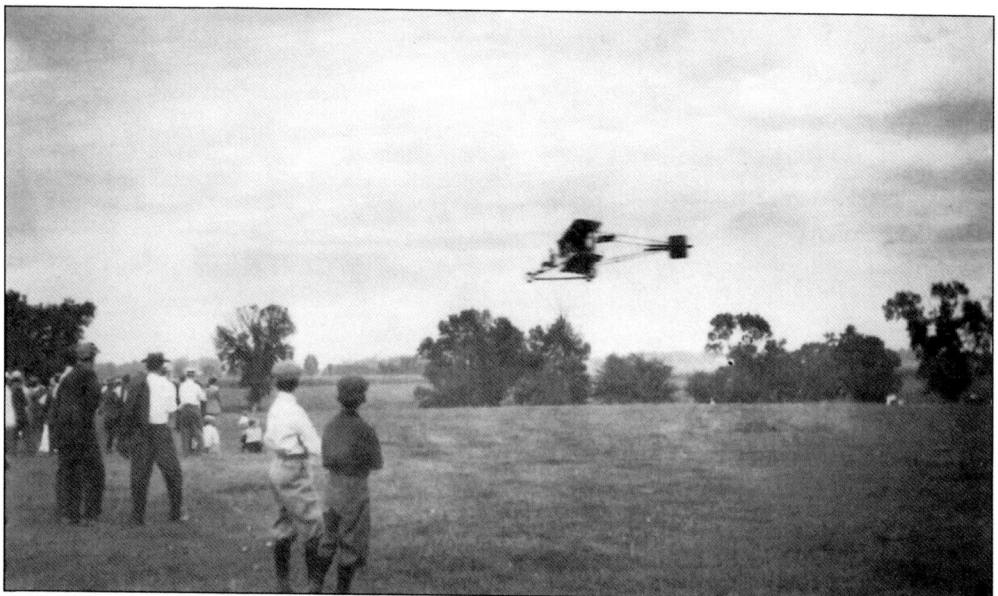

Dubuque and Cedar Falls were the sites of the first Iowa airmail deliveries, with Lincoln Beachey as one of the pilots. In September 1912, the postmaster stamped each piece of mail with the inscription, "Aeroplane Mail Service, Cedar Falls, Iowa, Sept. 5 and 6, 1912." It was the first use of airmail "covers" to commemorate an event and became a common way to create mementos and generate revenue. (Courtesy of the Cedar Falls Historical Society.)

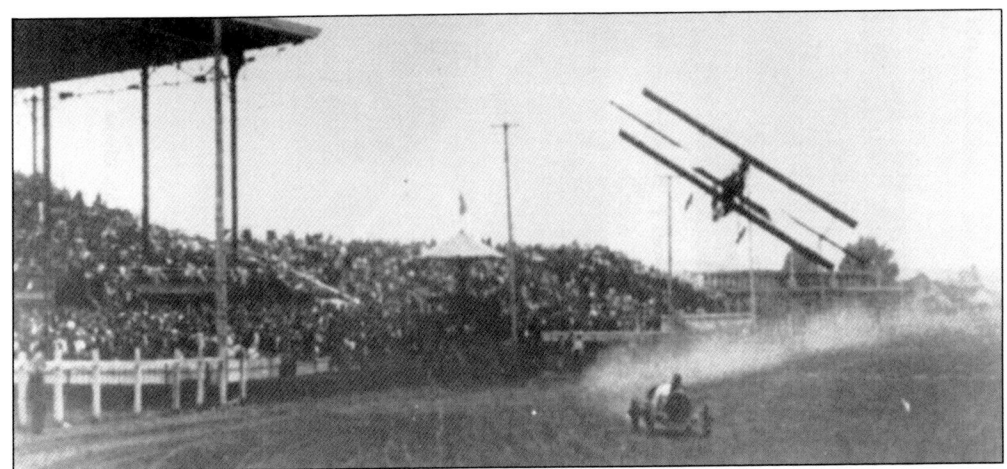

Lincoln Beachey was a great showman. Iowa promoters paid him $1,500 or more for each performance, which could occur several times daily because they knew he would perform regardless of weather conditions. In this photograph, Beachey races his Curtiss biplane against famed racing celebrity Eddie Rickenbacker, who later became America's pursuit pilot ace in World War I. Beachey also choreographed "battles" with soldiers on the ground firing blanks at him while he dropped "bombs" that were loaves of bread. When another aircraft was available, Beachey coordinated air-to-air "combat" as the two pilots fired blanks from pistols at each other, with Beachey as "hero" flying rings around the other aircraft. Orville Wright, a Curtiss rival, said, "He's the most wonderful flyer I ever saw. He's the greatest aviator of all." (Courtesy of the Antique Airplane Association.)

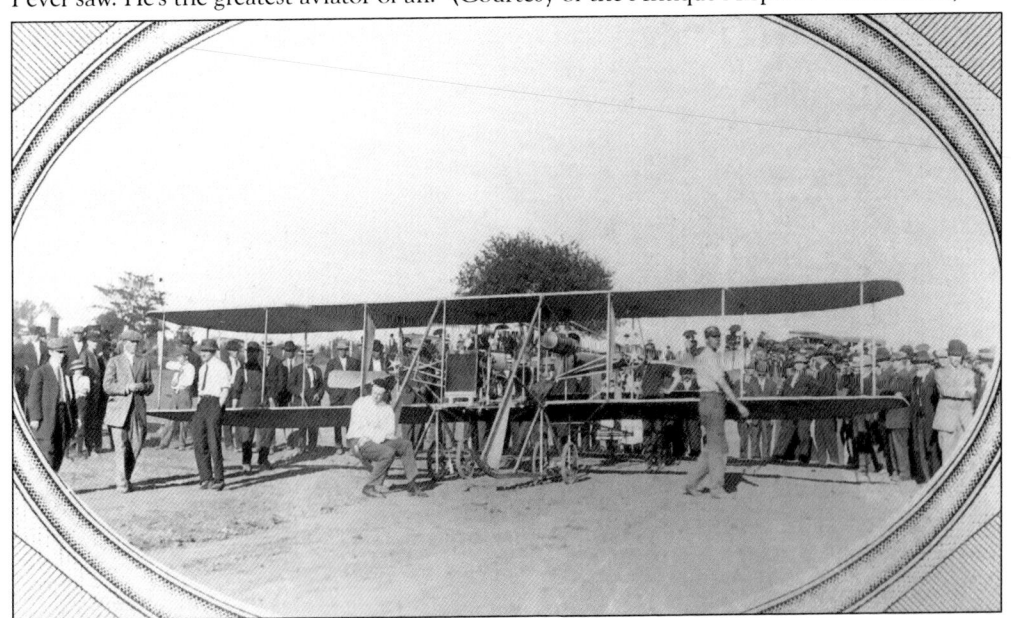

The Wright brothers were also very active in promoting aviation across the country with an exhibition team of their own. Here at the Eastern Iowa Exposition in Cedar Rapids in October 1911, Phil O. Parmalee and his YCR Wright Flyer prepare for a series of flights over four days that drew crowds of more than 15,000 on most days, with people watching from trees and nearby rooftops. A sharp contrast to other fliers, Parmalee's routines demonstrated smooth maneuvering skills, and his courteous manner encouraged people to ask questions and even take an occasional ride. (Courtesy of the Carl and Mary Koehler History Center, Linn County Historical Society.)

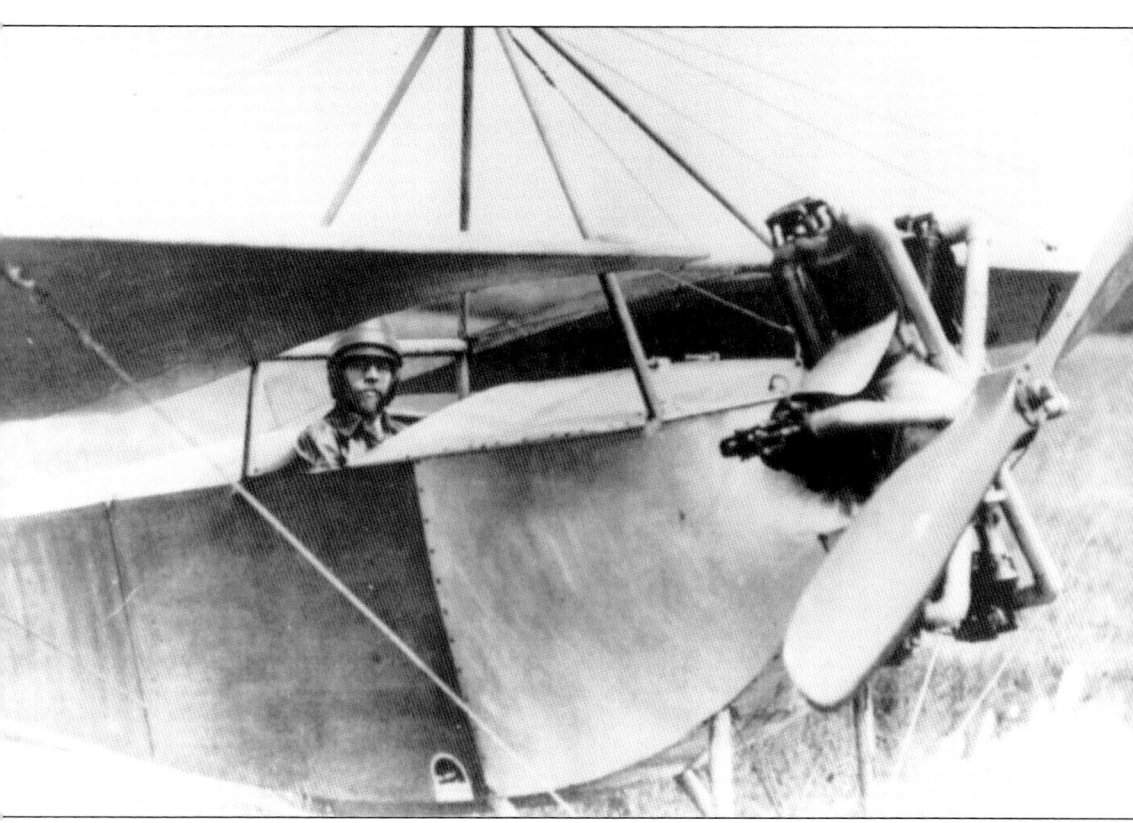

Billy Robinson of Grinnell was driven to break records on his own terms, even though he suffered from a weak heart. He quit school in order to help support his widowed mother, working as an automobile mechanic. With the help of Grinnell businessmen, Robinson started the Grinnell Aeroplane Company manufacturing monoplanes and biplanes of his own design. He also developed one of the first air-cooled radial aircraft engines. In October 1914, Robinson attempted to break the American flying distance record of 125 miles. After skirting the clouds that had formed over Chicago, he landed in Kentland, Indiana—a distance of 390 miles. His fame brought notoriety to the Grinnell community where, by now, Robinson had a wife and three children. A little more than a year later, Robinson attempted to break the American altitude record of 17,000 feet, which his business backers urgently opposed because of his health issues. Nobody knows if his homemade biplane actually reached that height. Crashing in a spectacular fireball near Ewart, Robinson died instantly and the barograph that recorded his altitude was destroyed. (Courtesy of the State Historical Society of Iowa at Iowa City.)

```
Ewart is in Poweshiek
County, 7 miles N W
of Montezuma...
```

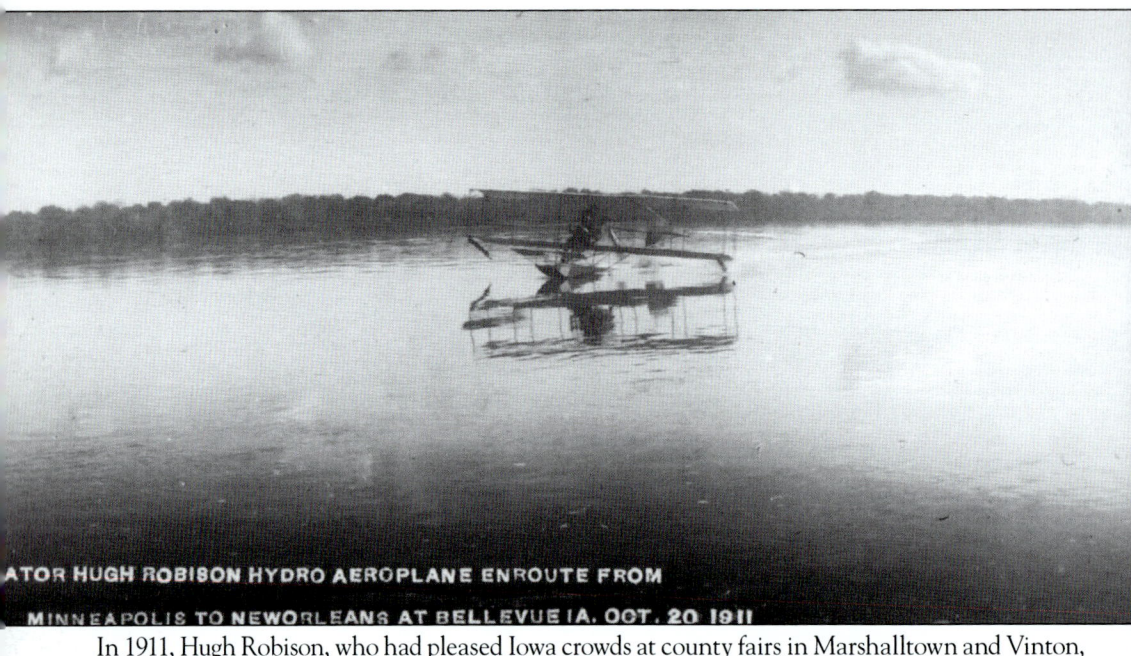

In 1911, Hugh Robison, who had pleased Iowa crowds at county fairs in Marshalltown and Vinton, decided to demonstrate the practicality of flight on a larger scale. He wanted to show people who lived along the Mississippi River that air flight could be just as safe and useful as barge, steamboat, and railroad traffic in these agricultural and industrial towns. Starting in Minneapolis, Robison flew his Curtiss hydro-aeroplane downriver, performing as he went, with an ultimate destination of New Orleans. Wherever there was a bridge, he flew under it. Wherever he spotted people gathered at a dam or boat launch area, he landed to cheers and offers of refreshment. (Courtesy of the State Historical Society of Iowa at Iowa City.)

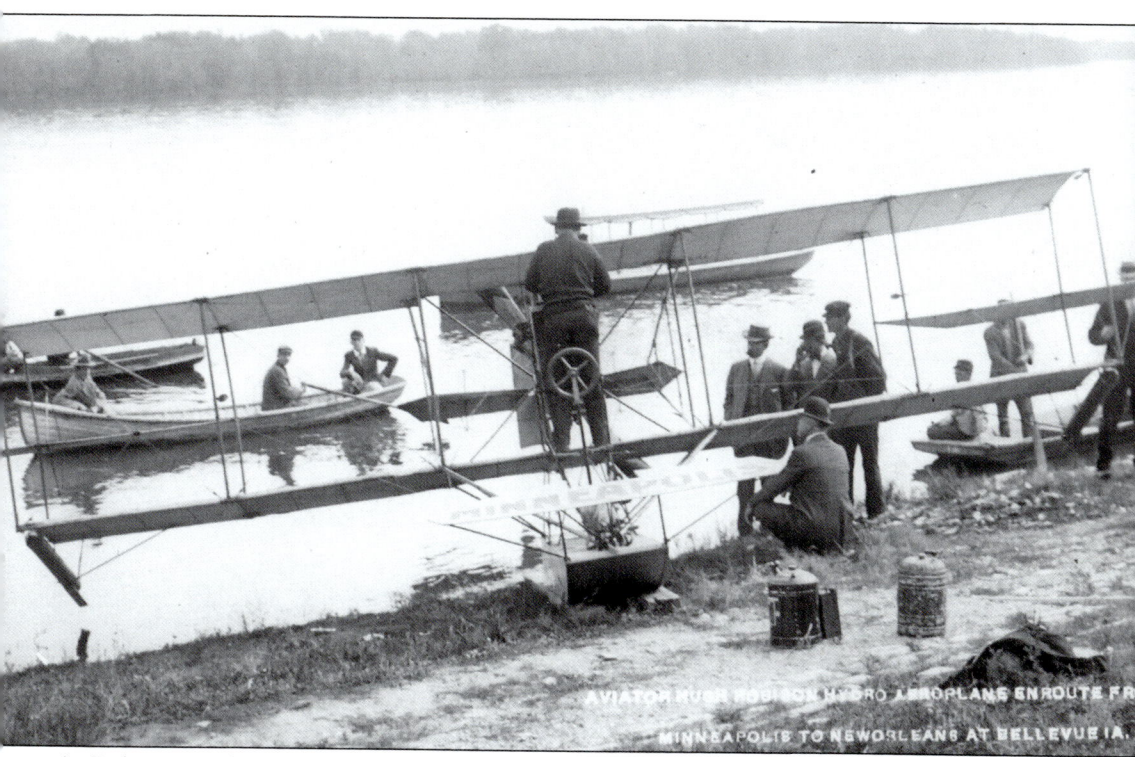

At Dubuque, Robison was met by a crowd of 5,000 people; many of them asked to write their names on the wings of his aircraft. After a night's rest, he continued to Bellevue. He went on to Clinton, then Davenport, and was always met by thousands of people, most of whom had never seen a "flying machine" before. His flight ended in Davenport because of a lack of funding, but his vision had served his desired purpose: creating awareness in aviation. (Courtesy of the State Historical Society of Iowa at Iowa City.)

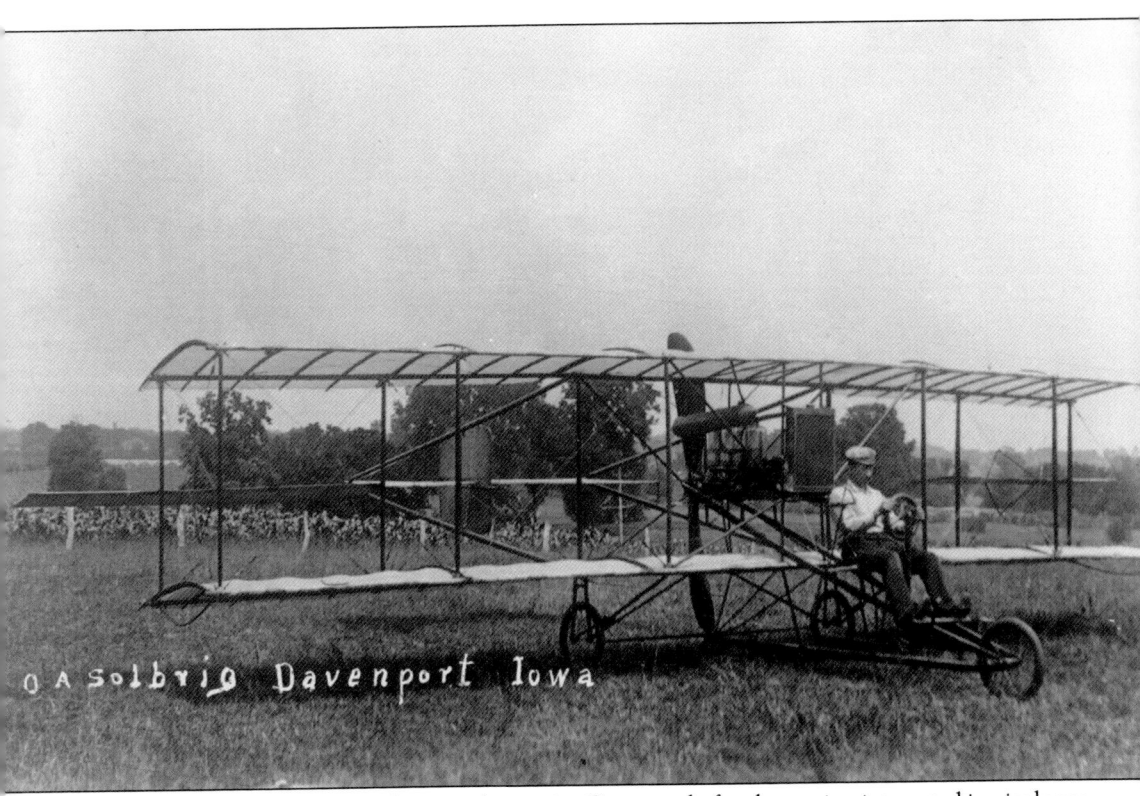

Oscar Solbrig had been a machinist in his native Germany before becoming interested in airplanes while working in a shop in Washington, Iowa, after marrying Davenport native Mary Heidenreich. He studied at the Curtiss aviation schools in both San Diego and New York. After purchasing about half the materials from Curtiss, the couple began constructing a Curtiss-type pusher biplane in their Davenport living room with Oscar fabricating the rest of the parts. Powered by a Roberts 50-horsepower engine, the Solbrigs designed their airplane with fittings that allowed the aircraft to be easily assembled and disassembled. Test flights were made at the Davenport racetrack with Oscar at the controls and Mary as the chief "mechanician," as she preferred to be called. As the aircraft's performance improved, flights were made down to the Mississippi River area to Suburban Island (now Credit Island). Oscar and Mary Solbrig were the first couple to be awarded the golden pin of the Early Birds, a group of aviation pioneers recognized for their flights or work on aircraft prior to World War I. (Courtesy of the Putnum Museum at Davenport.)

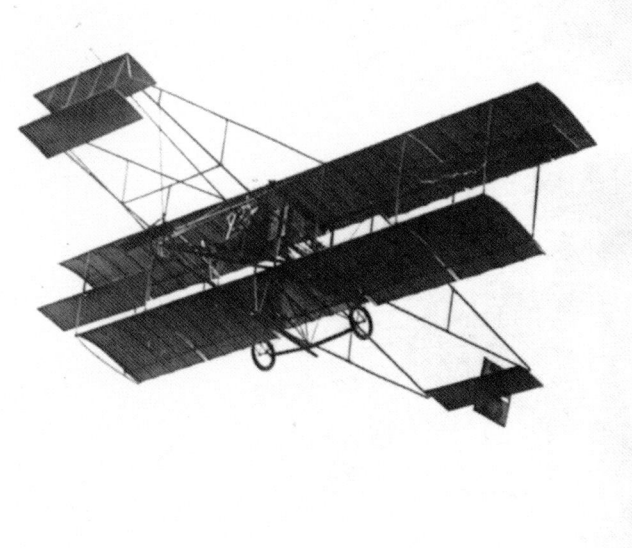
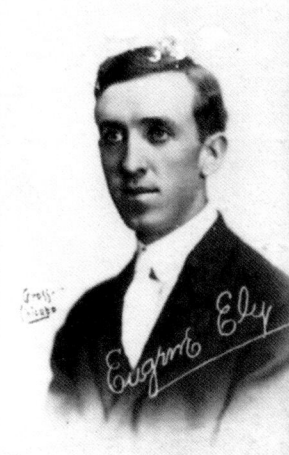

Another Davenport resident and aviation pioneer was Eugene Ely. Dropping out of high school to work on and race automobiles, Ely moved to San Francisco in 1909 to open a West Coast automobile stage line. There he met Glenn Curtiss, who convinced Ely to join his Curtiss Exhibition Team. From that time on, Ely was obsessed with breaking speed records and performing well-choreographed, precision aerial demonstrations all over the country, including his native Iowa. In 1910, after making one of the first powered flights in Iowa, Ely was assigned by Glenn Curtiss to work with the Navy in developing flying techniques that would allow airplanes to take off from and land on ships. Ely performed the first takeoff from a ship on November 14, 1910, in Virginia and the first landing of an aircraft onto a ship in San Francisco two months later. A year later, Ely made his final Iowa flight demonstration in Davenport, thrilling many of his childhood friends and family members. Two weeks later, he was killed during an exhibition in Macon, Georgia. (Courtesy of the State Historical Society of Iowa at Iowa City.)

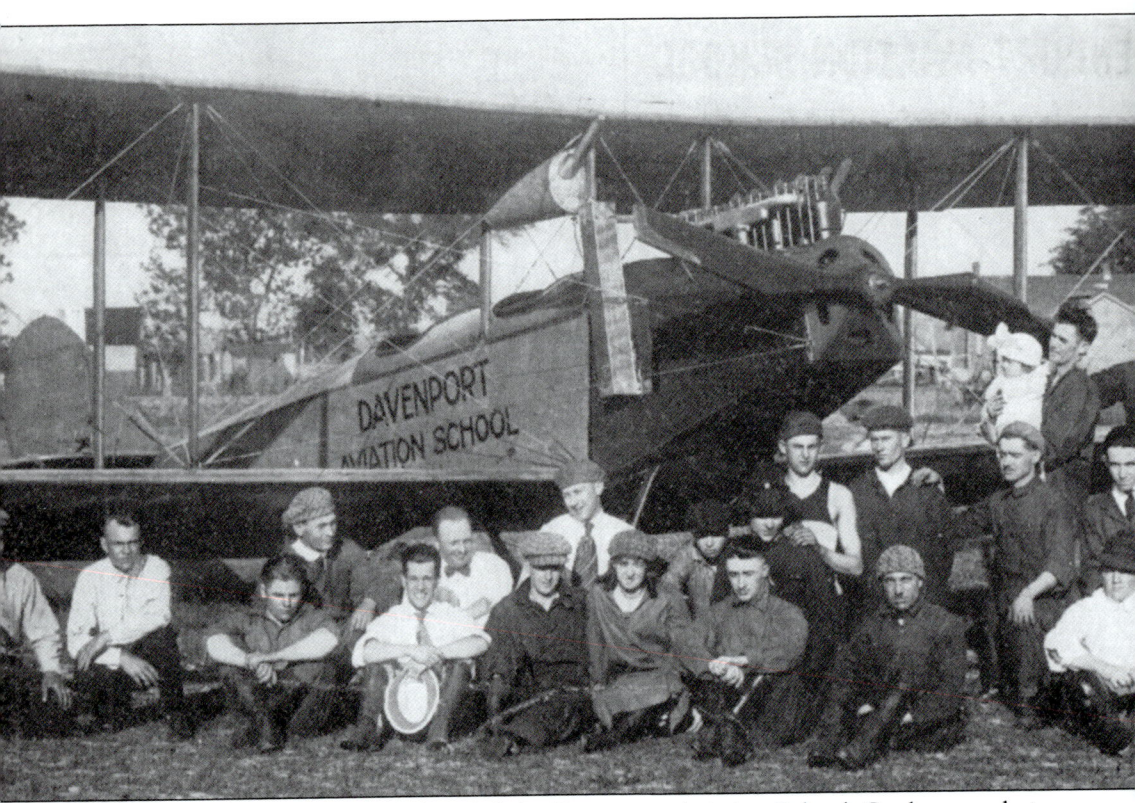

In 1916, William "Billy" Cook founded the Davenport Aviation School. Cook was a designer and pilot of several hydro-aeroplanes that performed up and down the Mississippi River, often teaming up with Katherine Stinson and her Partridge-Keller biplane to entertain large crowds. Cook had no problem when Neta Snook (first row, center) from Ames applied for admission to his new school. She was nicknamed "Curly" by her fellow students and later taught Amelia Earhart to fly. The school guaranteed each student first-rate instruction and success at earning his or her wings for a tuition fee of $400. Students came from all across the country, including a future Iowa barnstormer, Clifton P "Ole" Oleson. The instructional staff included accomplished pilots J.R. Hutchinson and Louis Boudor, along with local craftsmen like Oscar Solbrig, who guided the students with aircraft construction. (Courtesy of the Putnam Museum at Davenport.)

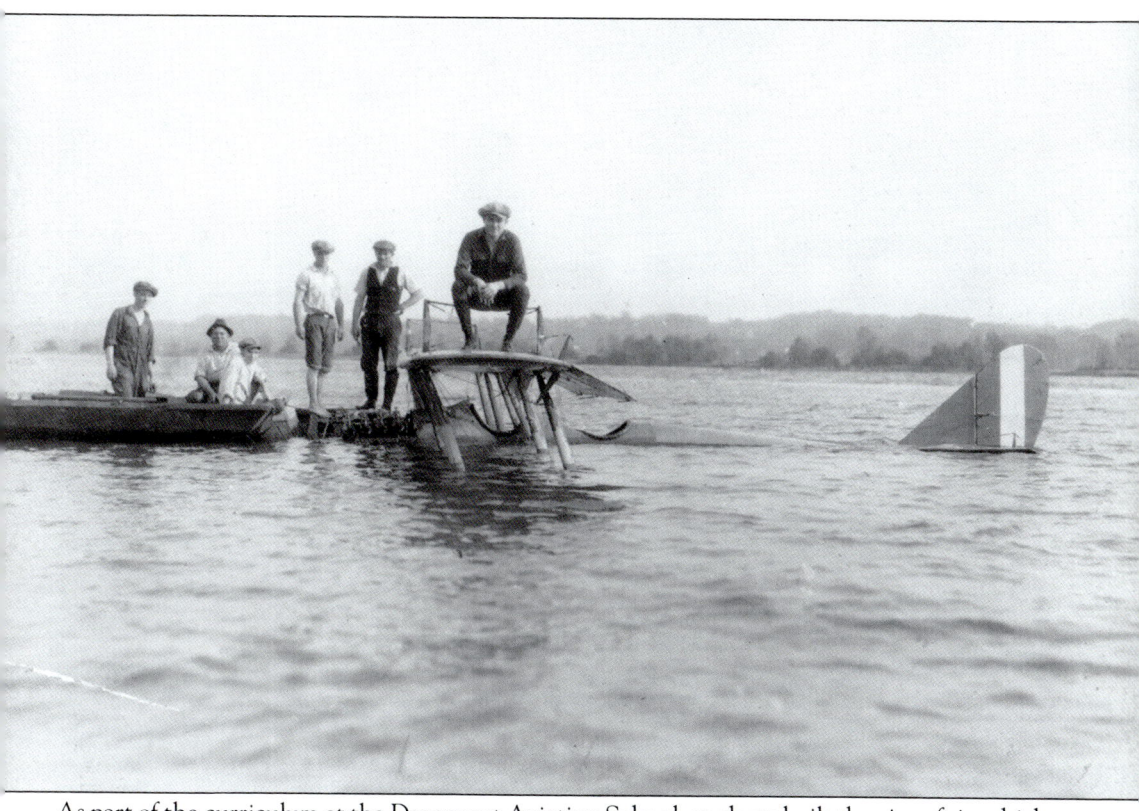

As part of the curriculum at the Davenport Aviation School, students built the aircraft in which they would gain their flight experience. The school's biplane design was based on the Curtiss JN-4 Jenny. When Curtiss refused to sell Billy Cook the plans, Cook toured the Curtiss factory, took some measurements, then hired Walter "Tex" Frey, a Curtiss worker, to help construct parts from memory. Oscar Solbrig made many of the parts in his local blacksmith shop. Louis Boudor was the test pilot, flying the biplane from Suburban Island (now Credit Island) on the Mississippi River. Each student got the opportunity for flight instruction with "Mr. Louie" as they called him. There were the occasional mishaps and even some "wet landings," as shown here, but soon the first dozen students each had 100 minutes of flight instruction. Cook, needing money, sought new investors. Unfortunately, on September 9, 1917, the school biplane crashed, killing a potential and very overweight investor and critically injuring Boudor. The school closed, but Cook was able to refund each student part of the tuition. (Courtesy of the Putnum Museum at Davenport.)

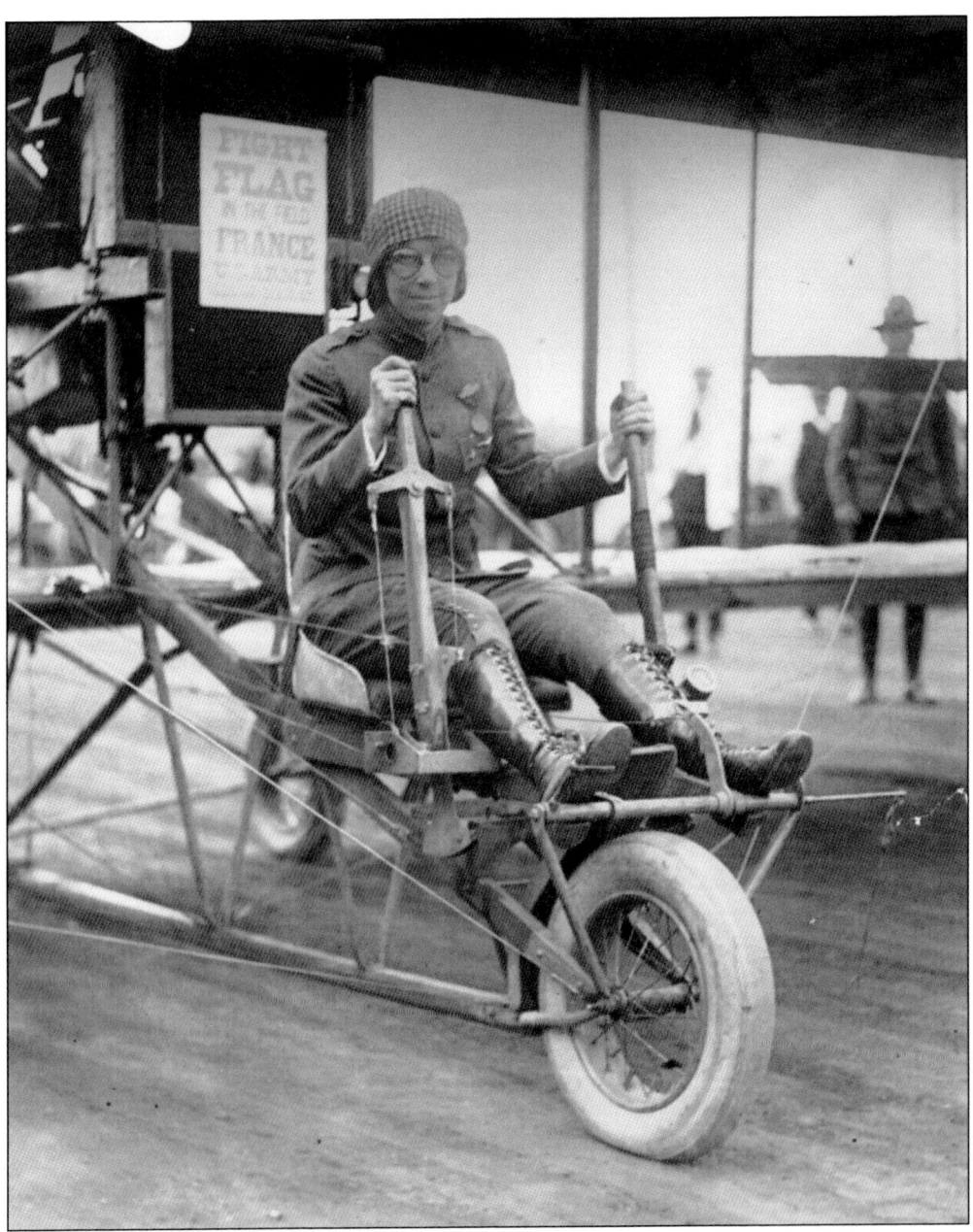

Ruth Law was another female aviation pioneer who enjoyed flying for large Iowa crowds in the days just before and during World War I. Taught to fly by Army instructors in Boston in 1912, she held the women's altitude record and taught herself to do loops. She started flying a Wright biplane before switching to a Curtiss pusher that had Wright controls installed on it, as seen in this 1917 photograph. She was a favorite at the Burlington Fair in 1916, where she carried parachutists in addition to her flying demonstration. During the Keokuk Fall Festival of 1916, Law thrilled the crowd by attaching torches to her airplane's wingtips and fireworks to the frame and flew above the town at night, creating a spectacular scene complete with steep dives and loops. Each of her three-day performances attracted huge crowds that cheered wildly and later held a reception for the young aviatrix. (Courtesy of the State Historical Society of Iowa at Iowa City.)

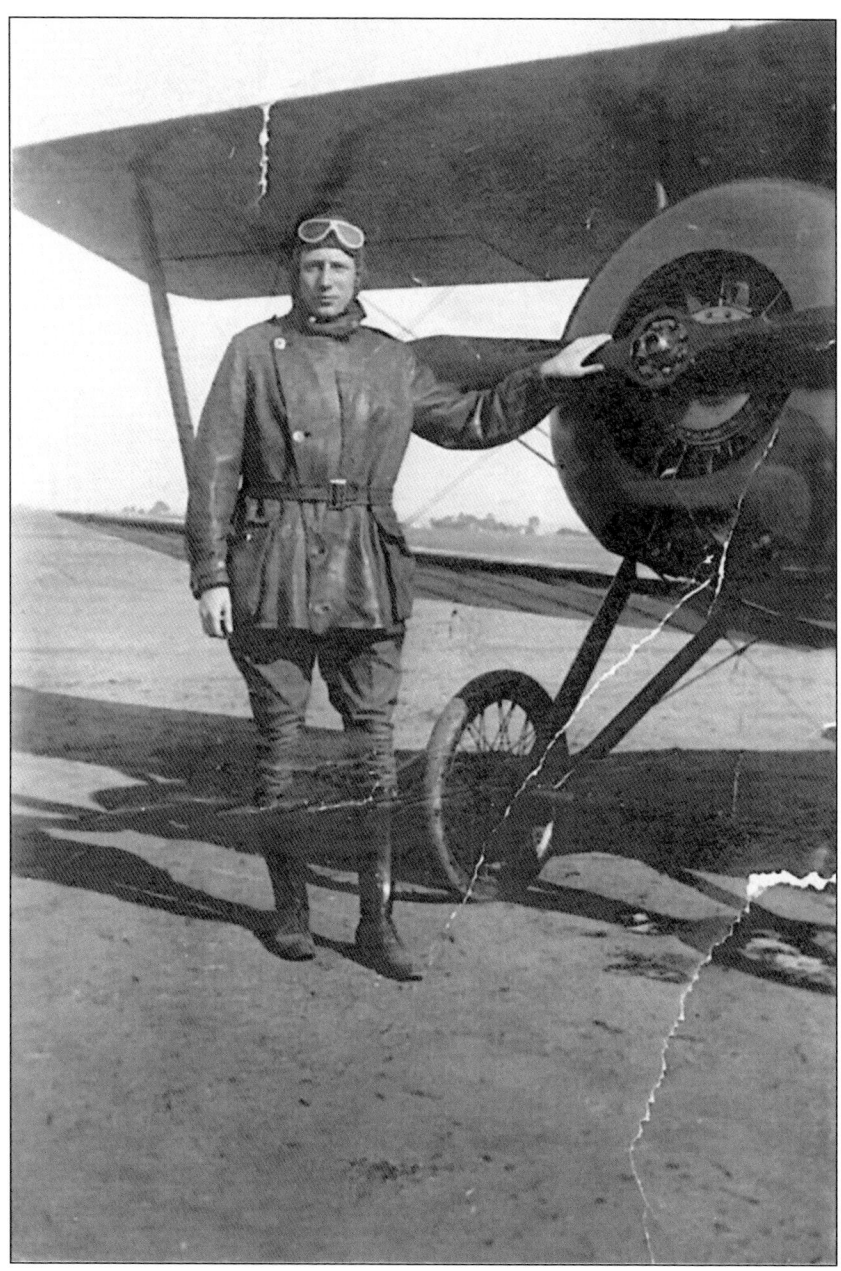

Some veteran fliers of World War I returned home to Iowa after the armistice, hoping to make a career in aviation. Dan Hunter of Cedar Rapids had been a lieutenant in the US Army Air Corps, teaching students aerial gunnery among other duties. He created his own flying service south of the city, offering everything, including aircraft maintenance, sales, freight hauling, and flight instruction. He used his military experiences to train civilian students. He said, "I give my students 15 hours of flying after which they are able to fly alone. Of this, 10 hours are in dual instruction on the fields and five hours of cross-country. Besides that, I give a course in the theory of aerodonetics, aero-construction and design, repair, and engine construction and maintenance." Hunter Aviation went on to become one of the largest aviation businesses in the state. (Courtesy of the Carl and Mary History Center, Linn County Historical Society.)

1919 -- 1920

Miller-Scales Aero Co.
Aeroplanes—Aeroplane Supplies
Aerial Activities

. F. Scales   WATERLOO, IOWA

Partnerships between returning Army fliers and local businessmen who were enthusiastic about being a part of this new aviation field started up all over Iowa. Another World War I veteran who came home to start a career in aviation was Lt. Milo Miller of Waterloo. He convinced local contractor George Scales that a fortune could be made by offering "all things related to aeroplanes" to northeastern Iowa citizens and businesses. Together they formed the Miller-Scales Aero Company, starting with three surplus Curtiss OX-5 Jennys that they kept in tents in a field between Waterloo and Cedar Falls. Offering 10-minute rides at $20 each, they soon had to hire another pilot, Earl "Rusty" Campbell, who later started an airport in Moline, Illinois. They also hired John Livingston, a young mechanic who later became one of Iowa's premier aviation celebrities. (Courtesy of the Cedar Falls Historical Society.)

Three
BARNSTORMERS AND VISIONARIES
1920 TO 1930

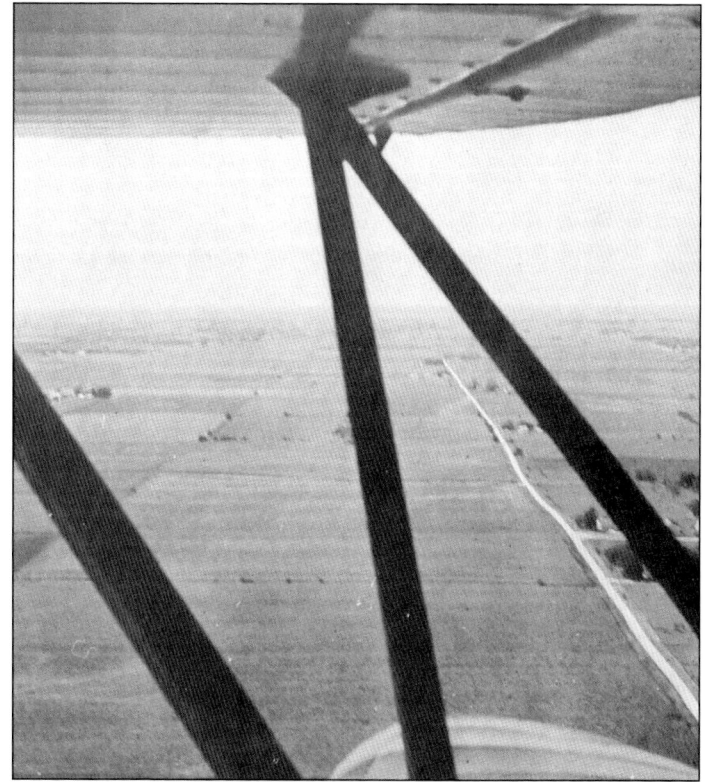

By the end of World War I, the era of "motorized crates" had given way to larger, faster, more powerful flying machines. Wartime experimentation produced airplanes that could make long cross-country flights and a new breed of dreamers who saw no limit to what air travel could accomplish. Iowans were about to witness a dramatic increase in aviation's influence on their lives. (Courtesy of the Antique Airplane Association.)

Big Air Meet and Circus
—AT—
FARLEY, IOWA
Sunday, Sept. 25th
SKY FULL OF SHIPS
Every Stunt Known To Aviation Will Be Shown

SHORTY AIKINS, DUBUQUE'S "HUMAN FLY"—Playing Leap Frog from Plane to Plane and Acrobatic Stunts in Mid-air. Several parachute Jumps.

SEE THE DUBUQUE YOUNG LADY IN HER FIRST PARACHUTE LEAP.

CAPT. MULLEN in his 4,000 foot leap. Aarron Rowe the flying Dare Devil hangs by his teeth and by his toes from landing gear, standing on top of plane while looping the loop.

Plenty of lunch and refreshments on the field.
Free parking space for autos and picnicing parties
Special Train Service On Illinois Central.

BAND CONCERT
Admission To Field—Adults 50c / Children 25c

Come Early.   Something Doing all the Time
SPECIAL TRAIN LEAVES 10:30 A. M.

There was a new generation of pilots, many of them ex-military fliers, who enjoyed traveling the countryside, often sleeping under the wings of their airplanes or in a generous farmer's barn at night. These barnstormers often combined to form "aerial circuses" that created entertainment and local heroes, as described in posters such as this one advertising an event in Farley, Iowa. (Courtesy of the State Historical Society of Iowa at Iowa City.)

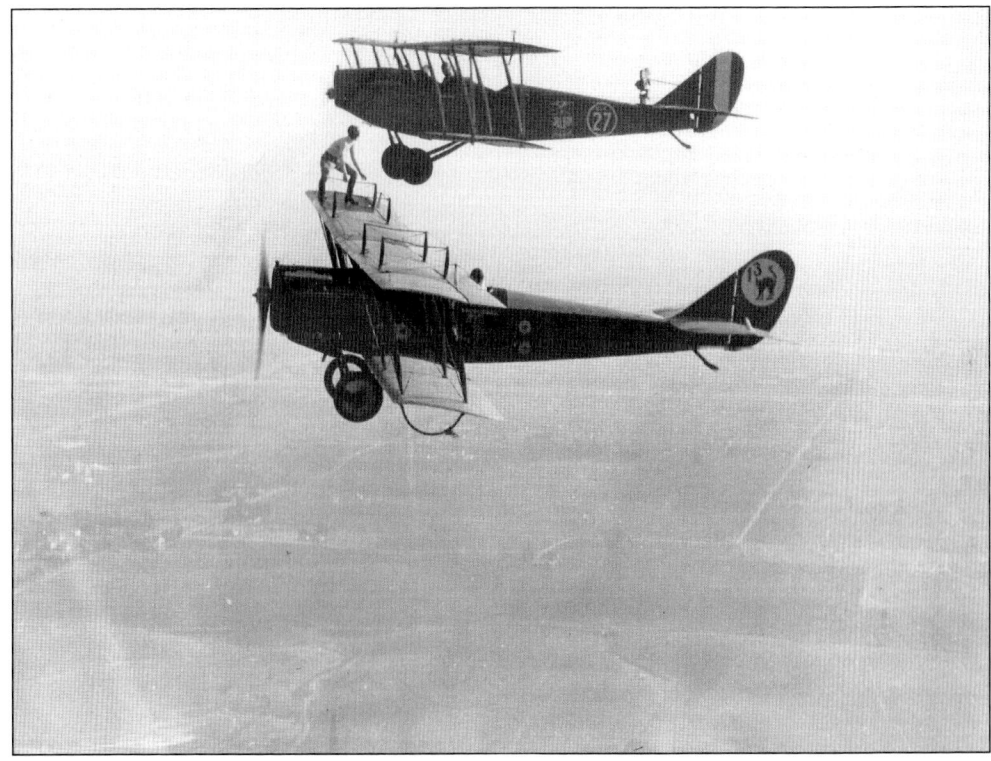

Competition among aerial circuses and barnstormers guaranteed Midwestern crowds increasingly elaborate stunts. Parachute drops and wing walking were some of the more common performances. A person transferring between an automobile to an airplane or between two airplanes, such as these two Curtiss Jennys, were big crowd-pleasers. (Courtesy of the Cedar Falls Historical Society.)

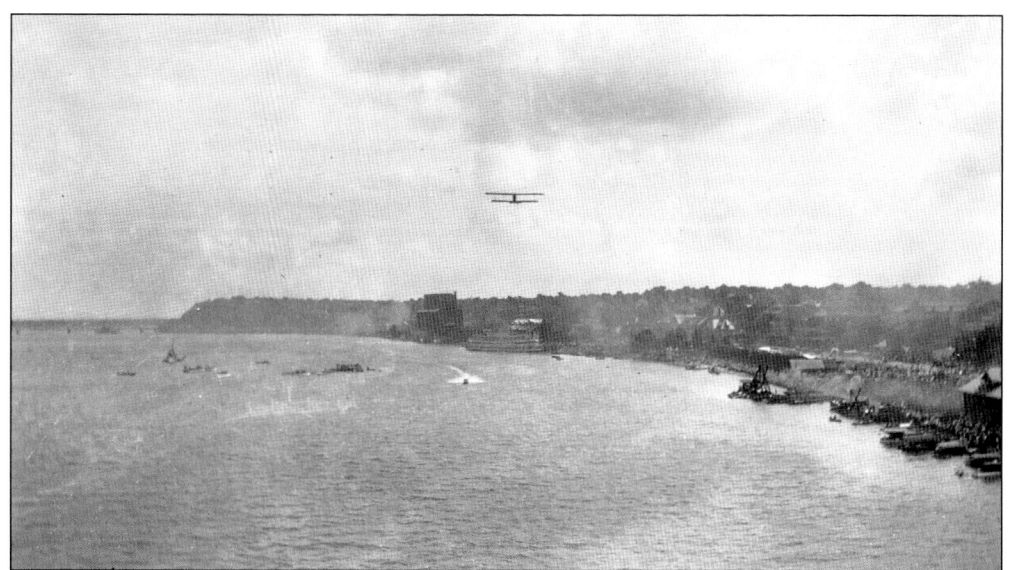

Along the Mississippi River, races between airplanes and high-powered speedboats entertained large audiences. Here, a biplane flown by a man named Nofzinger races a speedboat named Miss Toronto up the Mississippi River at a Burlington regatta festival. (Courtesy of the Des Moines County Historical Society at Burlington.)

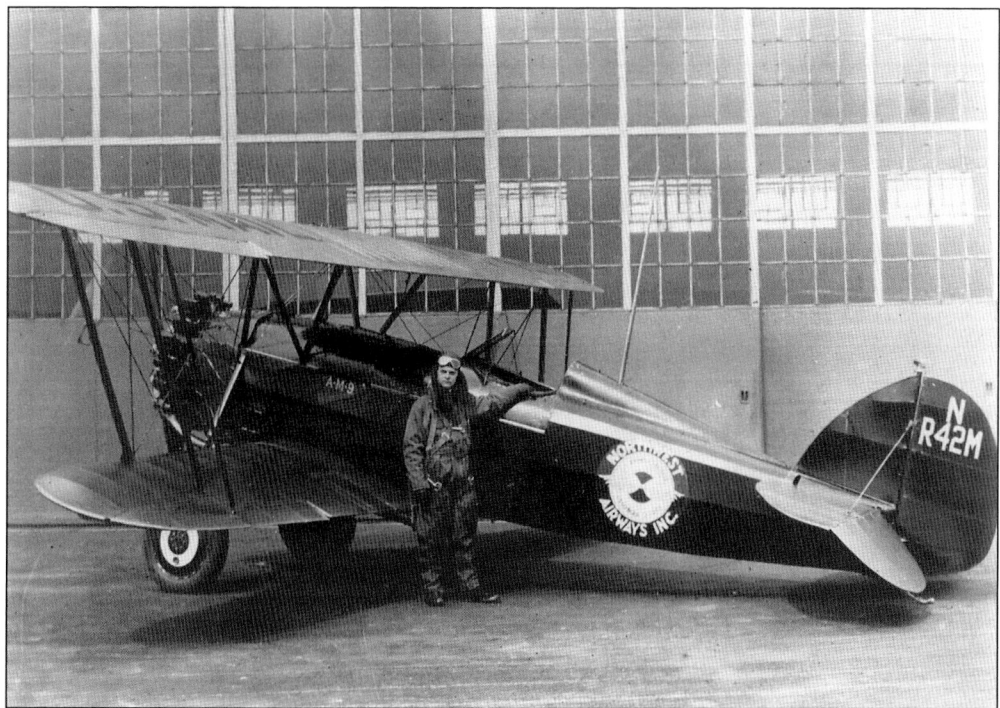

Instead of barnstorming or racing, some pilots started up small airlines, carrying both passengers and freight—often with just one airplane—operating from rural grass airstrips and well-established airports. Most of the airplanes, like this Waco J-6, were open-cockpit biplanes that carried only one or two passengers at a time and performed many other services, like flying the mail or whatever could pay the fuel bills. (Courtesy of the Antique Airplane Association.)

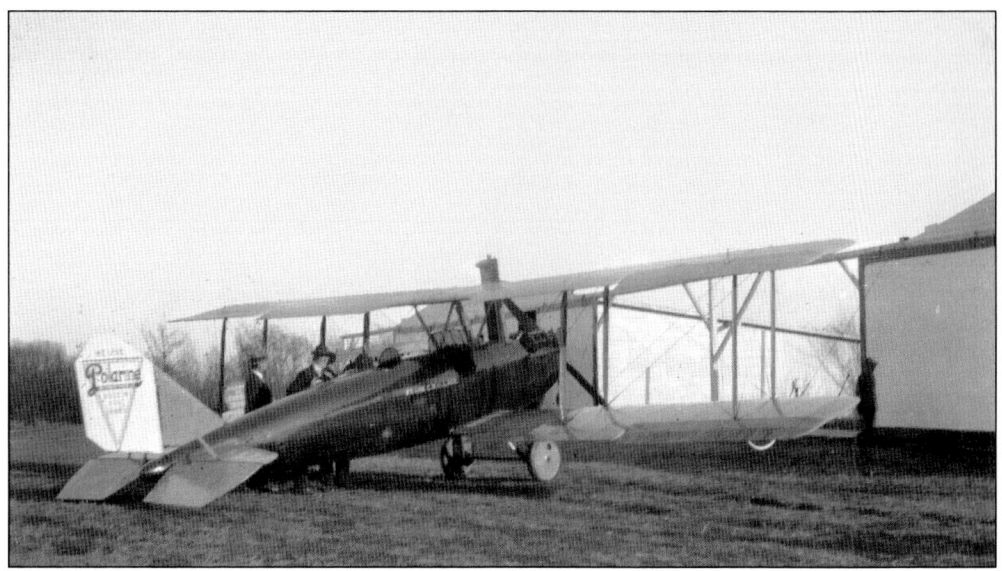

In 1919, brothers Frank and Frederick Wallace established Wallace Field, an airstrip on a 117-acre parcel of land north of Bettendorf along the Mississippi River. Their flight school was very popular and was where many Quad City citizens had their first airplane rides and later obtained pilot's licenses. The brothers also provided aircraft sales and repair service for several makes and models. (Courtesy of the Putnum Museum at Davenport.)

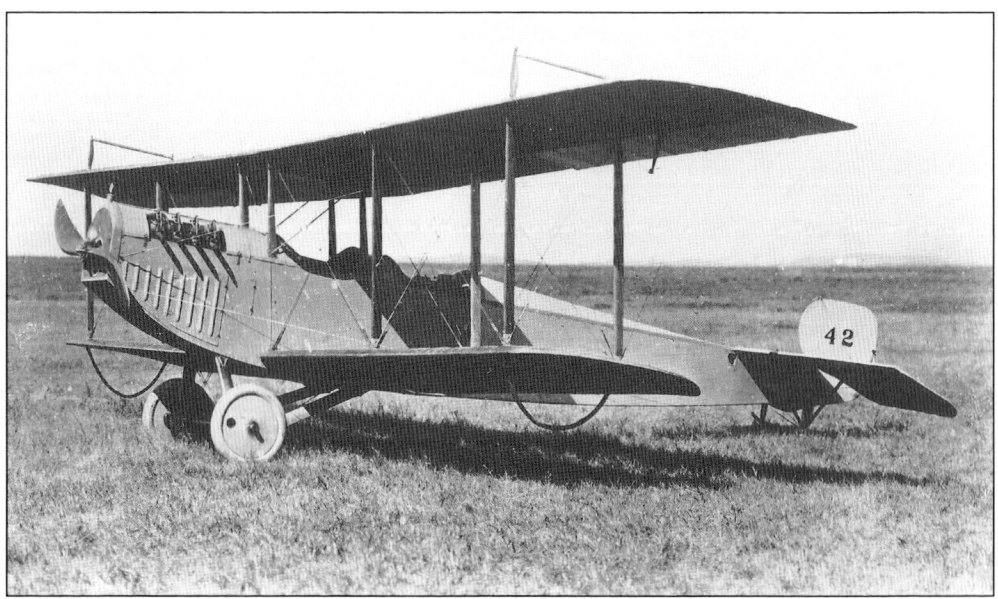

Many of the Wallace brothers' aircraft, like this Curtiss Jenny, were powered by the Curtiss V-style OX-5 and similar engines. The Wallaces installed new factory engines for their customers, promising to either sell the old engine for the aircraft owner or purchase and rebuild it for their own training aircraft. Frank later helped design and build the Monocoupe with Clayton Folkerts and Don Luscombe, eventually moving that venture across the river to Moline. (Courtesy of the Antique Airplane Association.)

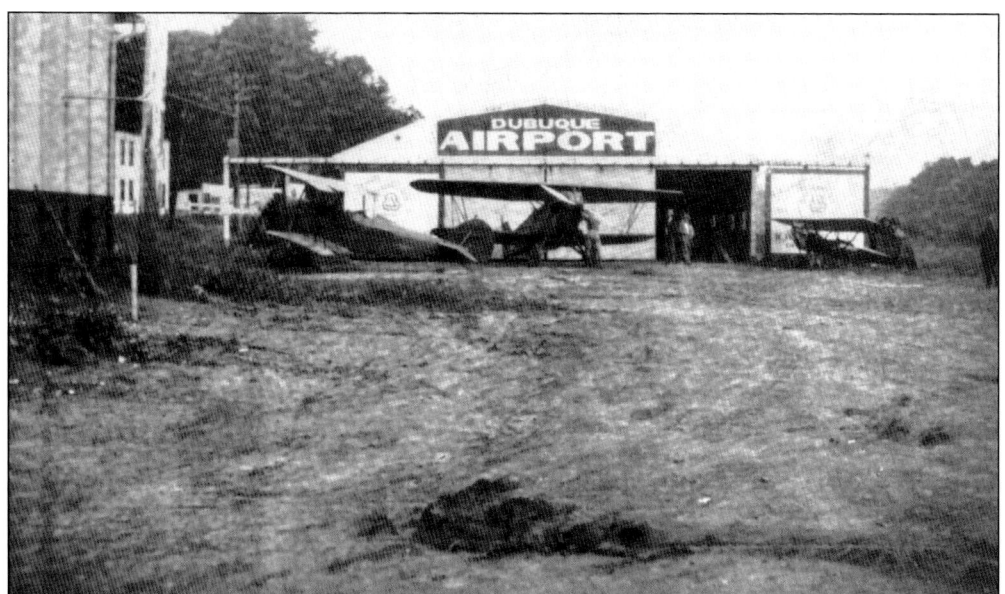

Dubuque Airfield was located at Nutwood Park. The 1,200-foot strip was shielded by high hills along its length and electrical wires across each end of the runway. Lincoln Beachey's performances there in the early years inspired an entire generation of barnstormers, including Lewis Boxleiter, Harry Chambers, Ralph Reed, DeWitt Collins, Harold Ownby, Ed Tegeler, and Clifton "Ole" Oleson. (Courtesy of the State Historical Society of Iowa at Iowa City.)

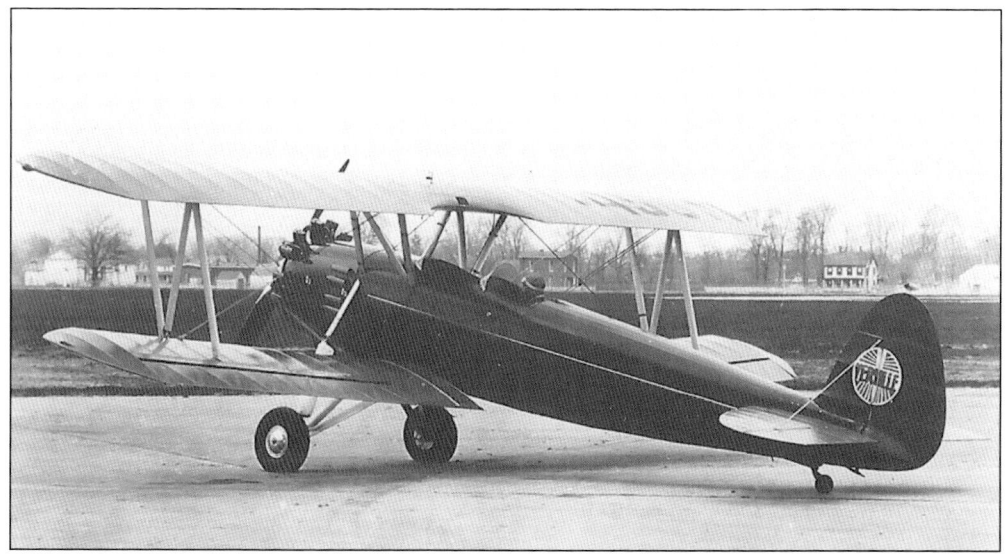

Harry Chambers was voted "Outstanding Flying Instructor for Iowa" after teaching his students in a variety of airplanes operating from Dubuque's treacherous grass strip, including the usual Jennys, Waco 10s, Waco 90s, Great Lakes 2T-1As, Travel Airs, and Verville Sport Trainers (pictured here), as well as a few hybrid aircraft constructed from various parts. (Courtesy of the Antique Airplane Association.)

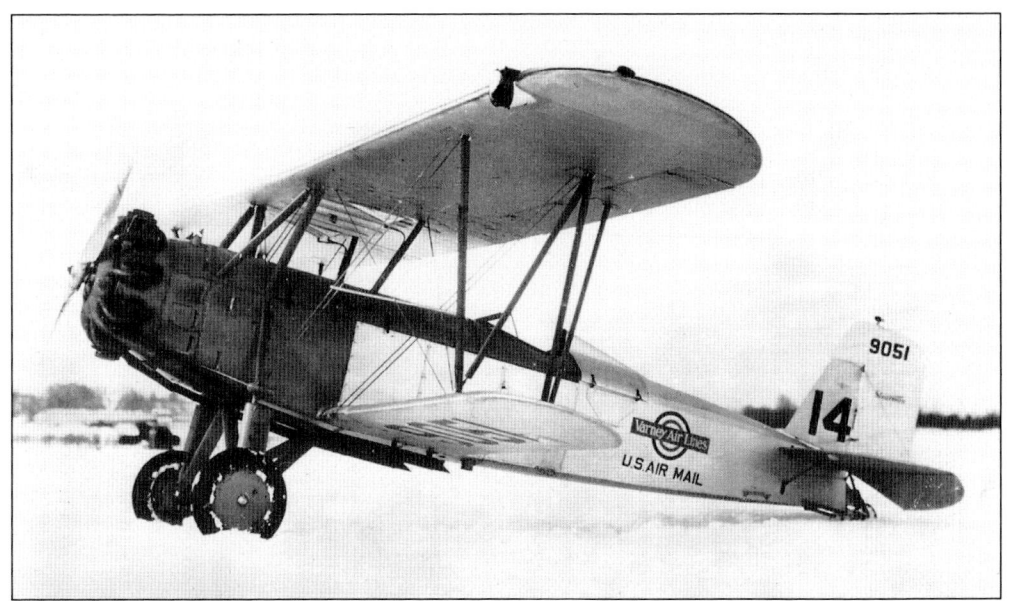

Regular airmail service had been a dream since early pioneers like Lincoln Beachey proved the airplane's effectiveness in making deliveries. The US Postal Service granted contracts to various businesses that wanted to serve regions in various parts of the country, but the service was fragmented and unreliable, often affected by bad weather. Airplanes like this Stearman biplane had an open cockpit at the rear with an enclosed cargo area up front for mail sacks. The cargo area could also be converted to carry passengers. (Courtesy of the Antique Airplane Association.)

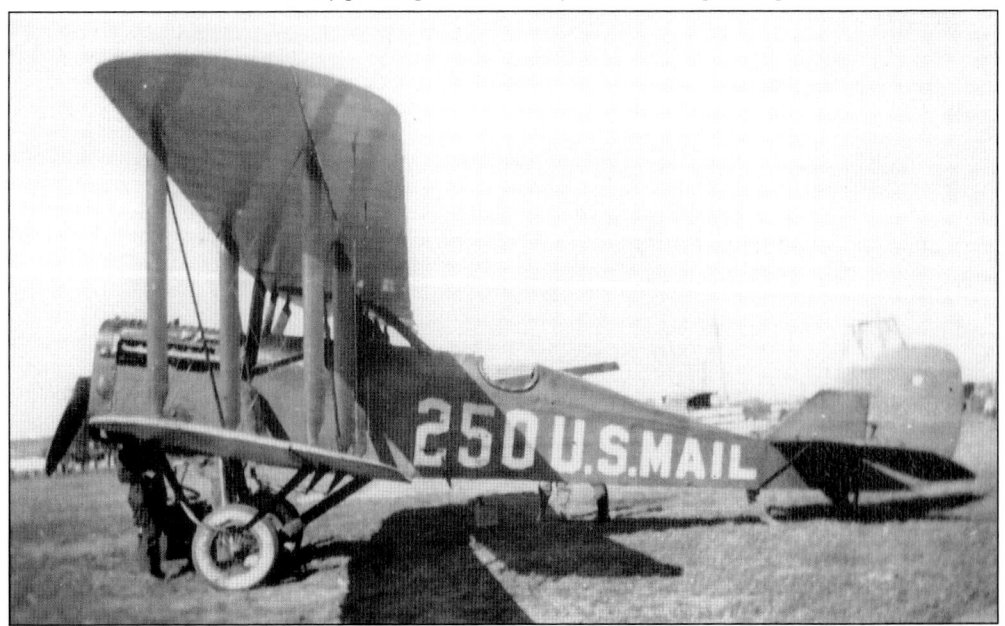

The long-awaited coast-to-coast US Air Mail Service made its inaugural flight in 1918. War surplus DeHavilland DH-4s made up most of the fleet. Iowa City was designated as one of the original alternate spur airports but got almost as much business as the main route field, as bad weather often forced pilots to land there to wait out a storm between Omaha and Chicago. (Courtesy of the Iowa City Municipal Airport.)

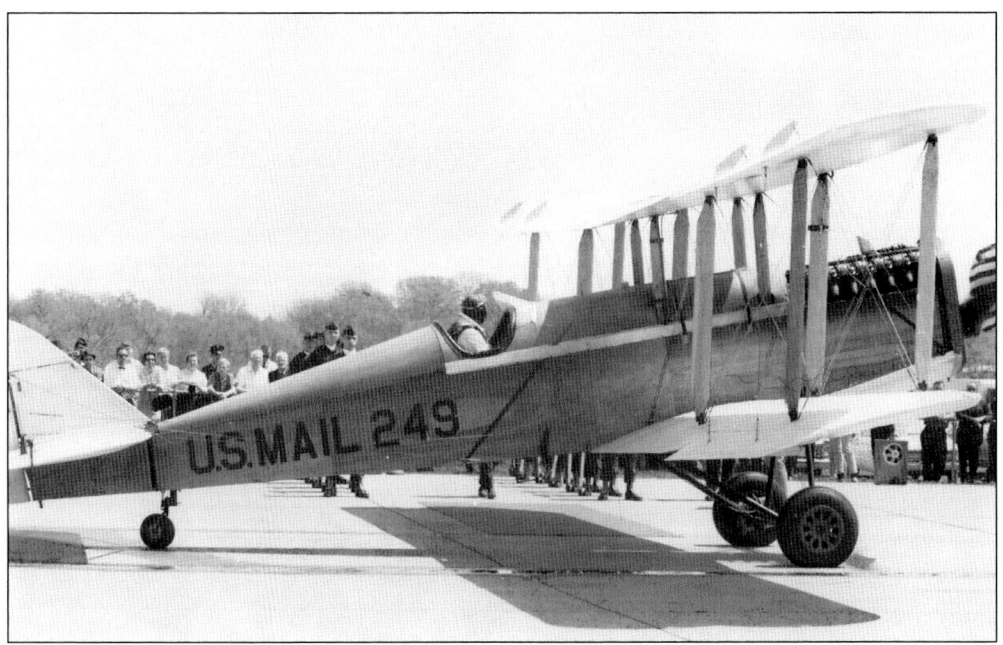

Iowa City citizens packed the airfield just to see one of the new mail planes, which were a novelty. The United States was divided into three main cross-country routes: New York to Chicago; Chicago to Cheyenne, Wyoming; and Cheyenne to San Francisco, covering a total of 2,665 miles. Each plane carried 400 pounds (about 16,000 letters). (Courtesy of the Iowa City Municipal Airport.)

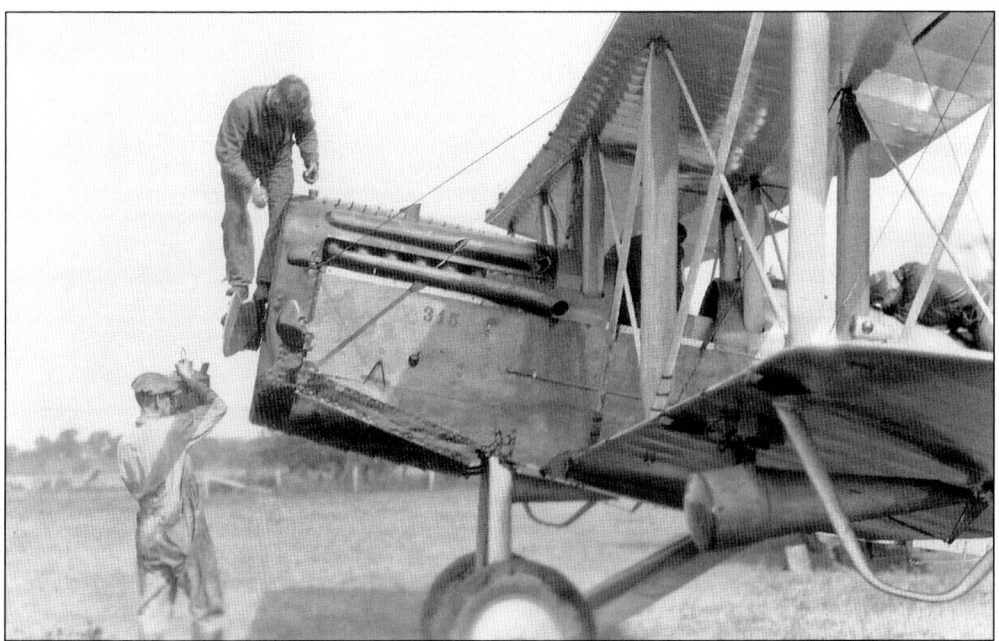

These "flying trucks" required constant maintenance and repairs. The "grease monkeys" (mechanics) and "beezers" (pilots) worked together, sometimes all night and often out in the open when necessary, knowing that the success or failure of the fledgling airmail service, as well as each pilot's life, rested on their shoulders. (Courtesy of the Iowa City Municipal Airport.)

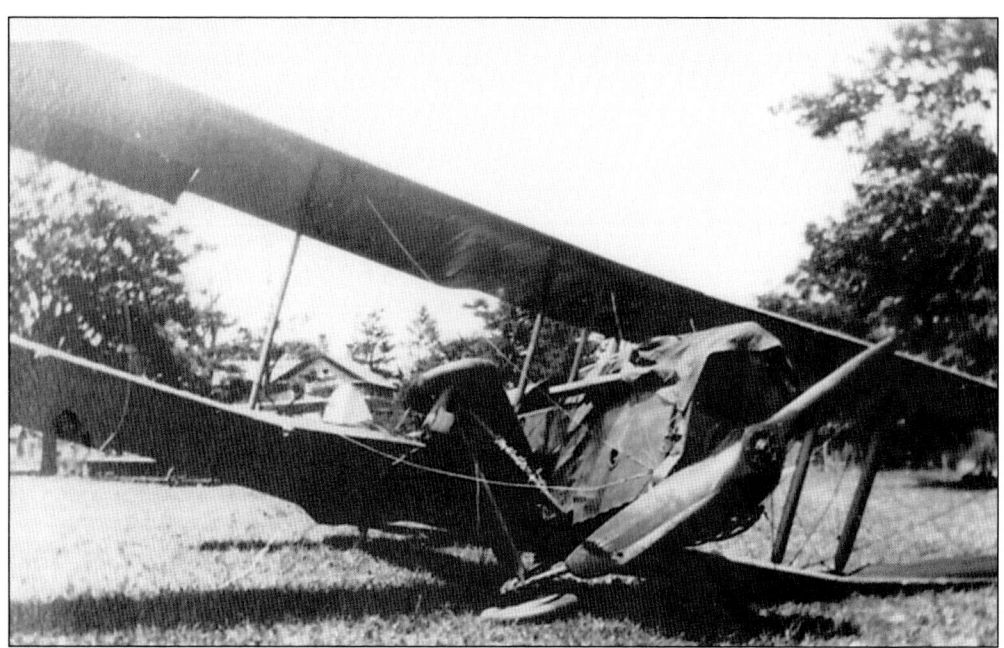

Forced landings were common all along the routes, and many pilots were lost in collisions with fog-shrouded trees and buildings, or they crashed because of fires resulting from leaky fuel lines. Of the 40 original airmail pilots, 30 died while flying the mail. Insurance companies would not cover pilots or ground crews, and stores refused to open charge accounts for pilots and their families. (Courtesy of the Antique Airplane Association.)

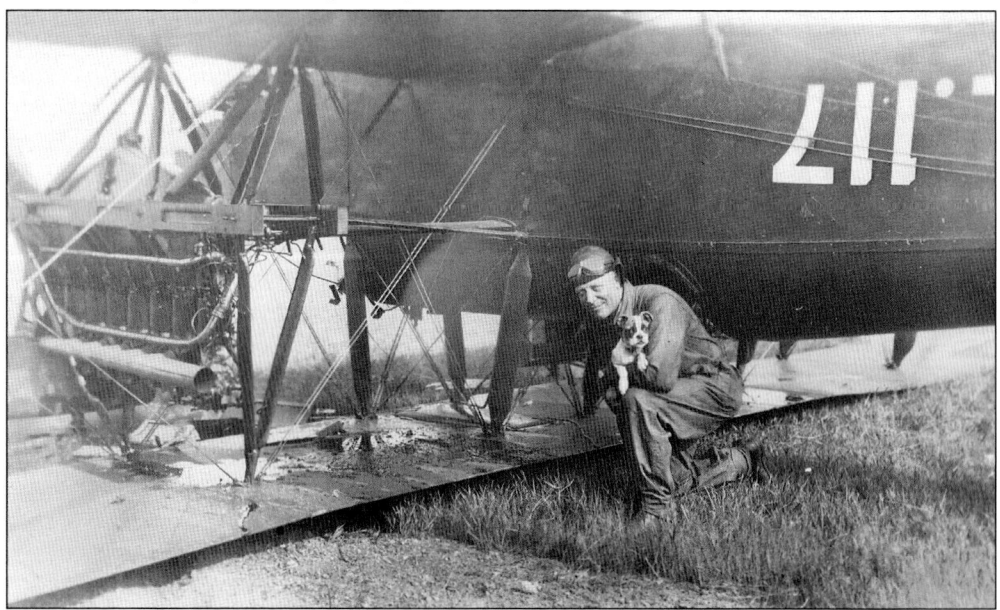

If a pilot was forced down, he was supposed to recover the mail, along with any "small passengers," and transport everything to the nearest town that had a railroad station. Each pilot used his own navigation methods. Some installed every conceivable new instrument, while others said, "An instrument panel is just something to clutter up the cockpit and distract my attention from the railroad or riverbed I'm following." (Courtesy of the Antique Airplane Association.)

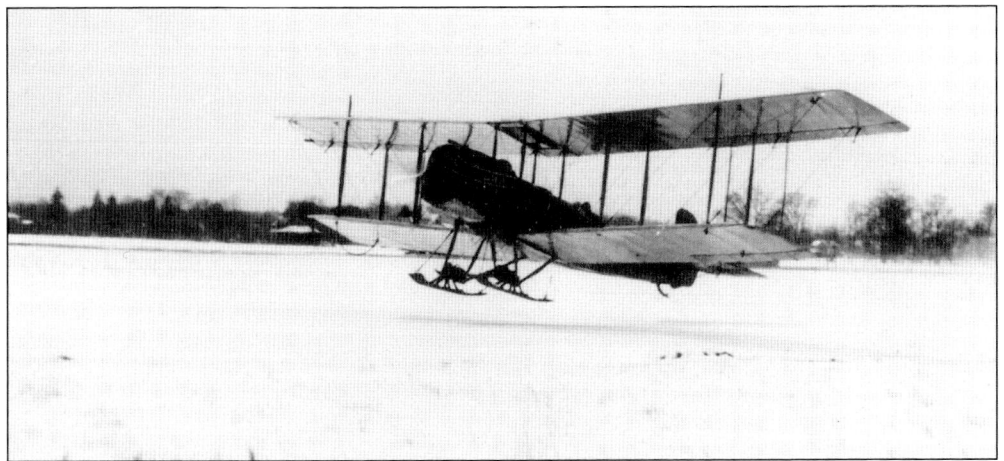

Airmail pilots were required to fly regardless of weather. This included unexpected snowstorms in early fall or late spring in the Midwest. Many pilots kept a notebook containing names and telephone numbers of farmers along the route, never knowing where they might be forced down. (Courtesy of the Antique Airplane Association.)

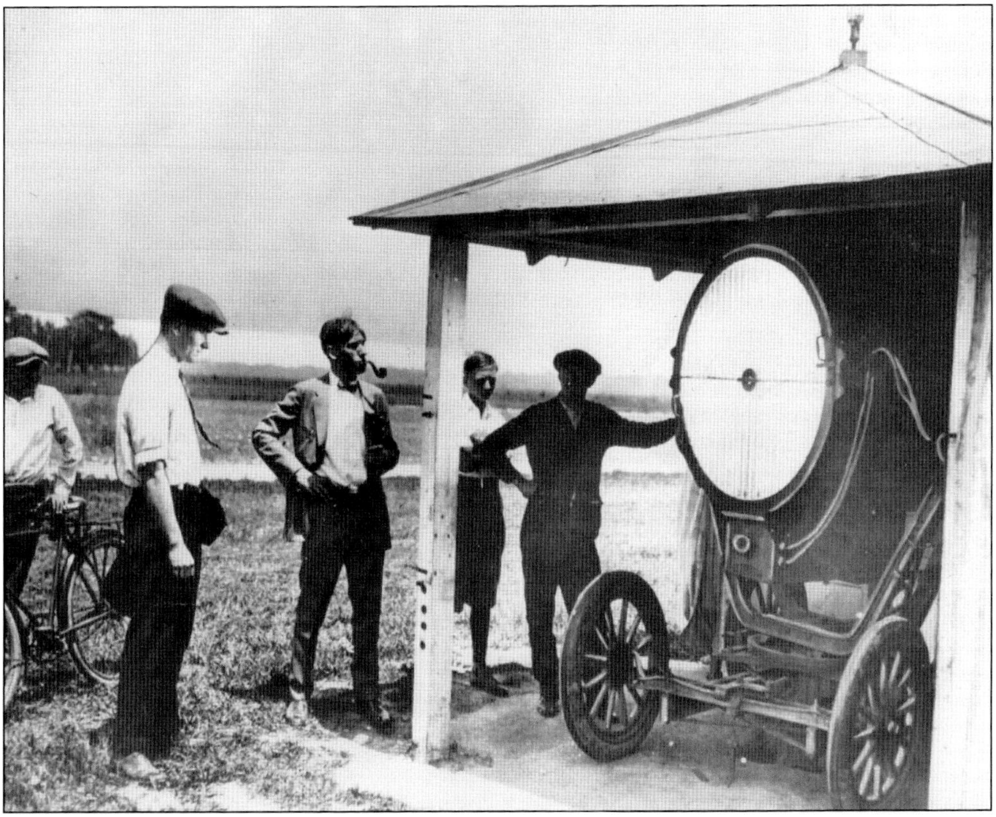

Since there was no established cross-country navigation or lighting system, pilots worked with airport operators to create effective, stronger, and better-placed lights at airports and strategically selected sites along each route. Citizens were recruited to light bonfires or turn on spotlights at specific times when a pilot might be flying overhead and in need of guidance to the next destination. (Courtesy of the Antique Airplane Association.)

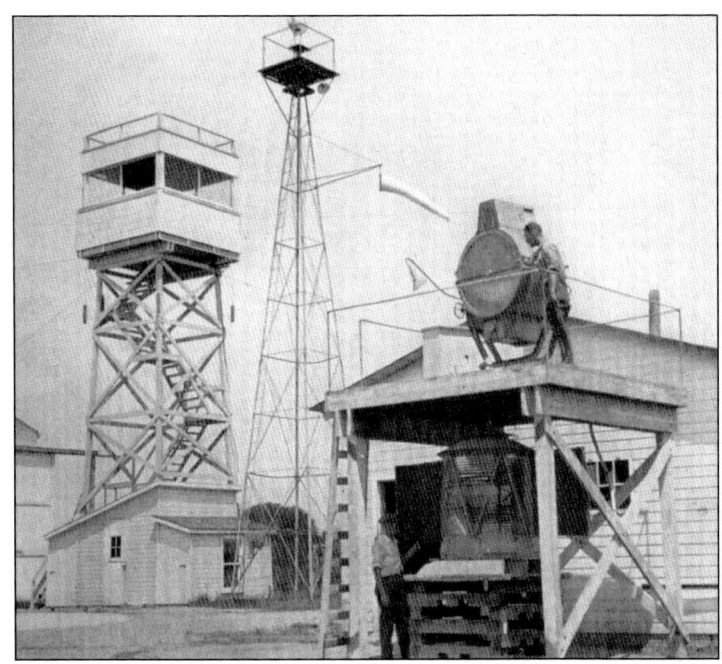

Iowa City's airport became one of the most reliable supporting nighttime airmail flights. A tall observation tower, elevated strong searchlight, and the latest weather information were available not only for airmail pilots, but for anyone flying across the Midwest. On a cold, February night in 1921, that system proved to be a crucial factor in saving the US Air Mail Service. (Courtesy of the Iowa City Municipal Airport.)

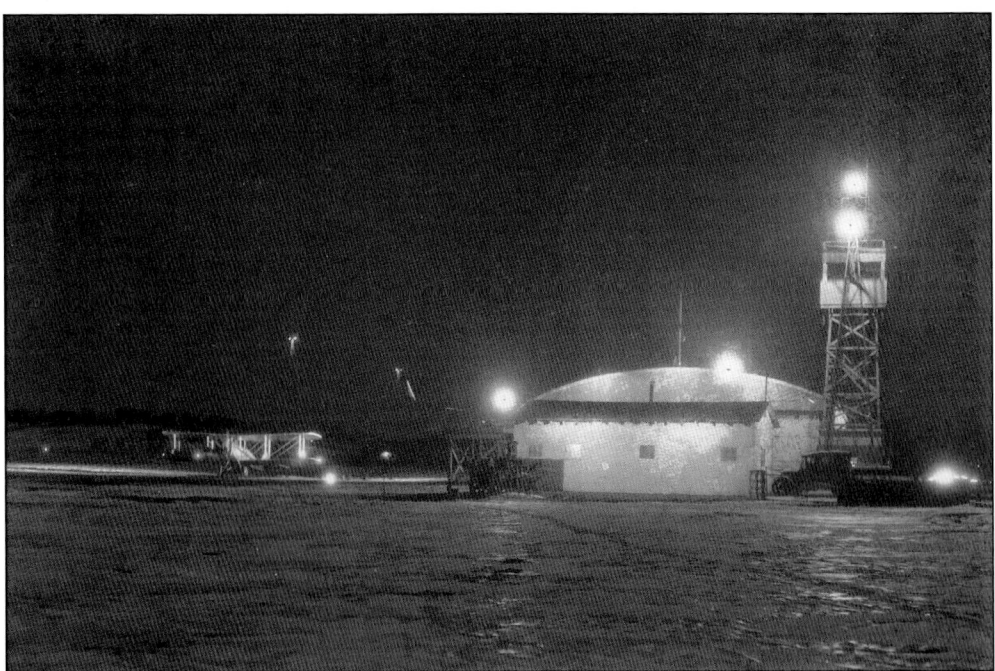

To persuade Congress to continue funding the expensive service, airmail executives planned a record-breaking, coast-to-coast demonstration flight. Two airplanes would leave from each coast and fly in a Pony Express–style relay system in both directions, intending to cover the distance in 36 hours, about one-third the time it took locomotives to cover the same distance. The future of the airmail service rested on this flight, with the nighttime legs being the most crucial. (Courtesy of the Iowa City Municipal Airport.)

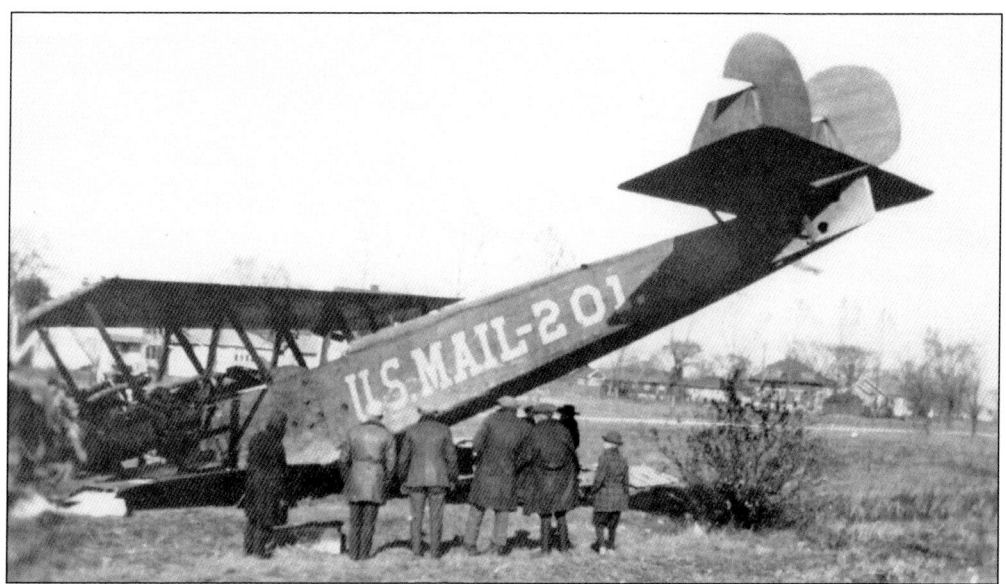

The date set for the "Big Relay" was February 22, 1921. The planes were to takeoff from each coast at dawn. There would be no radio communication for the nighttime legs of the relay, so citizens along the route were encouraged to light bonfires as guides for the pilots. The eastbound pilots, leaving from San Francisco, had good weather at first, but at Elko, Nevada, William Lewis, a young pilot who was to be married a week later, suddenly crashed and was killed. The other eastbound plane headed on to Cheyenne, Wyoming. (Courtesy of the Antique Airplane Association.)

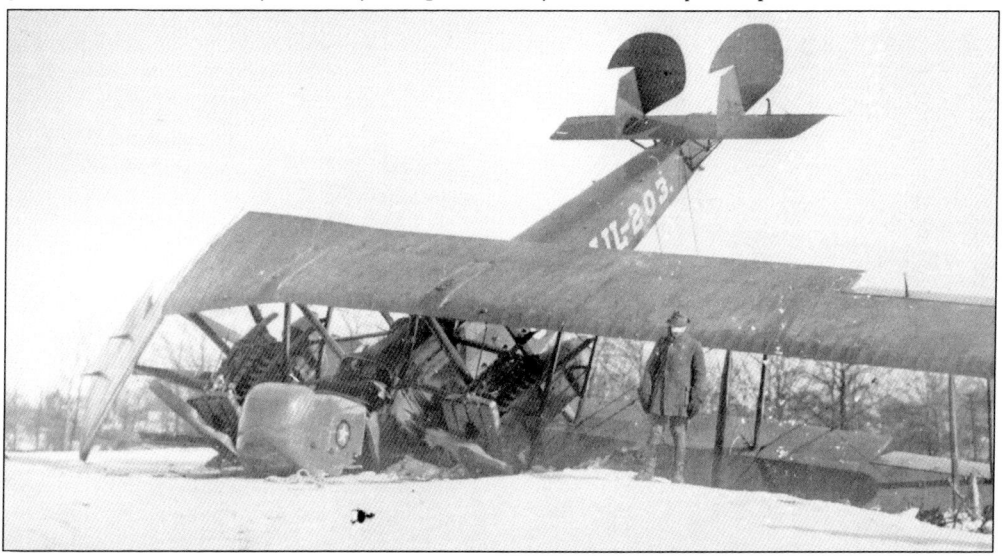

Meanwhile, the westbound planes, leaving from New York, encountered bad weather in the "Hell Stretch" of Pennsylvania. One plane was forced down in a snow squall. The other plane, trying to get to Chicago, was forced to wait in Cleveland for the weather to clear. The only mail plane left of the original four landed in darkness at North Platte, Nebraska, where veteran pilot Jack Knight took over. Knight had just flown his regular route from Omaha to North Platte earlier that day and was still stiff and sore from injuries he had received in a mountain crash the week before in Wyoming. Due to some repairs to the airplane, it was 11 p.m. before Knight took off for Omaha. (Courtesy of the Antique Airplane Association.)

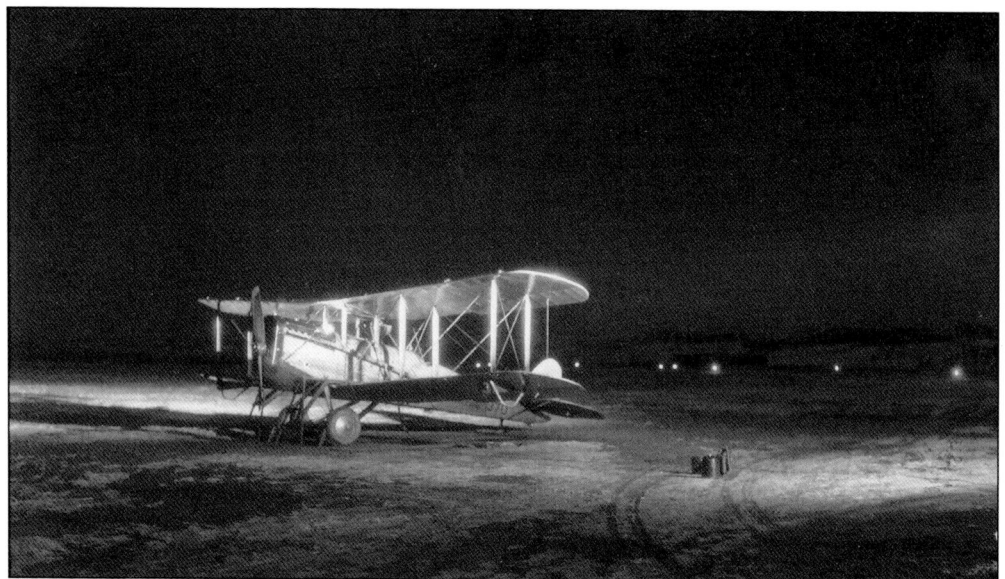

Reaching Omaha at 1:00 a.m., Knight was expecting to hand off his mail sacks to the westbound pilot from Chicago, who would make the return flight. But that airplane was still in Cleveland, and there was nobody left to get the mail across Iowa to Chicago. Knight told the airport manager, "It seems a shame to quit this flight when we've gotten the mail halfway. I'll take 'er on through to Chicago. If people will keep lighting bonfires, I can make it." By now it was 2:00 a.m., and a steady snow was falling along his route across Iowa. Knight took off and headed east. (Courtesy of the Antique Airplane Association.)

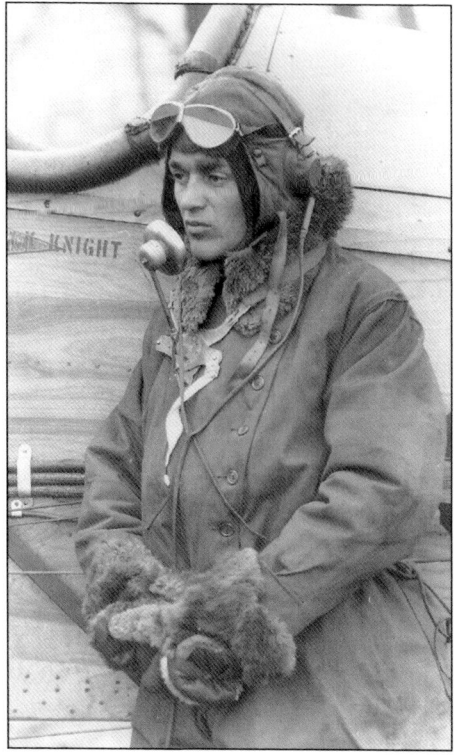

Knight could not pick out his Des Moines checkpoint through the snowy skies, but he could see railroad tracks, so he followed them eastward toward the Iowa City field. It was about 4:00 a.m. when Knight's DH-4 biplane, almost out of gas, arrived at Iowa City, which was completely dark. Knight circled the field, gunning his engine until the night watchman heard him and lit a signal fire. After the two men refueled the airplane, Knight took off and made it to Chicago, completely exhausted, just after sunrise, where the plane from Cleveland was waiting to take the mail on to New York. Knight always credited the Iowa City airfield with "saving the US Air Mail Service." (Courtesy of the Buchanan, Michigan, Historical Society.)

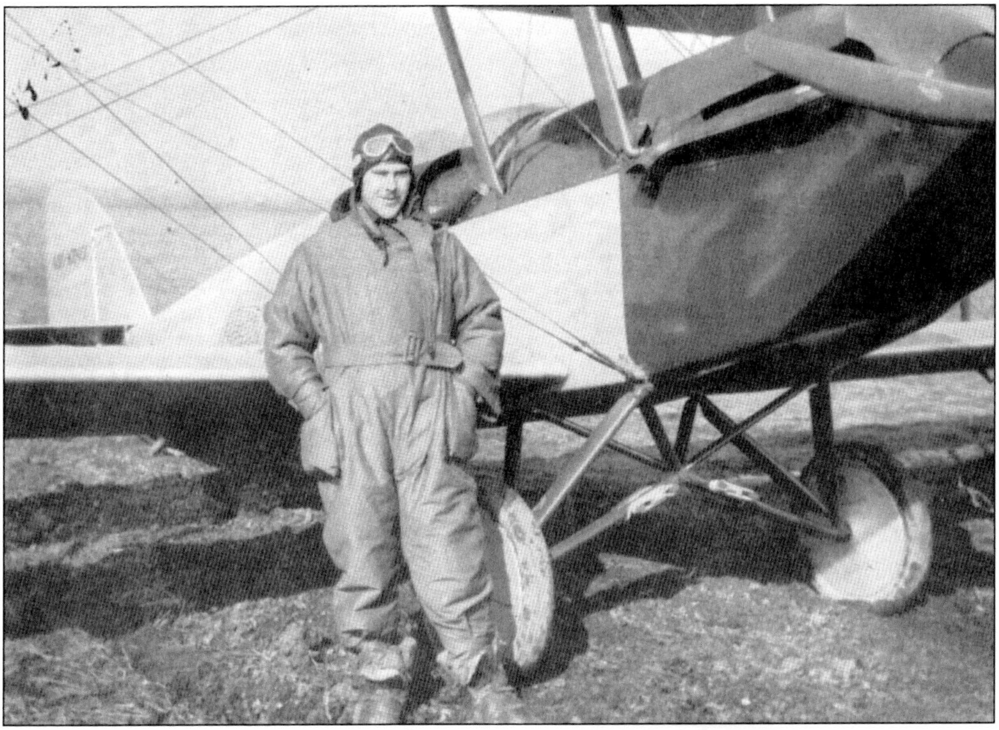

Burlington's Glen Romkey learned to fly Canucks and Avros while working for aircraft designer Ed Heath in Chicago. Teaming up with Glenn Conrad, Joe Earle, Tonkey Martin, and Al Wilson, along with female parachutists Vera Schoel and Edna Hayden, Romkey's air circus barnstormed across Iowa, Illinois, and Missouri. In 1921, he formed the Romkey Aviation Company in Burlington, starting out with three Boeing seaplanes based on the Mississippi River. (Courtesy of the Antique Airplane Association.)

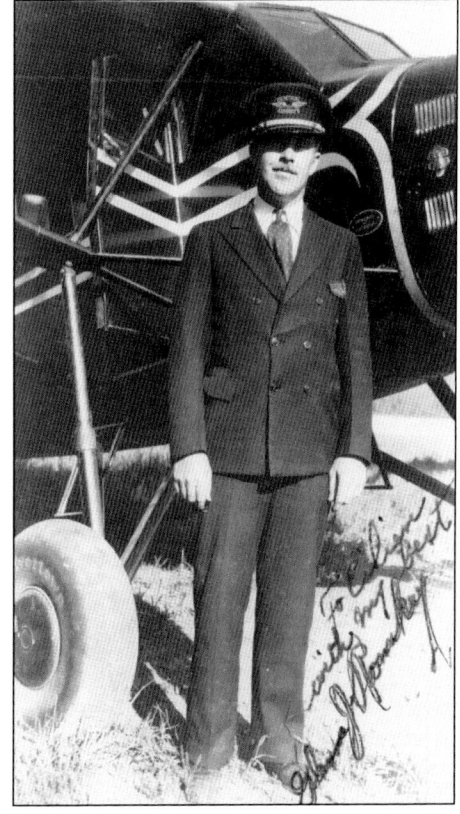

In the late 1920s, Romkey and SF Tannus formed the National Airways System. With design engineer Chet Cummings, the team built the Air-King Biplane, a three-place, open-cockpit plane powered by a Curtiss OX-5 engine. It was successful, creating many local jobs. Romkey and his group then built the Air Prince, a monoplane that was less successful, followed by the Air-King Monofour, another monoplane that used overhead controls, powered by a Wright Whirlwind engine. (Courtesy of the State of Iowa Historical Society at Iowa City.)

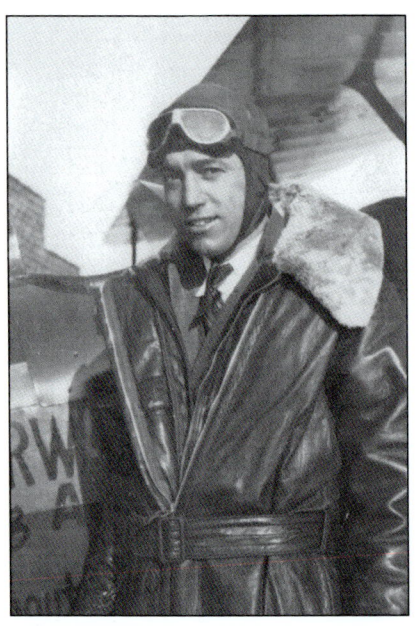

As a youngster, John Livingston's first love was building motorcycles and racing them on dirt tracks around his hometown of Cedar Falls. While working at Ike Albert's motorcycle shop in Waterloo, Livingston was offered better pay to work for the Miller Campbell Air Company (later the Miller-Scales Company) at the Byrnes Park airfield in Waterloo. Although he had never even seen an airplane engine before, he took the job, launching what would become one of the most celebrated careers in Iowa aviation. Teaching himself to fly by making faster and higher "engine tests" with the company aircraft he repaired, Livingston proved to be a natural pilot. In 1926, he entered his first cross-country air race. Even though he did not win, he impressed his competitors and the event sponsors with his clever modifications that made his airplane faster and more maneuverable. (Courtesy of the Cedar Falls Historical Society.)

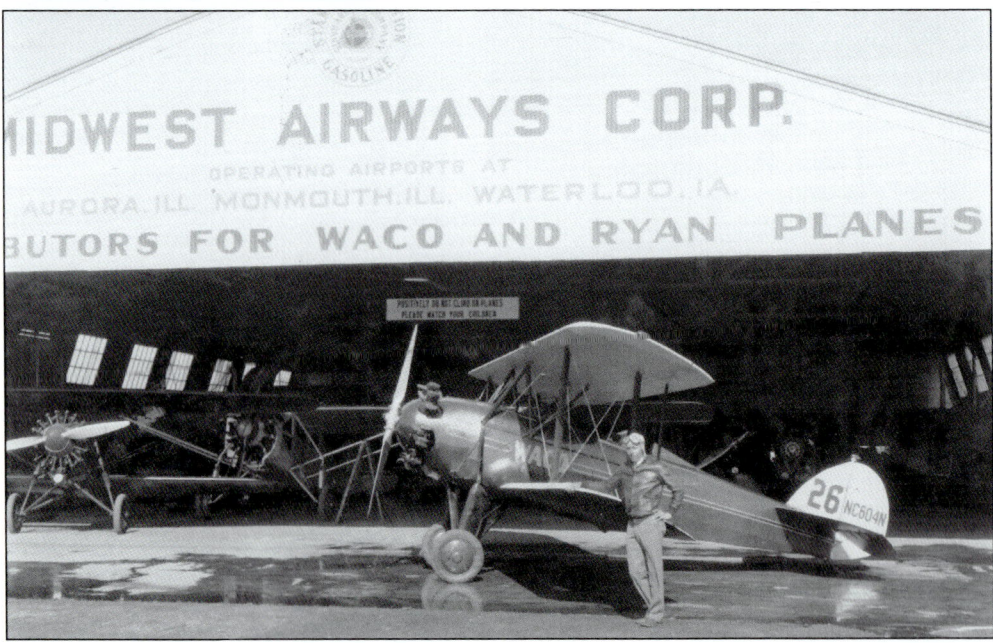

Teaming up with the Ohio-based Waco Aircraft Company, which provided parts and sponsorships, John Livingston began winning some of the biggest cross-country competitions. In 1928, he won the Transcontinental Air Race from New York to Los Angeles. When he wasn't competing, Livingston managed Midwest Airways Corporation, which was a distributor of Waco and Ryan airplanes in Illinois and Iowa. The company did a good business with new aircraft being delivered in crated pieces by rail to one of Livingston's three distributorships, where he and his employees assembled and test flew the new machines. Buyers were given several hours of familiarization instruction with their new airplane. Livingston also made trips to Troy, Ohio, to the Waco factory, where he worked test flying the new designs as they were developed. (Courtesy of the Cedar Falls Historical Society.)

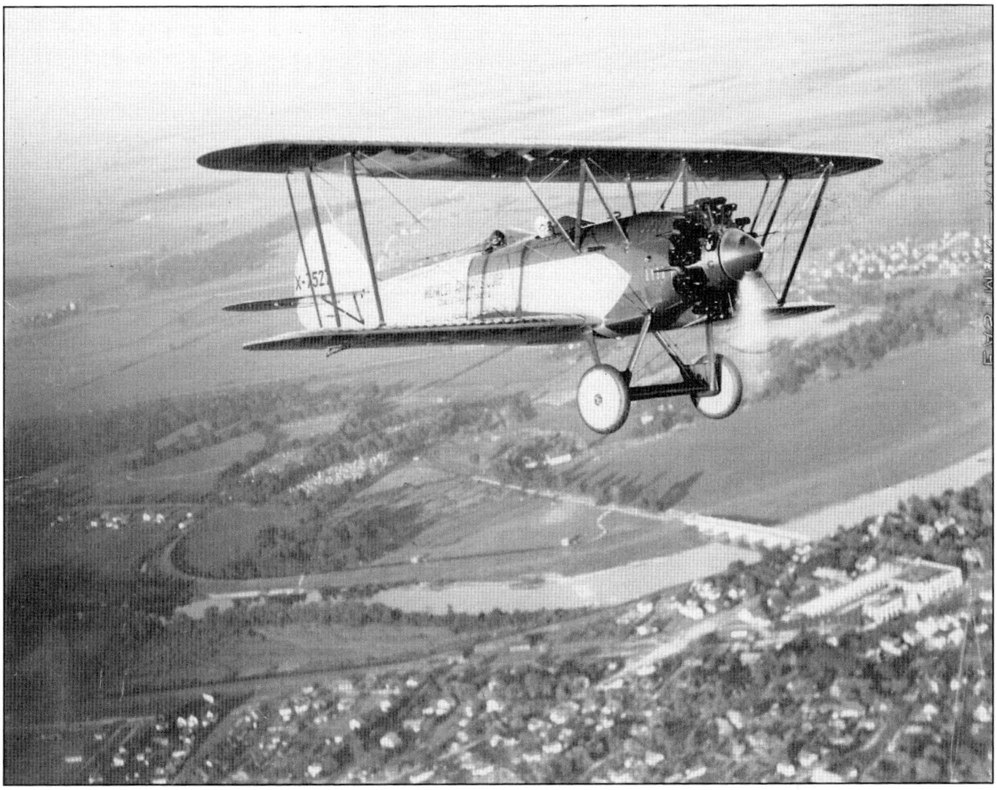

John Livingston's greatest passion was in air racing, especially when flying his Tiger Wing Waco, which contained all the latest factory-tested equipment, often modified by Livingston himself before taking the aircraft to competition. During his racing career, he finished in first place in 80 races, second place in 43, third place in 15, and fourth place three times. (Courtesy of the Cedar Falls Historical Society.)

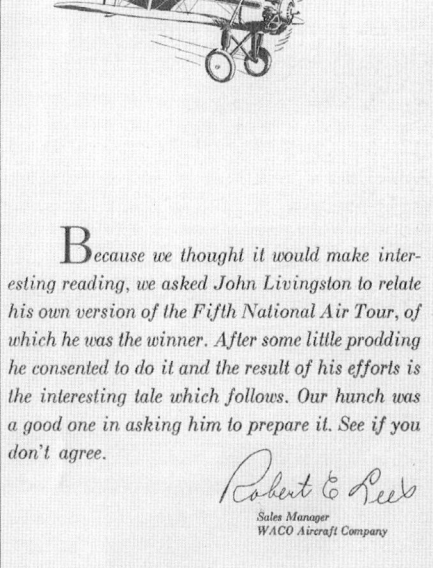

In 1929, John Livingston won the very prestigious National Air Tour, flying his modified Waco 225 Straight-Wing, powered by a seven-cylinder Wright J-6 Whirlwind engine. It was a great improvement over the Tiger Wing Waco he had flown in 1928. The company asked Livingston to author a booklet describing his magnificent victory. The publication was a huge success, and Livingston's celebrity status grew to international fame. (Courtesy of the Cedar Falls Historical Society.)

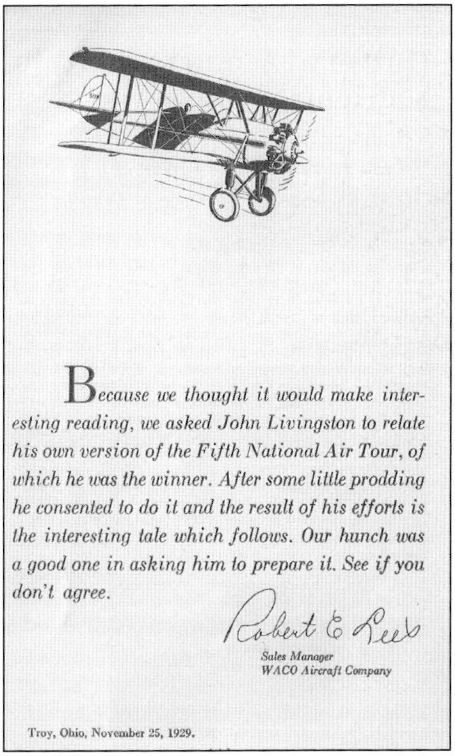

Because we thought it would make interesting reading, we asked John Livingston to relate his own version of the Fifth National Air Tour, of which he was the winner. After some little prodding he consented to do it and the result of his efforts is the interesting tale which follows. Our hunch was a good one in asking him to prepare it. See if you don't agree.

Robert E. Lee
Sales Manager
WACO Aircraft Company

Troy, Ohio, November 25, 1929.

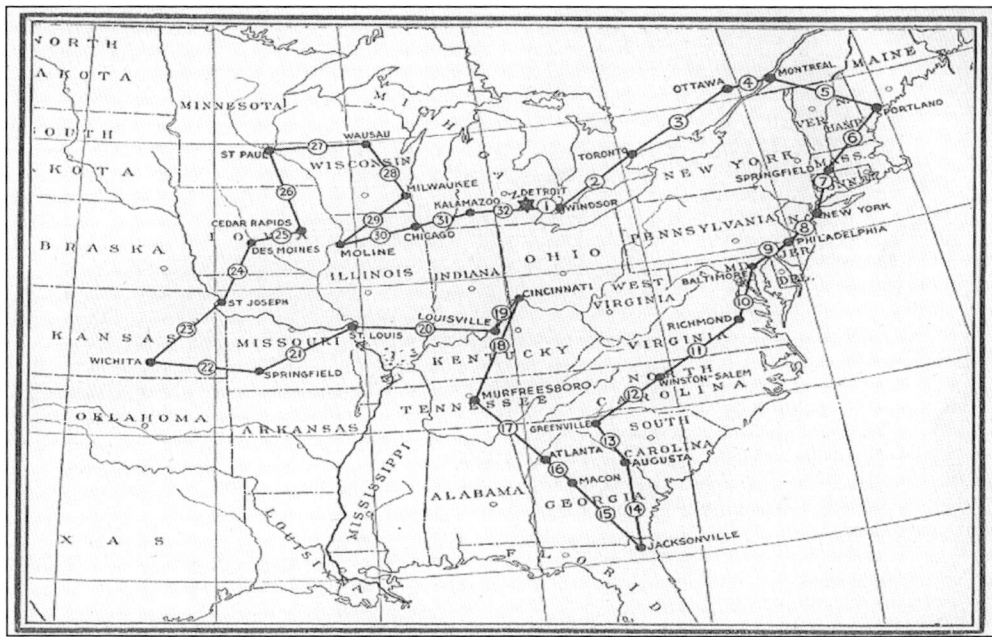

The route of the fifth National Air Tour covered 5,000 miles. Pilots accumulated points using a formula based on five factors: useful load, high speed, take-off time, time to dead-stop landing, and engine displacement. Starting in Dearborn, Michigan, on October 5, 1929, each competitor had to travel 32 legs (including two in Iowa). John Livingston maintained a perfect score on each leg, averaging over 130 miles per hour. (Courtesy of the Cedar Falls Historical Society.)

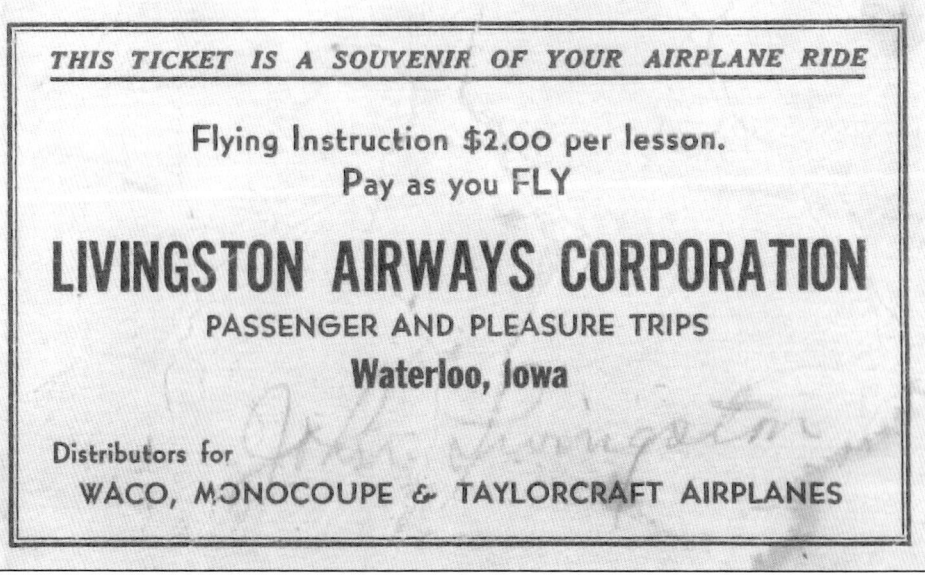

With his notoriety, Livingston could afford to expand his business ventures, buying out his original employer in Waterloo. Livingston Airways Corporation offered flight instruction, sightseeing, passenger services, and airfreight flights to existing aircraft sales and maintenance services. It also added the Monocoupe and Taylorcraft lines to its distributorships—it was just the beginning. (Courtesy of the Cedar Falls Historical Society.)

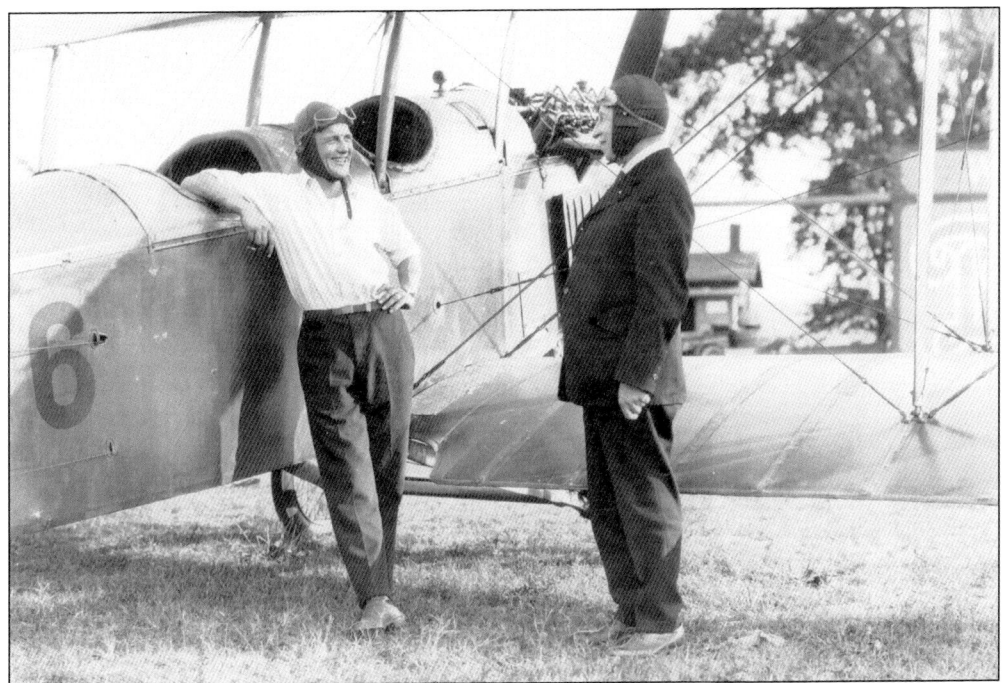

In Davenport, Ralph Cram (right), publisher of the *Davenport Morning Democrat*, was fulfilling a boyhood dream. Since his first airplane ride in the late 1910s, Cram wanted to be part of aviation. In 1923, he helped form the National Aeronautics Association. Seen here with pilot Freddie Carlson, Cram took over the development of a property on the west side of the city into an airfield. (Courtesy of the Putnum Museum of Davenport.)

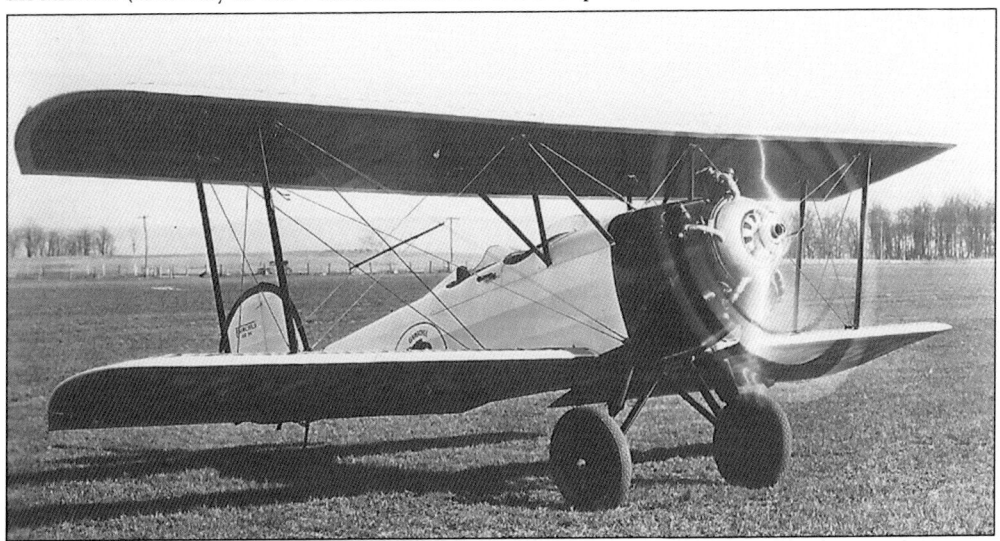

Cram Field was dedicated on November 12, 1928, and quickly became one of Iowa's busiest airports. Wade Rothwell opened a flying school there, and Lawrence Pedigo managed operations, offering seaplane instruction and a widely acclaimed mechanic school. Aircraft like this Fairchild KR-J4, as well as models produced by Waco, Stearman, Taylorcraft, and Piper, were used for flight instruction and passenger services. Ralph Cram finally soloed in 1931 on his 62nd birthday. (Courtesy of the Antique Airplane Association.)

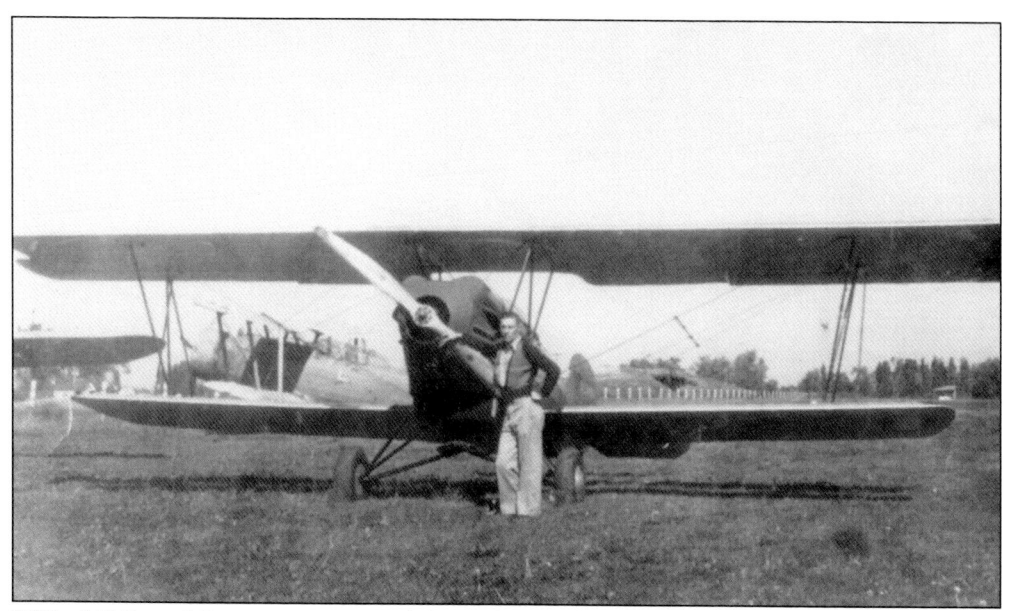

Willard Talley of Ottumwa was one of the early Iowa barnstormers and innovators. He started out flying J-1 Standards powered by Curtiss OX-5 engines. Shortly after his first solo flight, Talley joined a flying circus and performed loops, spins, and falling leaves, as well as doing his share of wing walking and transferring from cars to planes on a rope ladder. Talley attached fuses to his wingtips and rudder, which were lit before he took off. They created colorful trails as he performed loops and barrel rolls for the crowds. In addition to stunt flying, Talley also worked for Shell Oil Company, and, along with business partner John Thompson, used their Curtiss Jenny to drop handbills and carry passengers. (Courtesy of the Antique Airplane Association.)

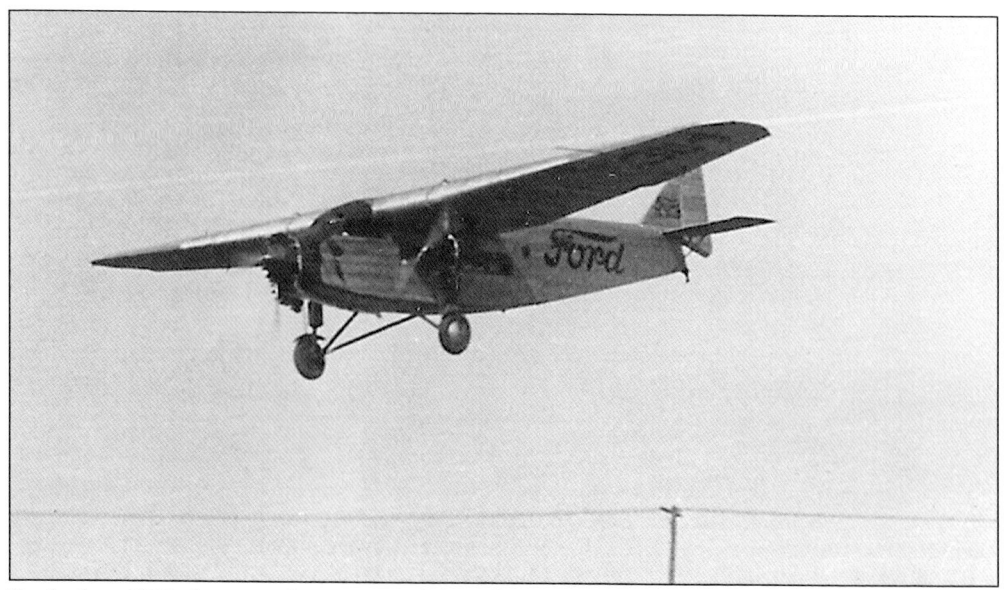

By the late 1920s, larger and more powerful airplanes began arriving in Iowa, carrying passengers in enclosed cabins, such as this Ford Tri-Motor. It was a reliable favorite with airlines that were starting to fly scheduled routes, using many of the original airmail fields to serve communities that were close to railroad lines. (Courtesy of the Antique Airplane Association.)

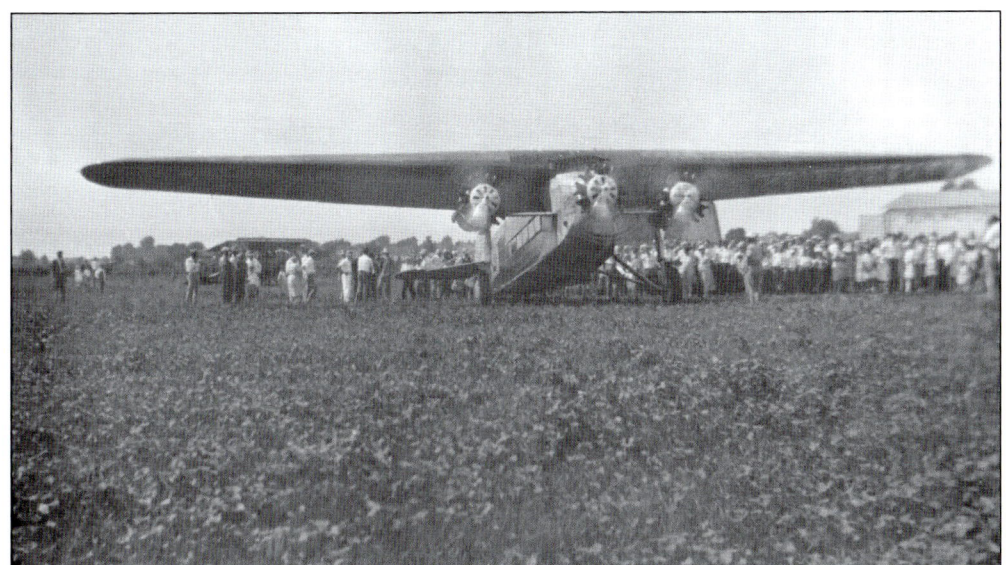

Just like the mail planes of the early 1920s, the bigger airliners drew large crowds in the late 1920s, such as this group gathered around a Ford Tri-Motor in Keokuk. While the early barnstormers had thrilled people with their stunts, these commercial pilots hoped to convince the average citizen that air travel was not only safe, but also comfortable and convenient. (Courtesy of the Antique Airplane Association.)

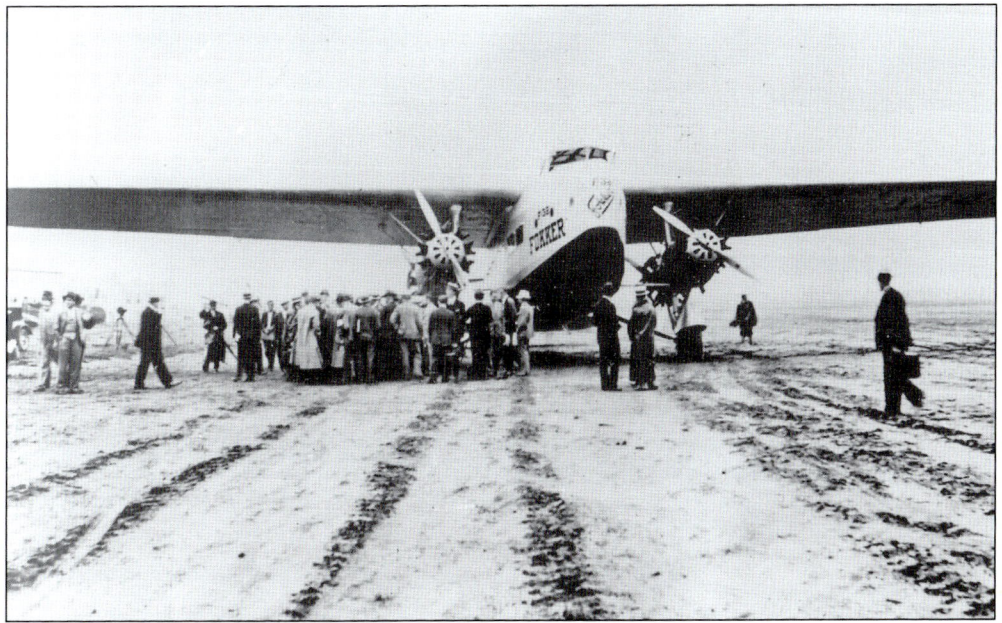

European countries were also developing their own fleets of powered aircraft and were anxious to show the world they could compete with American designs. Anthony Fokker, who had designed many of the best German fighter airplanes of World War I, produced several large passenger airplanes such as the Fokker F-32 (pictured) and the Fokker F-10, a trimotor aircraft that was a competitor with Ford's airliner until one crashed in a Kansas field, killing Notre Dame football coach Knute Rockne. After that, Fokker's days of selling airplanes in America were over. (Courtesy of the Antique Airplane Association.)

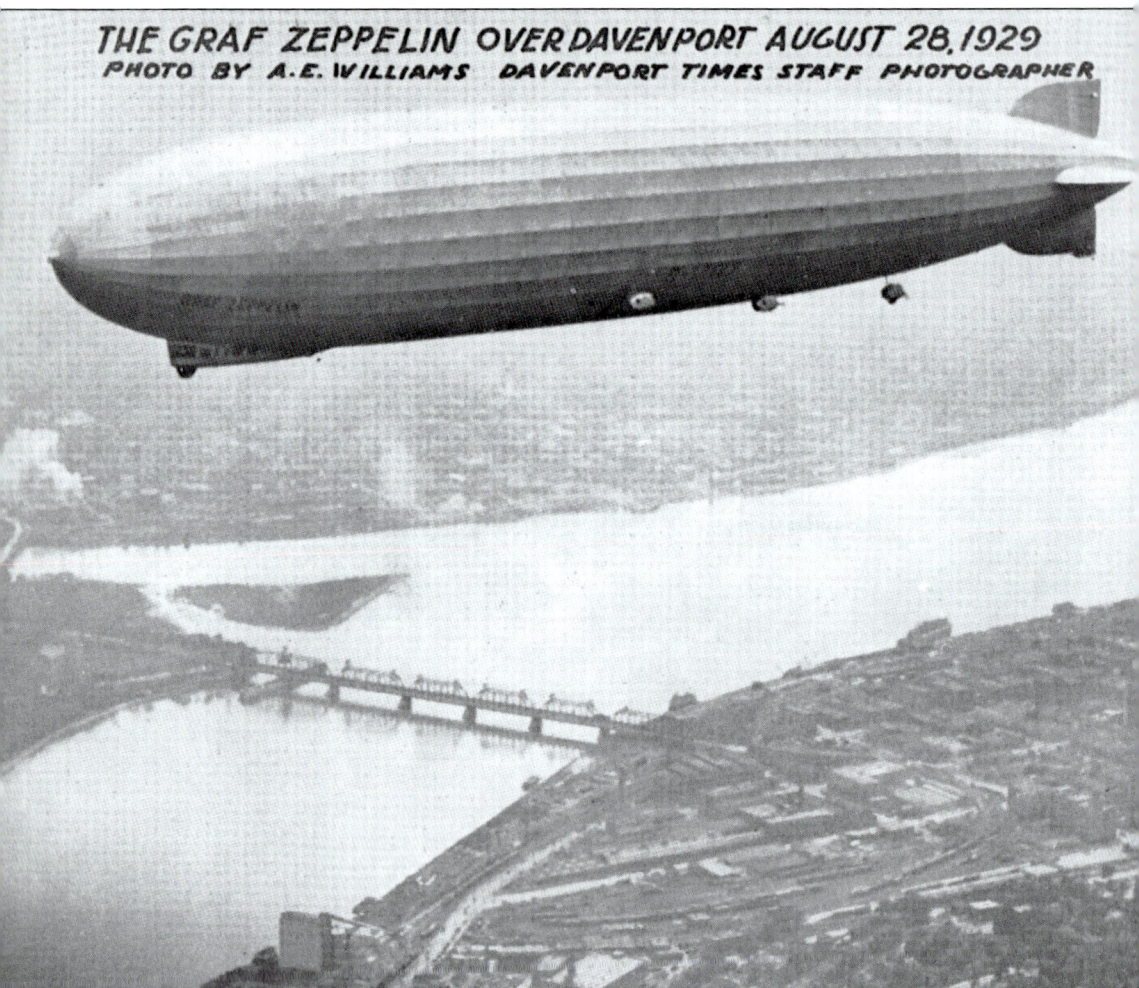

Germany also committed millions of dollars toward the development of lighter-than-air dirigibles and sent the mighty Graf Zeppelin on a worldwide tour to promote that style of air travel, as well as Germany's leadership in aviation engineering. Here, the Graf Zeppelin flies above Davenport's river levy area as the Roaring Twenties come to a close. Aviation was about to enter what would come to be called its Golden Age. (Courtesy of the *Quad City Times* at Davenport.)

Four

AVIATION'S GOLDEN AGE
1930 TO 1940

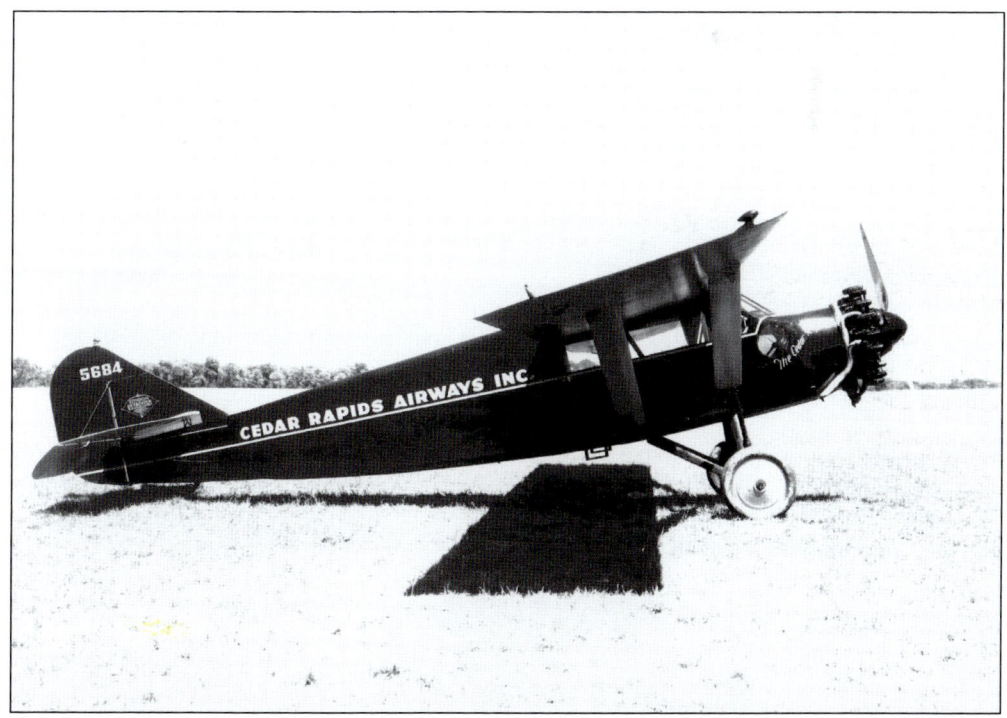

As Iowa began the 1930s, its barnstormers with their circus acts and stunts made room for the dreamers who envisioned air travel with less flamboyance. Aircraft with enclosed, heated cabins like Travel Airs, Howards, and this Stinson Detroiter were used at eastern Iowa airports to carry passengers and cargo to connecting flights at larger cities like Chicago, St. Louis, and Kansas City. (Courtesy of the Carl & Mary Koehler History Center, The Linn County Historical Society.)

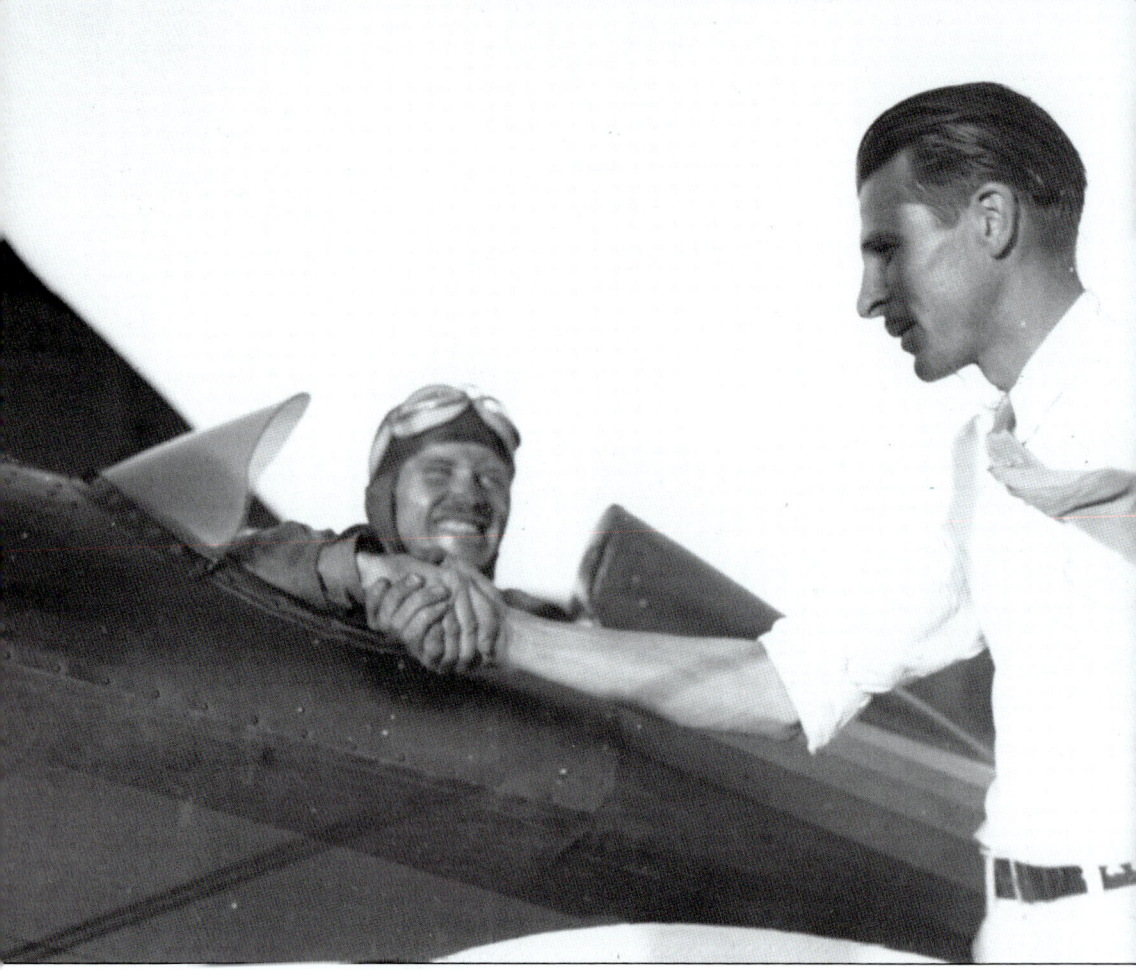

With the advent of commercial airline service, airports needed to expand. The old grass strips were replaced with concrete and asphalt surfaces that could accommodate larger, heavier aircraft as well as ground support equipment and navigational aids. In tough economic times, local commercial aviation supporters teamed up with some of the old barnstormers to attract attention and promote aviation. Local businessmen like Ed Tegeler (right), a Dubuque automobile dealer and private pilot, arranged air shows that often included free commercial aircraft rides for people after they had seen the show at the airport. Here, Tegeler congratulates performer Roy O. Hunt upon completion of his record-breaking flight on July 5, 1931, when Hunt flew 124 outside loops in 124 minutes. (Courtesy of the State of Iowa Historical Society at Iowa City.)

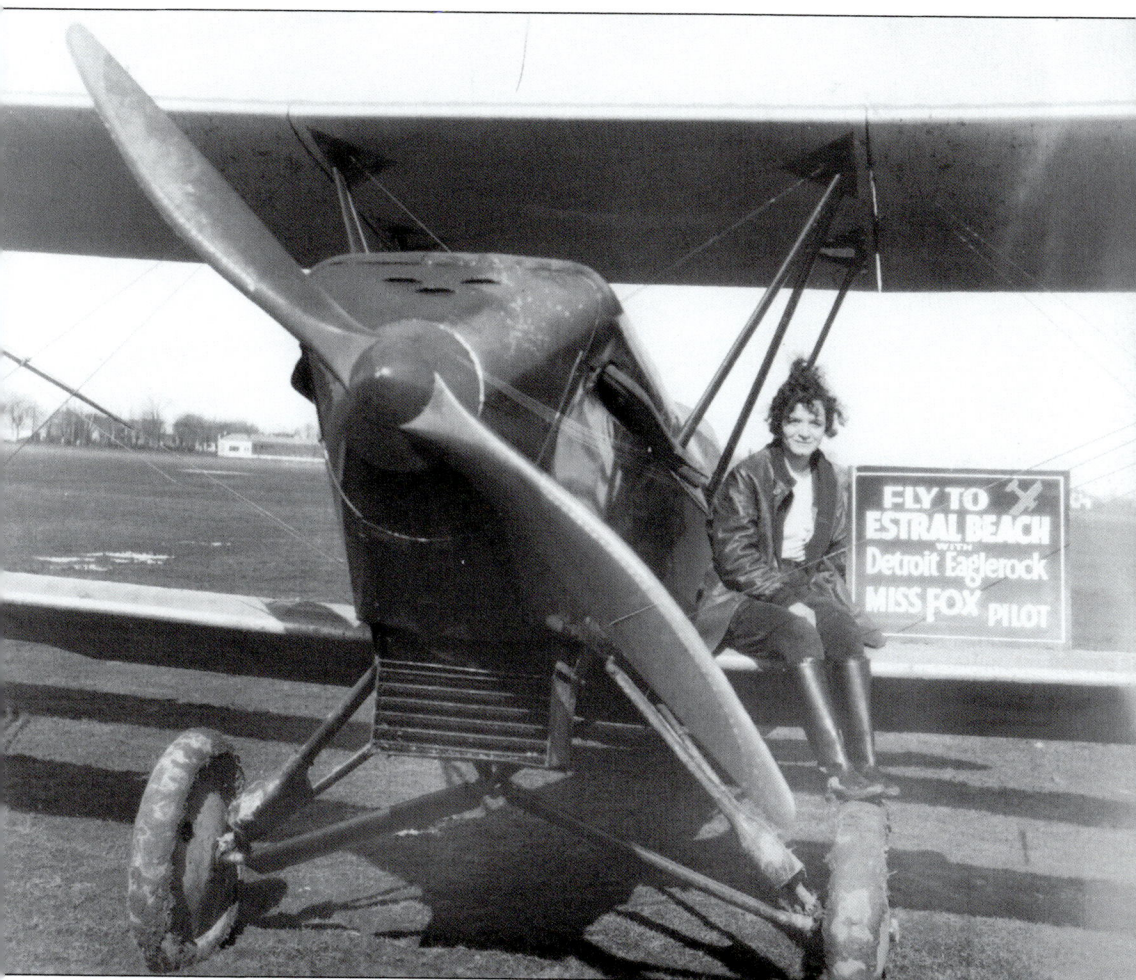

Ila Fox was from Pella, Iowa, attended Central College before going on and graduating from the University of Iowa. Upon moving to Davenport in the late 1920s, she began taking flying lessons from Leo Brennan at Cram Field. To supplement her income, Fox assisted Rusty Campbell in promoting aviation across the river at the Moline Airport, where she continued her flight instruction with Pat Miller. She often helped entertain weekend crowds by flying with Miller in the front seat and answering aviation questions afterwards. She dressed the part by wearing a white leather jacket, tight jodhpur breeches, and black riding boots. She kept all her flying exploits a secret from her family. When she soloed, becoming the first woman in the Davenport area to do so, it made all the newspapers, and her secret was out. To her surprise, her family was not only supportive but proud of her achievements and encouraged her to continue her training. When she received her pilot's license, Fox became the first Iowa woman to achieve that goal. (Courtesy of the State Historical Society of Iowa at Iowa City.)

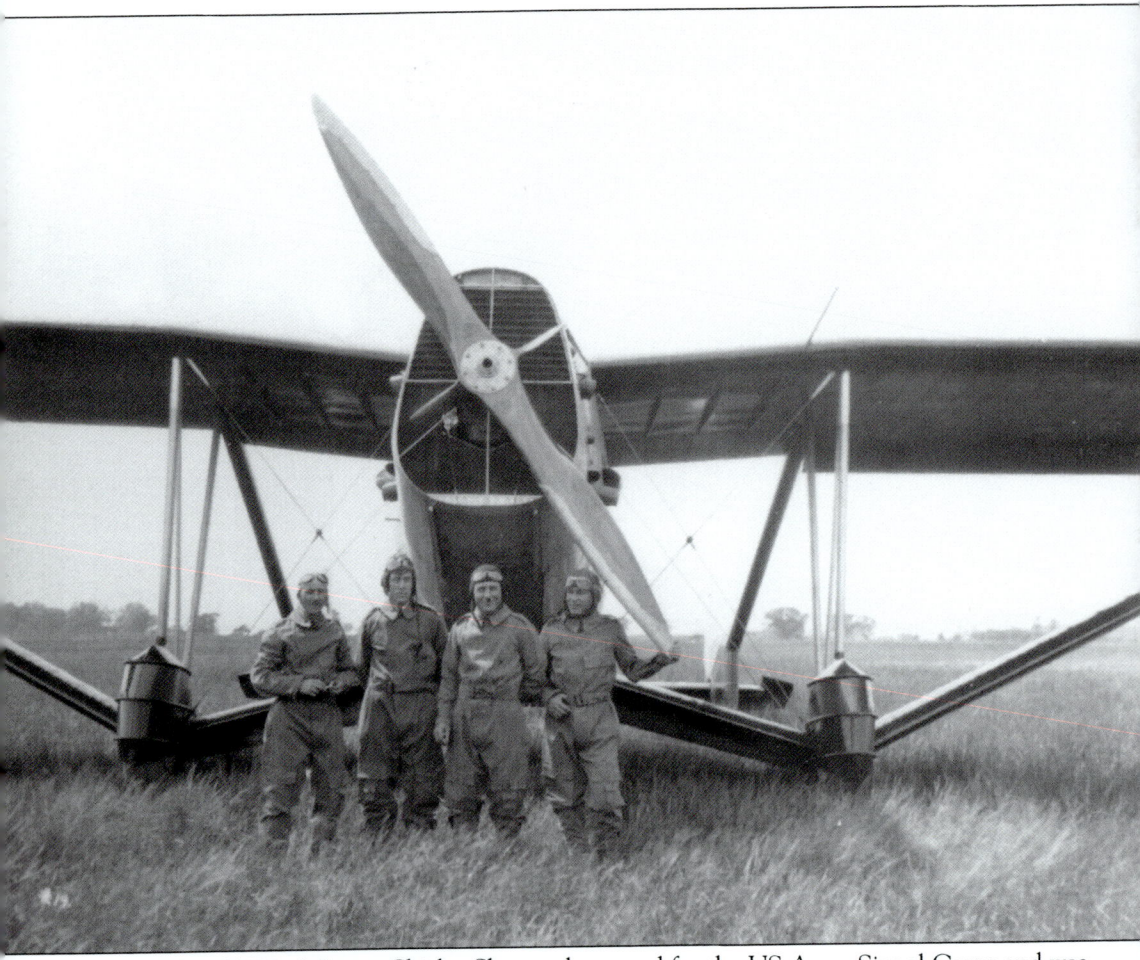

During World War I, Iowan Shirley Short volunteered for the US Army Signal Corps and was so gifted a pilot that he was kept in the country to train new pilots and perform acrobatics for students. In the early 1920s, Short managed Curtiss-Iowa Aircraft Corporation's auxiliary airfield at Oelwein while performing in the Great American Flying Circus. In 1923, Short began transporting the mail, primarily along the hazardous Allegheny Mountains route. Later, he flew for the *Chicago Daily News*. In 1927, he was awarded the year's Harmon Trophy, given to the pilot who advanced aviation the most. In 1931, Short prepared for an around-the-world flight with a crew of three others who would join him in flying a gargantuan Bellanca biplane named the *Blue Streak*. The airplane had an 87-foot wingspan and used two large engines mounted in tandem, one in the front and one in the rear. On May 25, 1931, during a high-speed test flight that was to last 10 hours, the Bellanca crashed, killing all on board. (Courtesy of the State Historical Society of Iowa at Iowa City.)

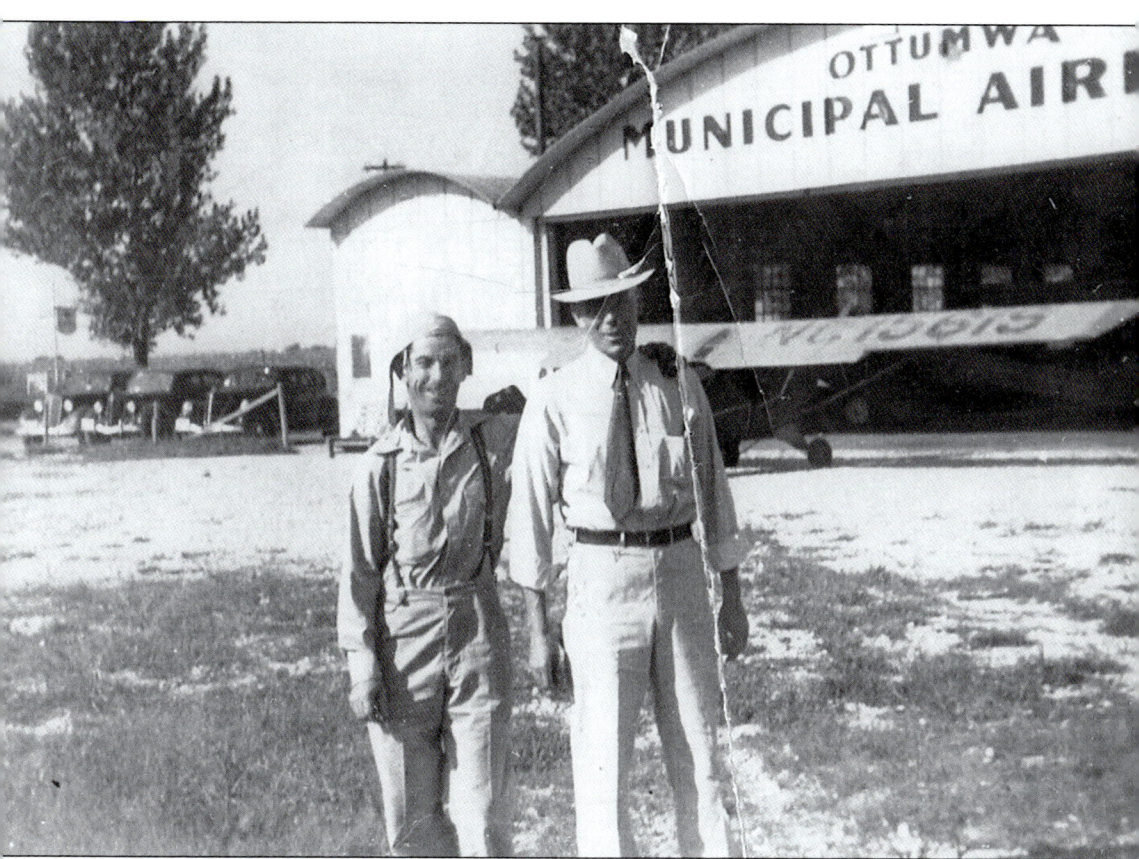

Another well-known Iowa barnstormer was Clifton P. "Ole" Oleson (left) born in McGregor. Oleson made his first flight in a homemade glider at the age of 12. Two years later, he received his pilot's license, becoming America's youngest flyer. For the next four years, he traveled the Midwest for the Curtiss Exhibition Team, flying stunts, wing walking, parachuting (sometimes with his pants on fire), transferring from plane to plane, and even hanging by his teeth. He said, "I always knew there was some sharpie down on the ground laying a bet that I'd never get down alive." During World War I, he served as an instructor in Texas and then flew for the US Air Mail Service. In the 1930s, he returned to Iowa, where he operated the old Ottumwa Airport and taught hundreds of people to fly at his Oleson School of Flight. Pictured with Oleson is Clair I. "Deke" Sherwood, another Iowa aviation pioneer who managed Ottumwa Airport until his death in a plane crash in 1938. (Courtesy of the Antique Airplane Association.)

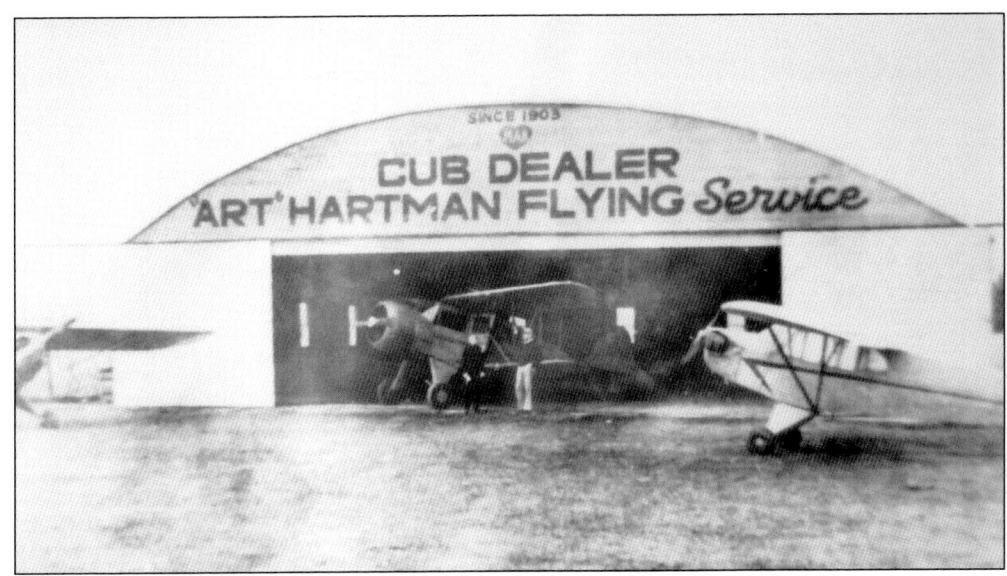

In Burlington, Art J. Hartman continued his work promoting aviation. Since 1911, he had built and flown his own designs, including a hydroplane that nearly killed him when it crashed during takeoff on the Mississippi River. After barnstorming his way around the Midwest as a stunt pilot, wing walker, and mechanic, in 1927 Hartman rented 50 acres of land near Burlington to create a true airport. Later, he obtained a loan to purchase the property. For more than 20 years, he managed the airport without receiving any salary. Instead, he received a percentage of the concessions and whatever he could make giving passenger rides after he gave the city 10 percent of his earnings. (Courtesy of the Burlington Regional Airport.)

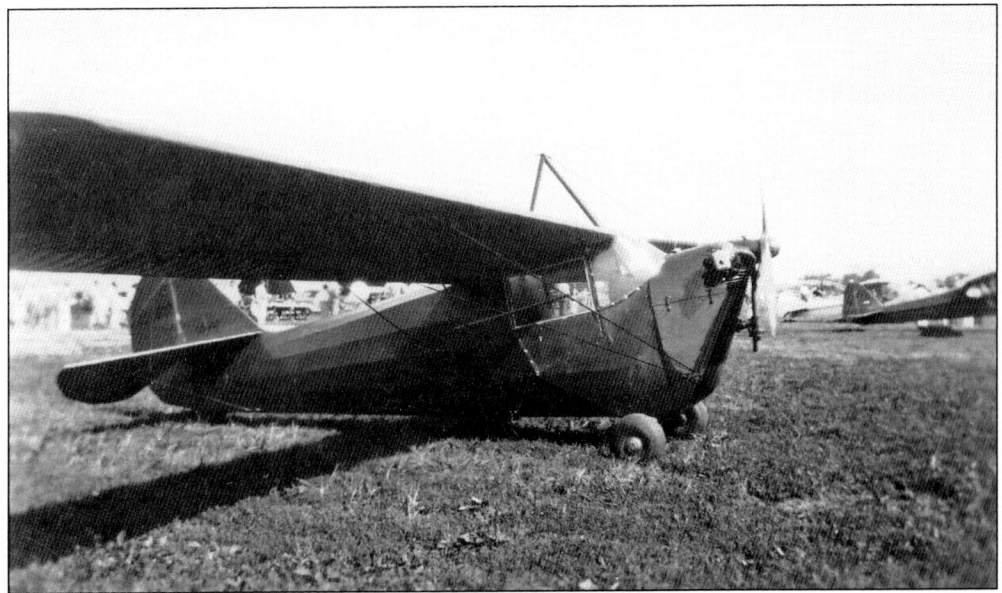

Hartman Flying Service provided flight instruction and was a distributor for several lines, including Taylorcraft and Piper, and serviced all kinds of aircraft, including this Aeronca C-3. Hartman's vision for aviation's future in southeast Iowa inspired others to provide the funding to improve the airport. Installing beacons and floodlights attracted airmail flights, which began in 1934 when the City of Burlington took over the airport. (Courtesy of the Antique Airplane Association.)

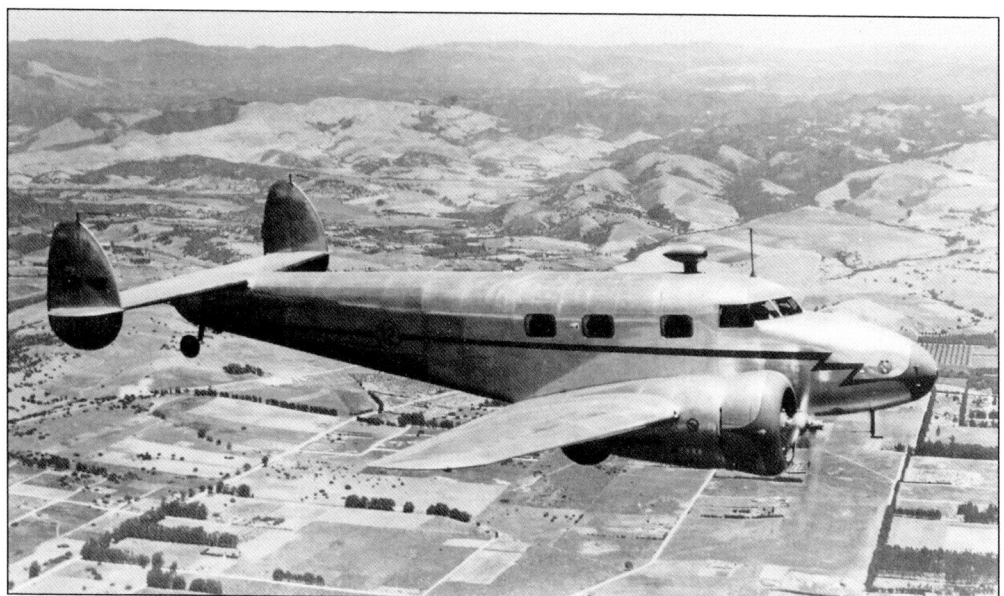

As airports modernized with better lighting, navigational aids, paved runways, taxiways, and terminal buildings, larger airplanes operated by regional and national airlines began serving eastern Iowa communities. During the early 1930s, large single-engine Travel Airs, Howards, and Stinsons were common at local airports. By the end of the 1930s, luxurious multiengine airplanes like this Lockheed Model 12 Electra took over the passenger market. (Courtesy of the Antique Airplane Association.)

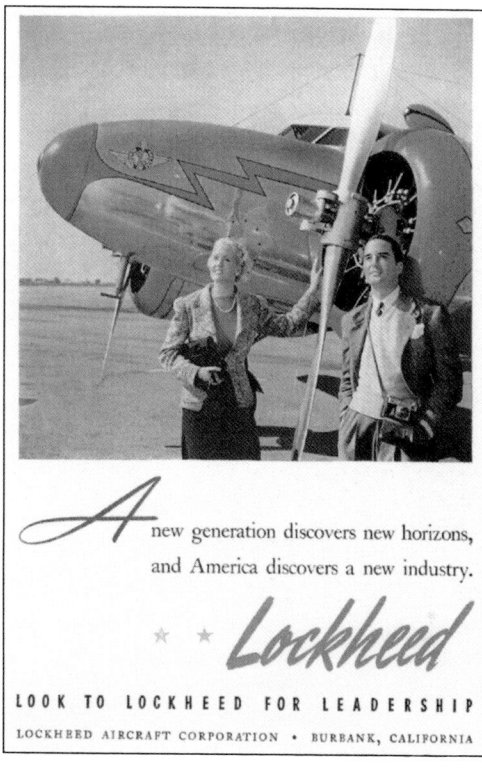

Lockheed did its part to promote customer comfort and convenience for both its Electra and Lodestar transport aircraft. Both had powerful twin radial engines and spacious cabins with food and beverages often served by the first flight attendants. One airline promised that a customer could "have breakfast at home, transact business 400 miles away, then dine at home—all in ONE day" by "discovering new horizons with Lockheed." (Courtesy of Irv Lindner.)

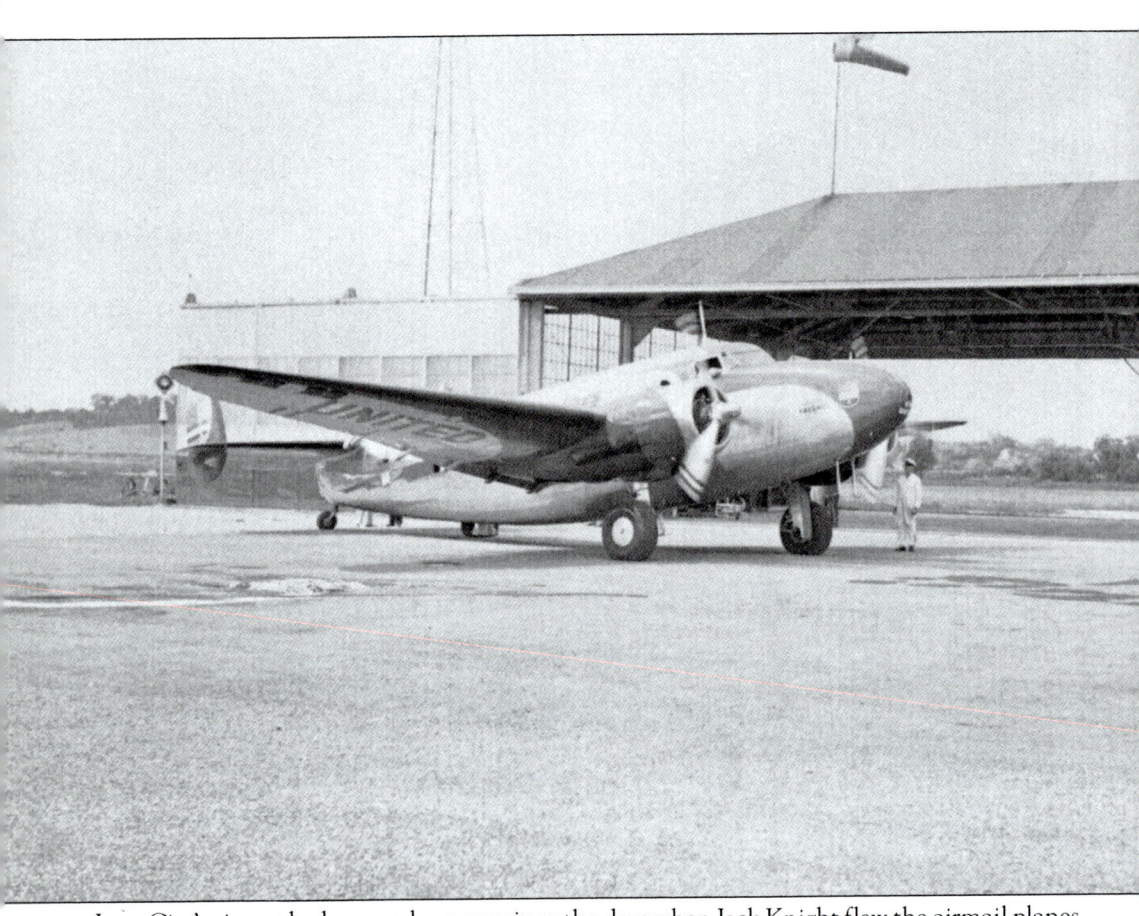

Iowa City's airport had come a long way since the days when Jack Knight flew the airmail planes. Its modern, well-equipped facility and large, spacious hangar was exactly what United Airlines needed for service from eastern Iowa to larger cities like Chicago, St. Louis, and Kansas City. United Airlines also leased ramp and hangar space at the Iowa City airport to other regional carriers like Mid-Continent Airlines, which transported both passengers and freight across the Midwest. (Courtesy of the Iowa State Historical Society at Iowa City.)

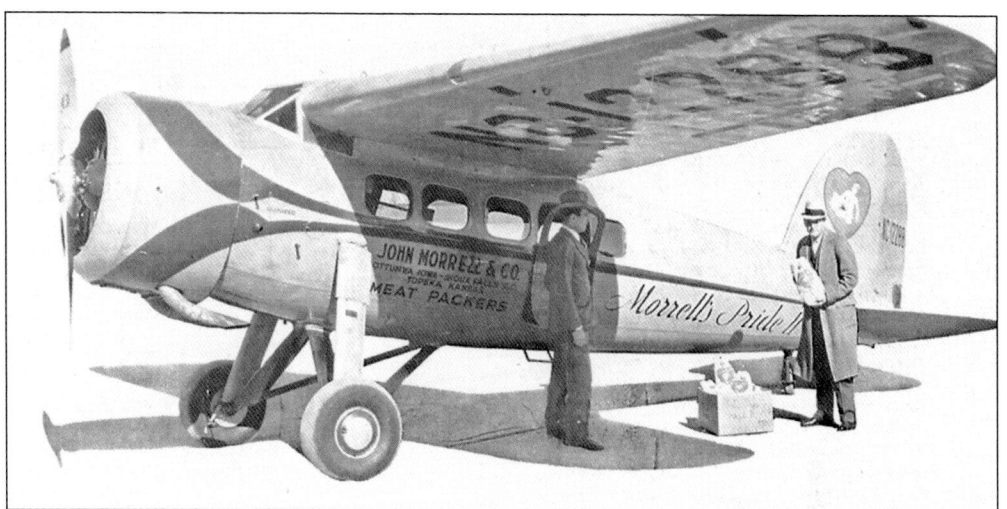

The John Morrell meatpacking company of Ottumwa started operating its own airplane around 1930—the first meatpacking company in the country to do so. The Morrell's Pride I was a six-passenger Travel Air, followed by the Morrell's Pride II (pictured), a unique Lockheed Von Hake Detroit Vega DL-1 with a metal fuselage built in Detroit that was then shipped to California for the installation of wooden wings. (Courtesy of the Antique Airplane Association.)

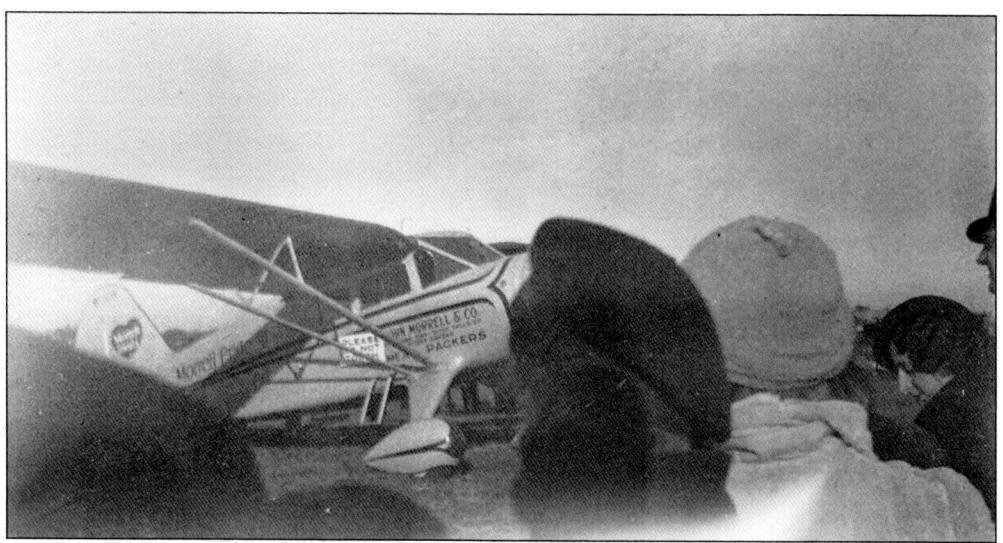

The Morrell's Pride III was a four-passenger Stinson Reliant, often seen at Midwest air shows to promote both business aviation and Morrell's products. All three of the first John Morrell & Co. airplanes spent most of their flying hours transporting executives and customers between the Ottumwa and Sioux Falls plants. Pilots included Cliff P. Kysor, Dan L. Carver, and J.J. Thompson. (Courtesy of the Antique Airplane Association.)

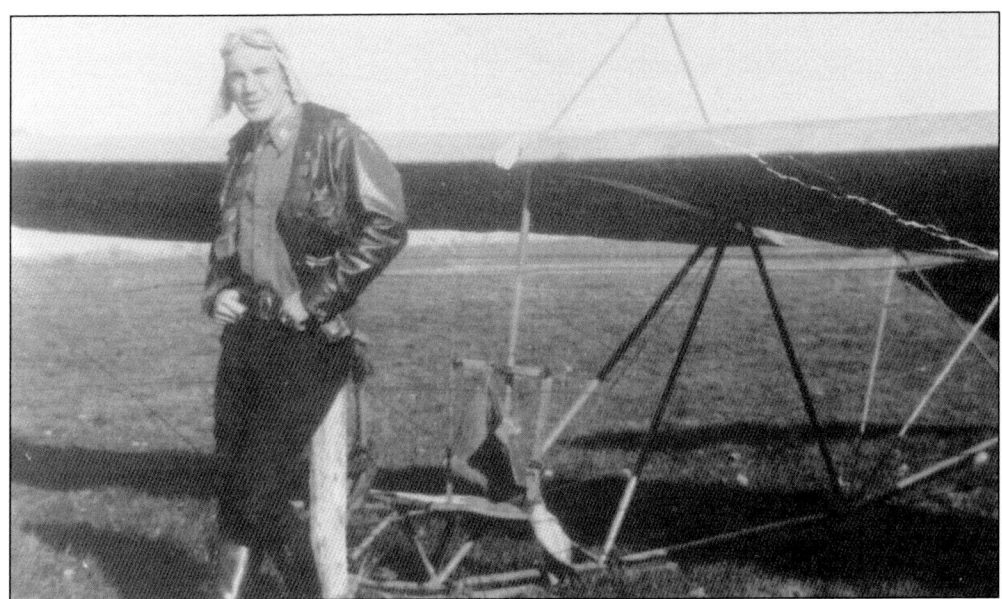

Even with the growing popularity of powered flight in Iowa, gliders were still being built and flown, especially by those on limited budgets and who lived in rural areas. By the mid-1930s, Iowa ranked 20th in the nation for having the largest number of licensed pilots (183), which included those with glider ratings. One of the men who enjoyed building and flying gliders was Stanley Carr of Ottumwa. Carr enjoyed flying his 240-pound Alexander Eaglerock primary glider. Like many glider pilots, he eventually made the transition to powered flight, taking lessons at the old Ottumwa Airport in the late 1930s. (Courtesy of the Antique Airplane Association.)

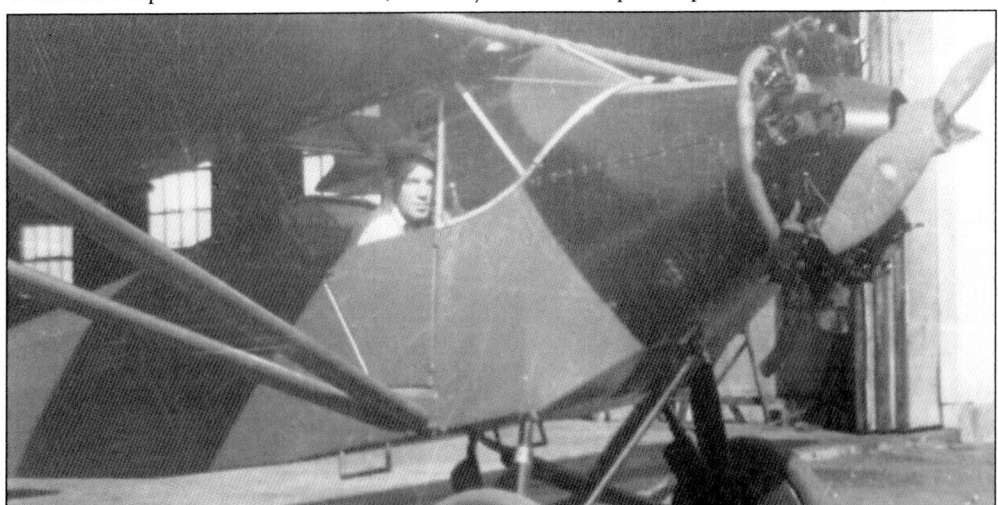

Stanley Carr was one of a large number of students who took lessons at the Ottumwa Airport instructed by Clifton "Ole" Oleson and Deke Shirwood. Carr was a member of the largest single group of students to receive solo licenses at one time. The others included Kenneth Morain, Noah Smith, Ray Suiter, Hugh Hilton, and Freeman McCoy. After obtaining his pilot's license, Carr barnstormed all over southeastern Iowa, flying all types of aircraft. Here, he is sitting in a Velie M5 Monoprep built by the company started by Don Luscombe in Bettendorf, which later moved across the river to Moline as part of the Velie Auto Company's manufacturing site. (Courtesy of the Antique Airplane Association.)

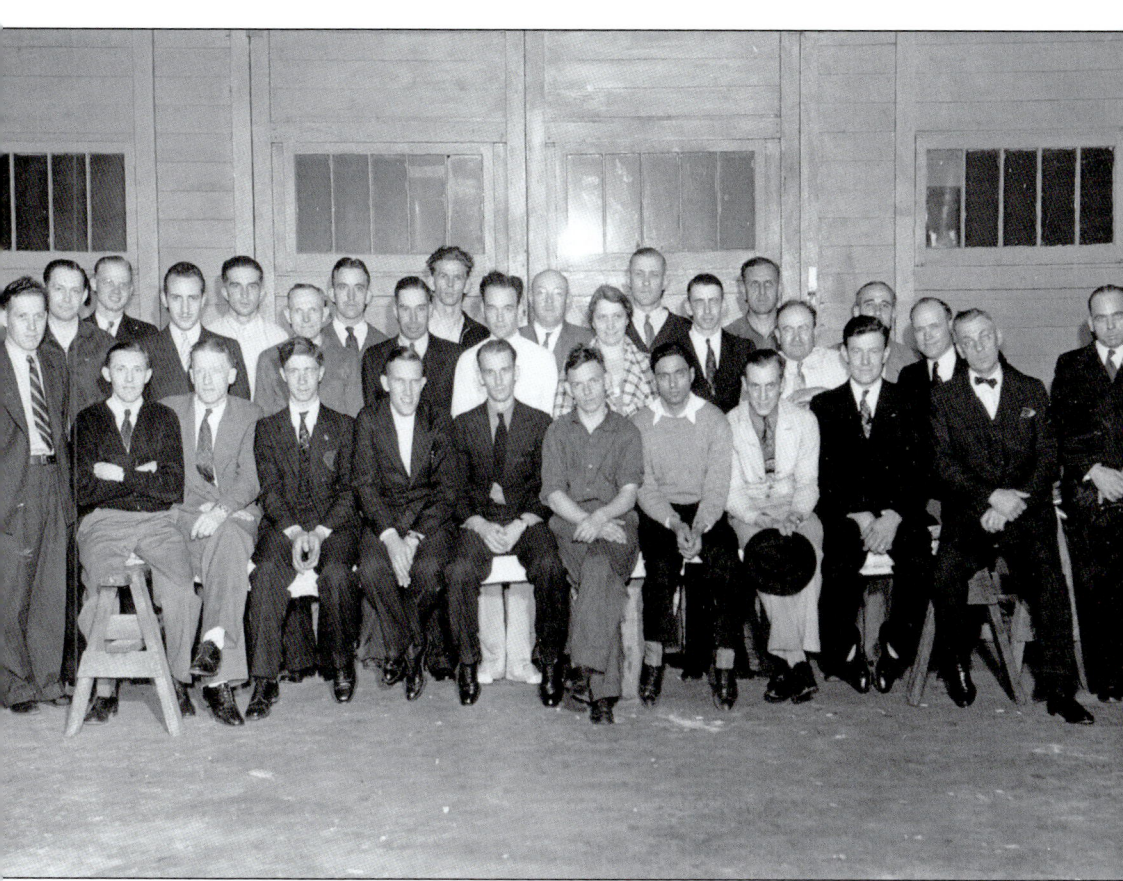

Community aviation organizations formed as more and more citizens became involved in flying and manufacturing aircraft. The Quad City Airmen's Association was one of the first and largest air associations in Iowa, formed in 1936. Original members included George Dickson, Vern Aten, Dr. W.R. Streed, Herb Schlicting, Delbert Clayton, George Willecke, Ed Andreson, Floyd Adams, Dwight Carlson, Joe Mieser, Glen Phelps, Ada Phelps (the first female member), Ed Schmidt, Al Frankhauser, Pat Miller, Gabe Mosenfelder, Clyde Shoemaker, Harold Mills, Stub Quinby, Ken Lee, Bill Ziegler, Des Erickson, Ralph Oakley, Ray Laverenze, Paul Bloom, Jim Corelis, Ed Greim, Clarence Paustin, and G.F. Jontz. (Courtesy of the Putnum Museum in Davenport.)

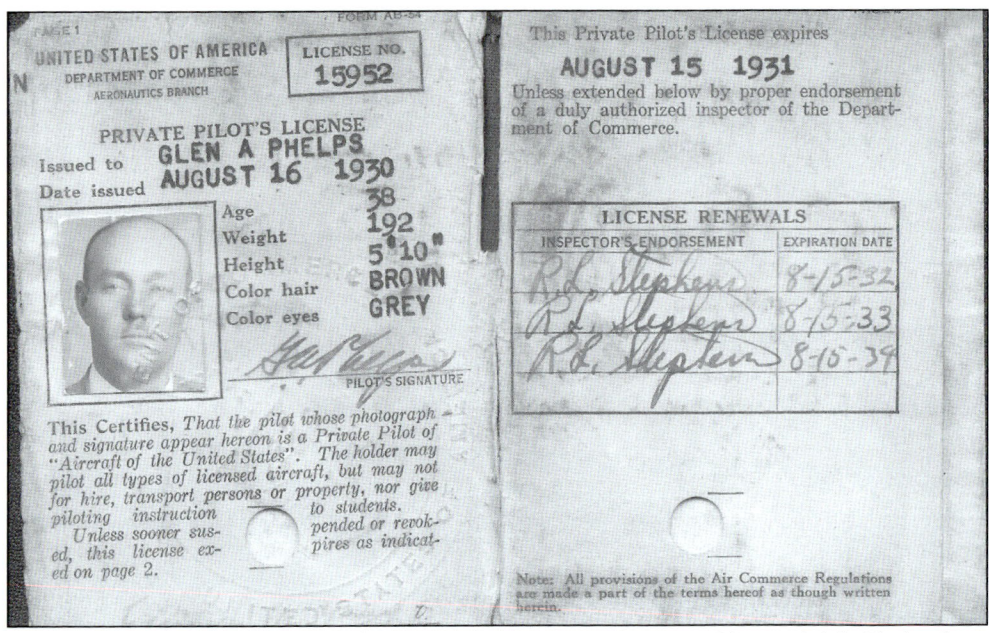

Two charter members of the Quad City Airmen's Association were Glen and Ada Phelps from Davenport. Glen became interested in aviation when he sold insurance to the Velie Company for its factory in Moline. Intrigued by watching the airplanes being built on the assembly line, then being flown away, he decided to learn how to fly. It was not the first time Glen had come up an unusual idea that he brought to Ada. (Courtesy of the Phelps family.)

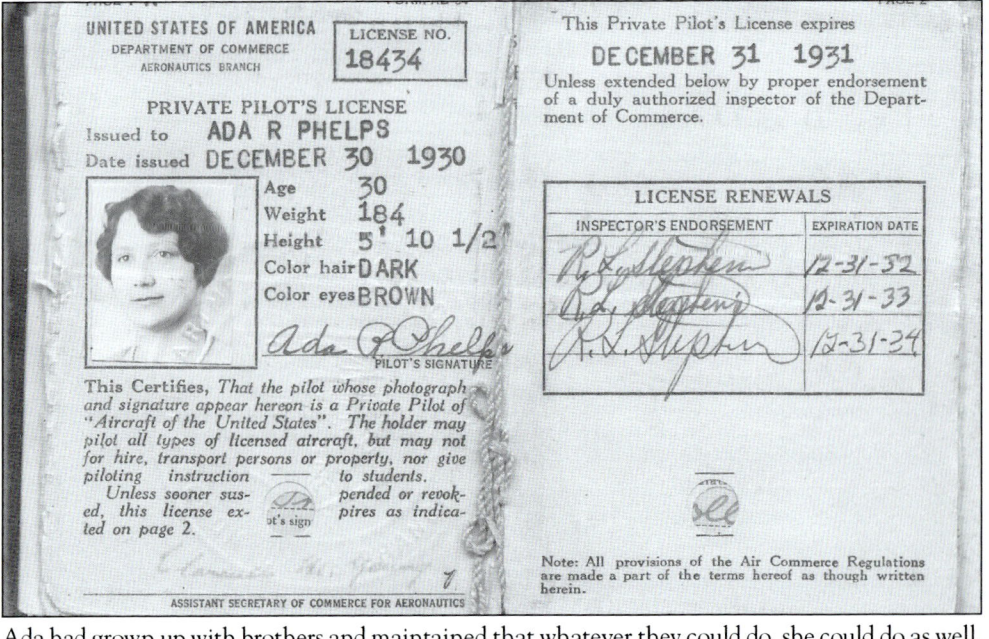

Ada had grown up with brothers and maintained that whatever they could do, she could do as well, so when Glen explained his plan, she declared that she would also learn to fly. The couple placed an order for a Velie monoplane. Ada suggested an orange color to impose their airplane's contrast against the blue sky. Their plan was to follow it along the factory assembly line as it was being built and then complete their lessons in their new airplane. (Courtesy of the Phelps family.)

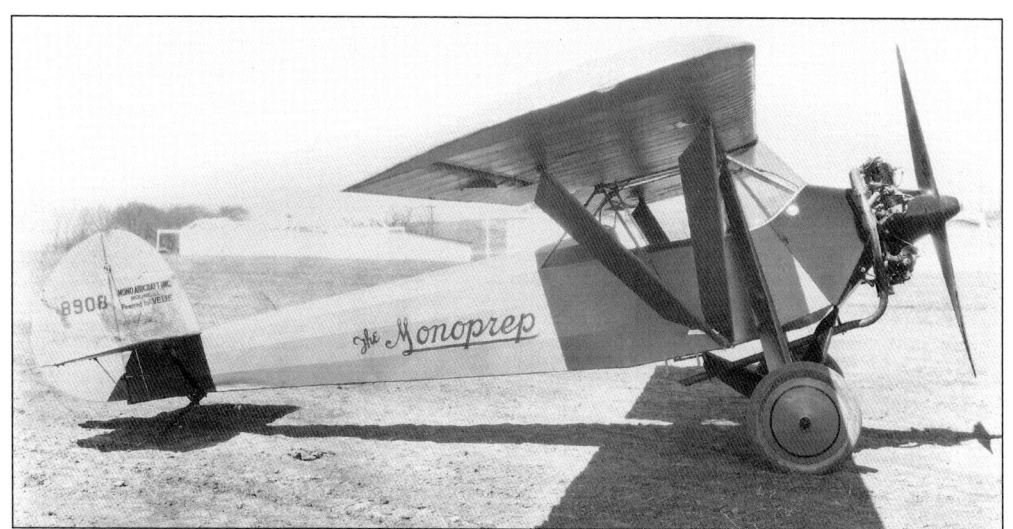

The Phelps's Monoprep was completed in March 1930 and flown to Davenport's Cram Field. Glen surprised Ada, who had not seen the completed airplane, pointing it out as they drove over the hill on Division Street toward the airport. "See that down there? That's ours," he said. George Dickson and O. Ray Hansen were private pilots trying to build flying hours toward their commercial licenses, so they agreed to be instructors at no charge in the Monoprep; Hansen was Glen's instructor and Dickson was Ada's mentor. (Courtesy of the Phelps family.)

The Monoprep M-5 was small and light, powered by Velie's own radial engine. Born from the original "Monocoupe" designed by Clayton Folkerts of Dubuque, who teamed up with Don Luscombe and Bettendorf's Wallace brothers, the company moved its operation to Velie's Moline factory to build the more conventional Monoprep. It was a good trainer and economical for cross-country flights. The company also produced the larger Monocoach and Monosport airplanes. (Courtesy of the Phelps family.)

Glen Phelps earned his pilot's license in August 1930. When Ada Phelps received her license in December, they became "Iowa's first flying couple." They bought some land on Jersey Ridge Road in Davenport and built a grass runway. Chet Loose, who worked at Cram Field, helped them with maintenance. During World War II, every airfield was required to have a 24-hour armed guard, so the Phelpses had to move the Monoprep to the Moline Airport where they soon lost hangar space. (Courtesy of the Phelps family.)

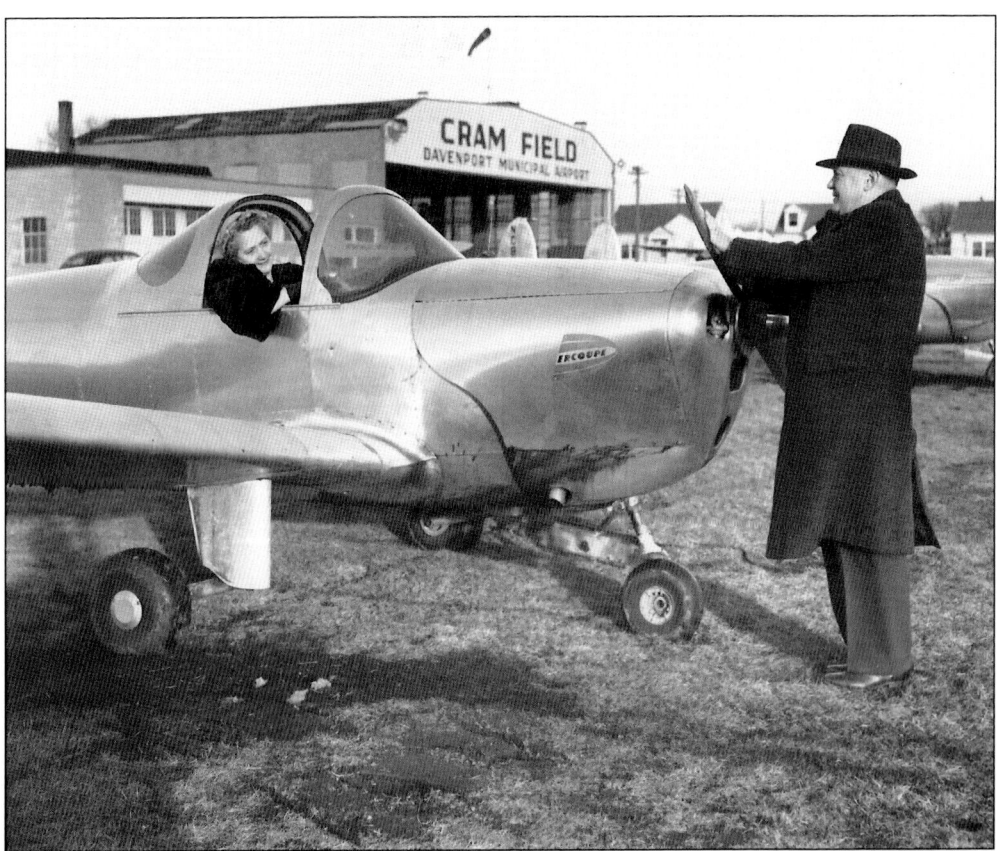

The Phelpses eventually sold the Monoprep but stayed very active in flying throughout the Quad Cities area. During 1932's Fourth of July weekend, Ada parents' car was hit by a drunk driver in Vinton. Ada flew herself from Davenport to Vinton in time to see her parents before they died. Ada stopped flying when her children were born but continued to promote aviation for the rest of her life, encouraging young people, especially girls, to become involved in aviation. (Courtesy of the Phelps family.)

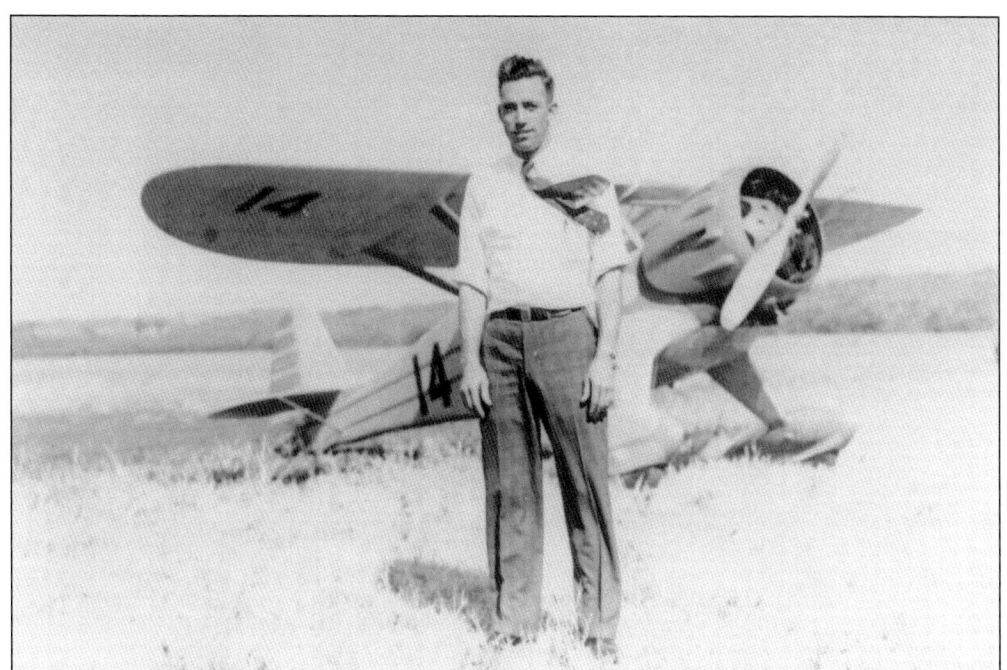

In northern Iowa, John Livingston continued to compete in air races, including the Cleveland Air Races, where in 1931 he won 9 out of the 12 events. He decided to give up racing in 1933, when he had to parachute from his airplane because the landing gear fell off. He continued to test new aircraft designs and systems for the Waco Aviation Company. (Courtesy of the Cedar Falls Historical Society.)

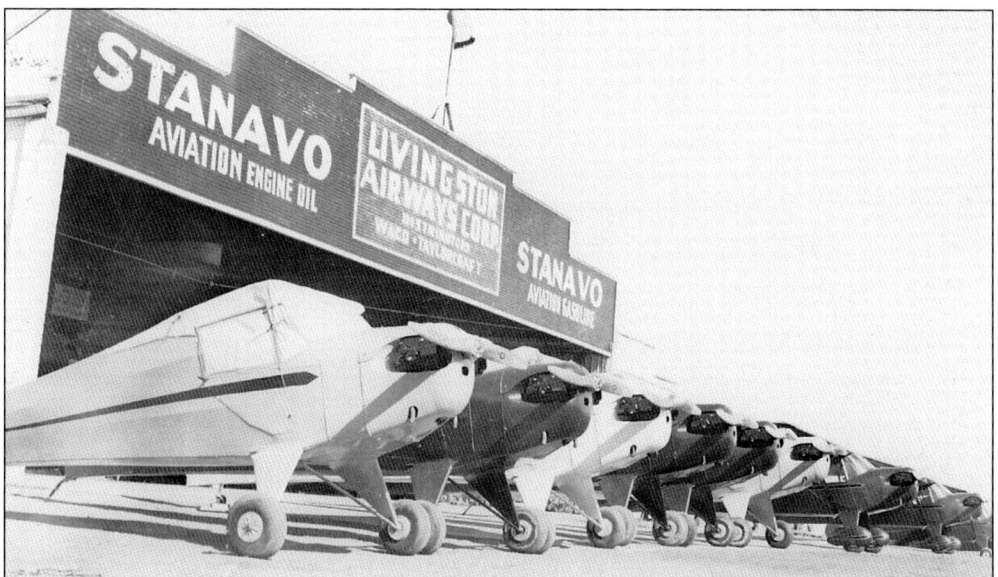

Livingston's business was thriving, even in the midst of the Great Depression. He continued to divide his time between his Waterloo-based flight instruction and aircraft maintenance facility and his other distributorships in Iowa and Illinois. Here, a row of Cubs, delivered by rail, wait for final assembly before being available for sale at Livingston Airways Corporation. (Courtesy of the Cedar Falls Historical Society.)

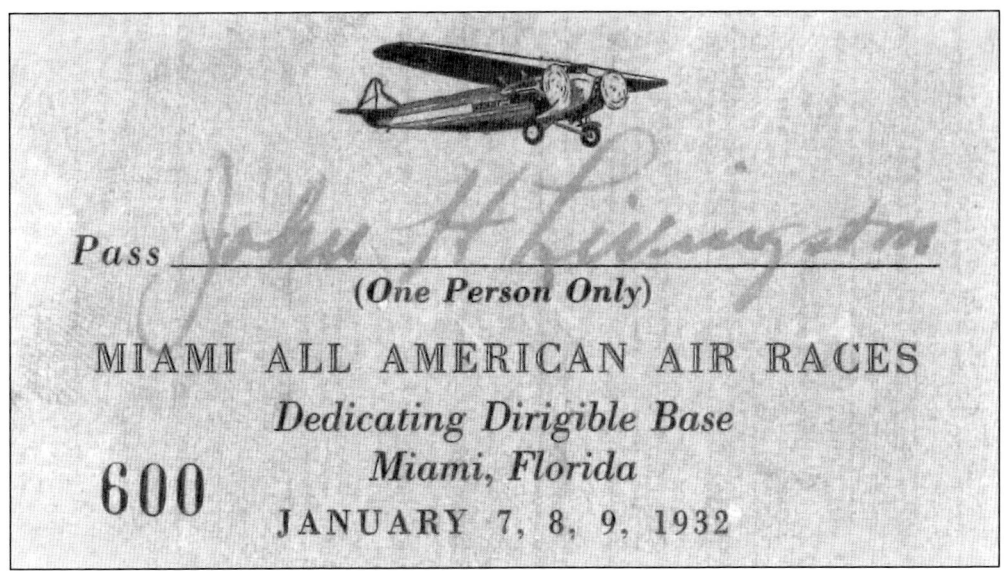

The Miami All American Air Races had been one of John Livingston's favorite events since 1932 when it dedicated the dirigible base in Miami. In 1939, even though he had officially retired from competition, Livingston entered and won the Glenn Curtiss Trophy in Miami, flying at 156.806 miles per hour, which was far faster than the runner-up airplane. (Courtesy of the Cedar Falls Historical Society.)

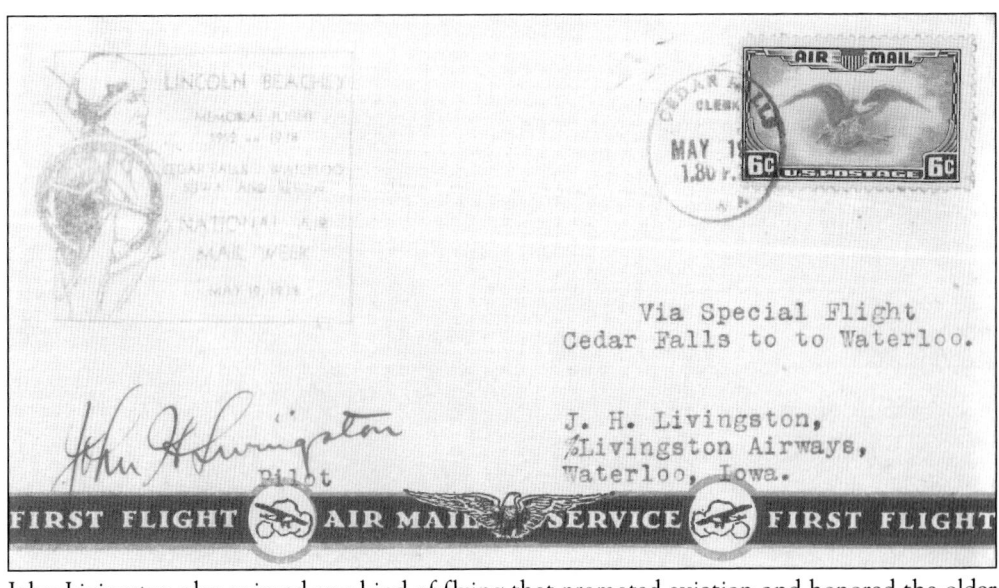

John Livingston also enjoyed any kind of flying that promoted aviation and honored the older pioneers. In May 1938, during National Air Mail Week, Livingston flew a reenactment of Lincoln Beachey's historic 1912 flight from Cedar Falls to Waterloo and back, carrying the these covers (at 6¢ for an airmail letter!) to commemorate that special event. (Courtesy of the Cedar Falls Historical Society.)

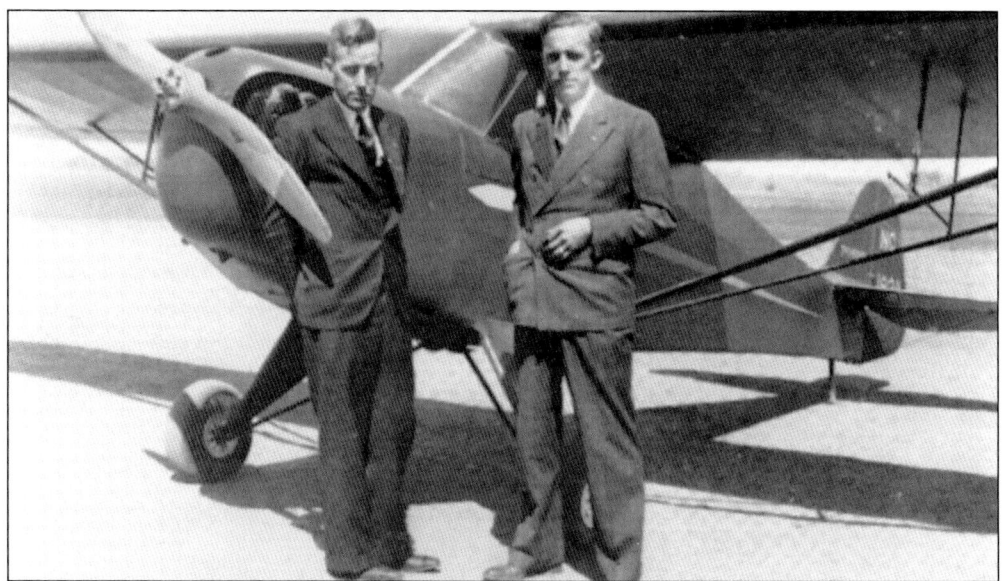

John Livingston had a younger brother named Aden, whose nickname was "Bite." The Livingstons' mother forbade Bite from anything related to flying, but when Bite announced that he was moving to San Diego to accept a job, his mother agreed to let him learn to fly. He helped John operate the airport as he worked to earn his pilot's license. Here, Bite (left) poses in front of a 1937 Taylorcraft Cub. (Courtesy of the Antique Airplane Association.)

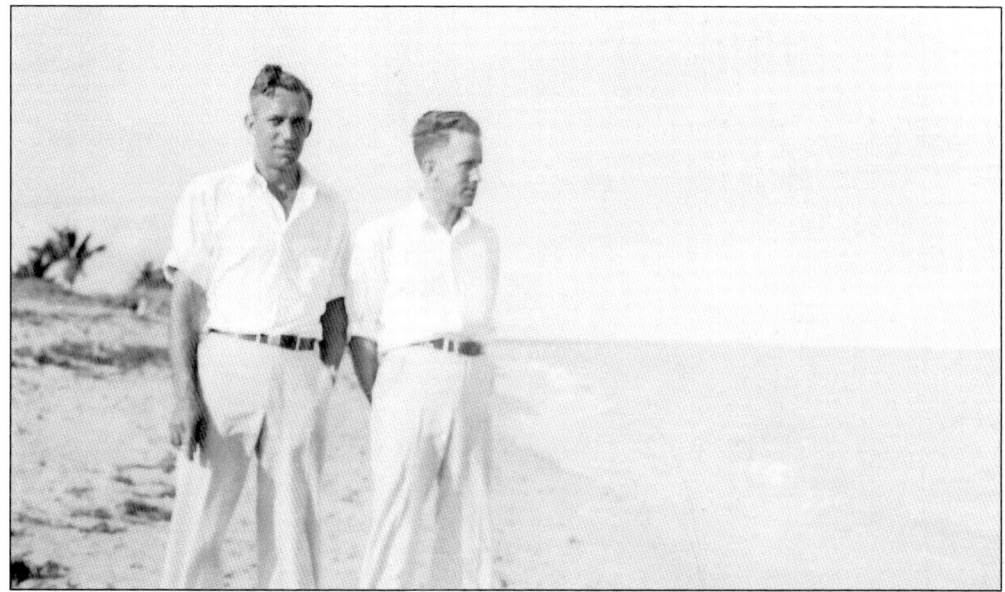

Bite Livingston described his early flying experiences: "I went down to Monmouth where John operated an airport and he taught me to fly in a 'Jenny.' It held 12 gallons of gas, used eight an hour, and flew at 65 miles per hour. You couldn't go far in that thing. I was 23 years old." (Courtesy of the Cedar Falls Historical Society.)

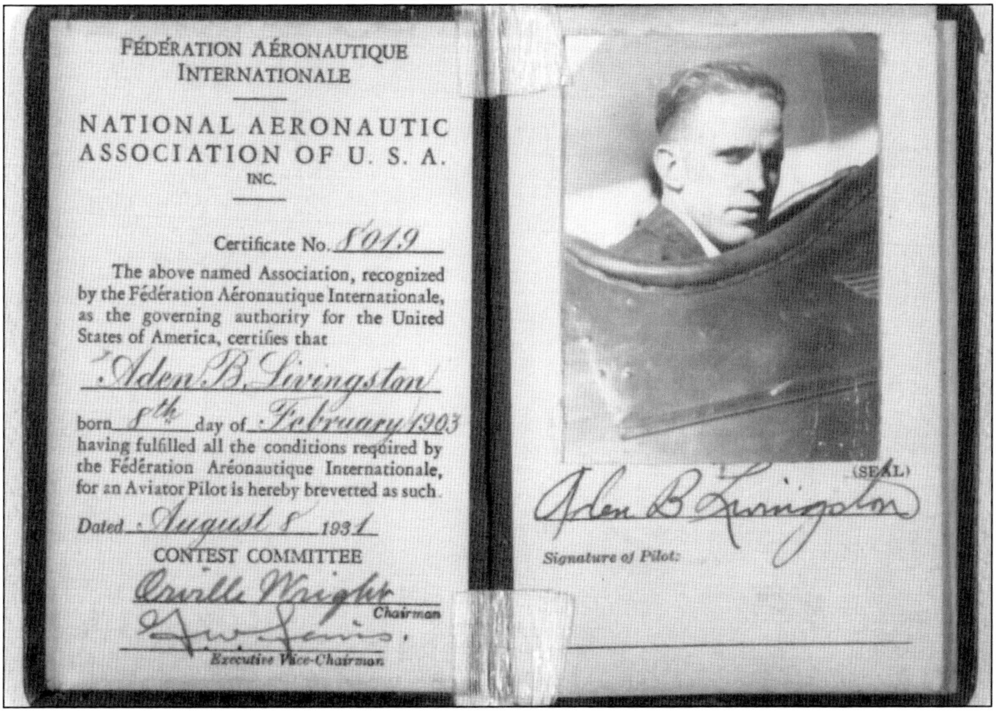

Bite Livingston received his license in 1927, which had a glider rating—the first in Iowa. When he renewed the license (pictured) in 1931, it was signed by Orville Wright. The brothers operated an airline carrying passengers from Waterloo to Des Moines daily. Bite recalled, "It was called 'Ryan Airline.' We had a plane like the one Lindbergh used to cross the Atlantic, a Ryan Brougham. The fee was $10 one-way and $18 round-trip." (Courtesy of the Cedar Falls Historical Society.)

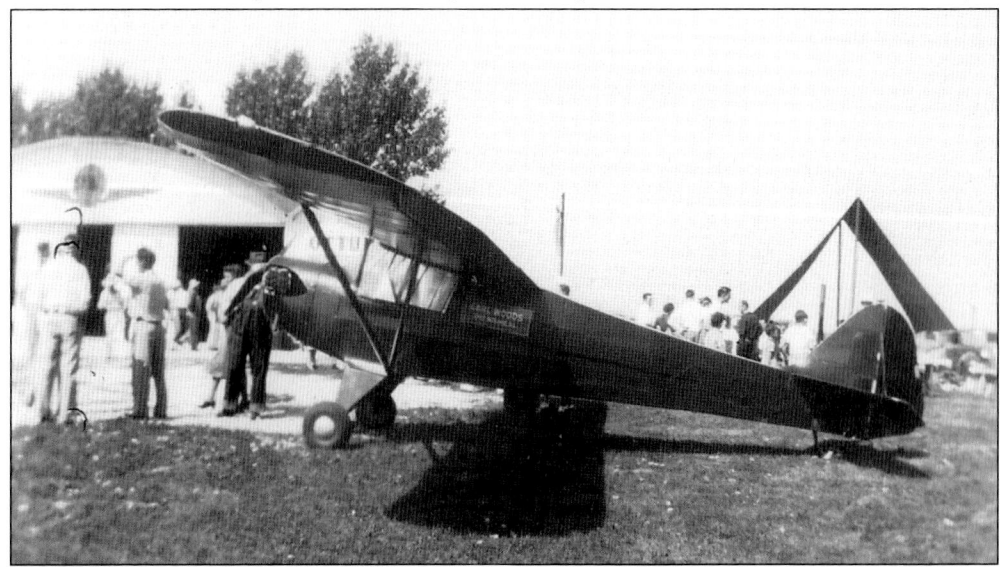

Bite's favorite airplane to fly was the Cub, which had originally been designed and built by Taylorcraft Corporation, like the airplane pictured here. Later, Piper became the large manufacturer and distributor of the Cub type. Bite flew his Cub well into his 80s, always preferring its sparse cockpit and instrument panel. (Courtesy of the Antique Airplane Association.)

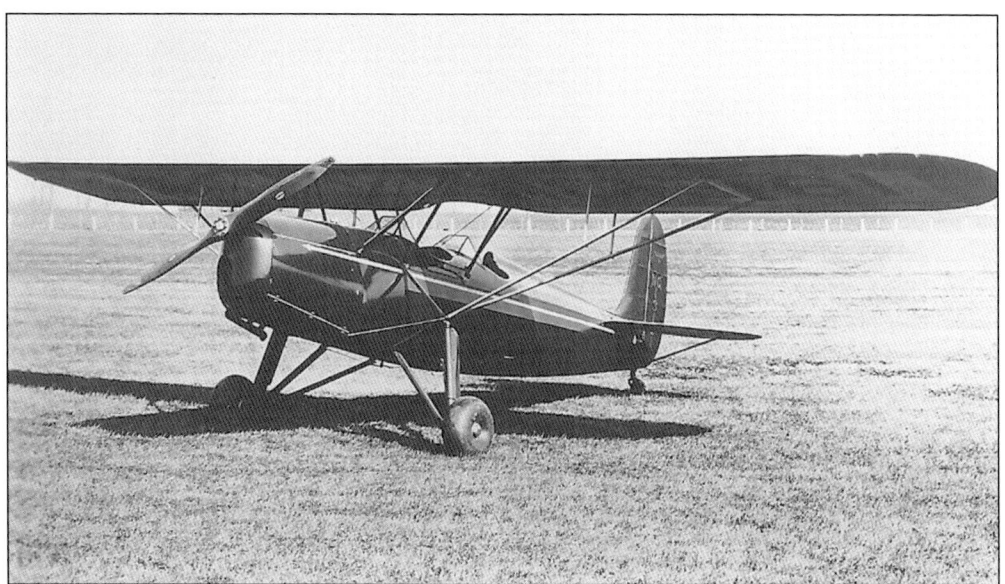

Another popular airplane used for flight instruction at the Livingston fields, as well as most other small strips, during the 1930s was this Fairchild F-22 "parasol" model. It was light and maneuverable and very forgiving for fledgling pilots. (Courtesy of the Antique Airplane Association.)

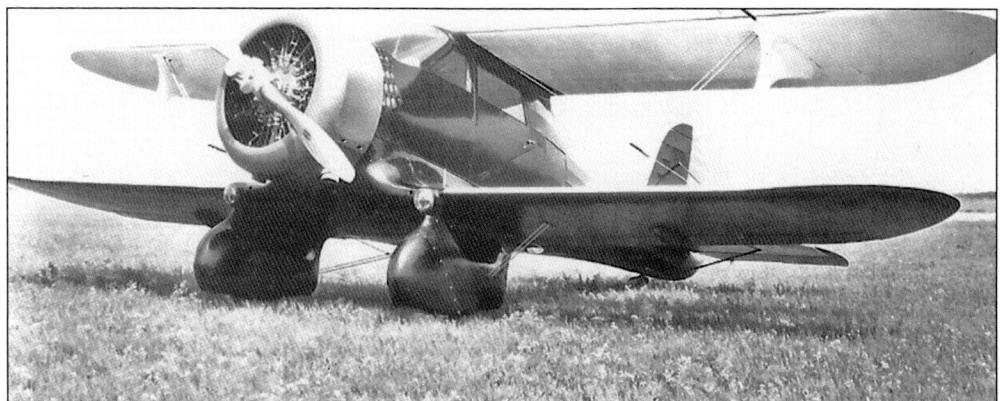

As the decade of the 1930s came to a close, a visitor to an eastern Iowa airport was treated to a wide range of airplanes. There were still old Jennys and Wacos that were mostly used for air shows and low-cost flight instruction. The newer, larger biplanes, like this Beechcraft A-17F Staggerwing were the ultimate in private and corporate flying comfort, using longer, enclosed cabins with massive wing areas and powerful radial engines. (Courtesy of the Antique Airplane Association.)

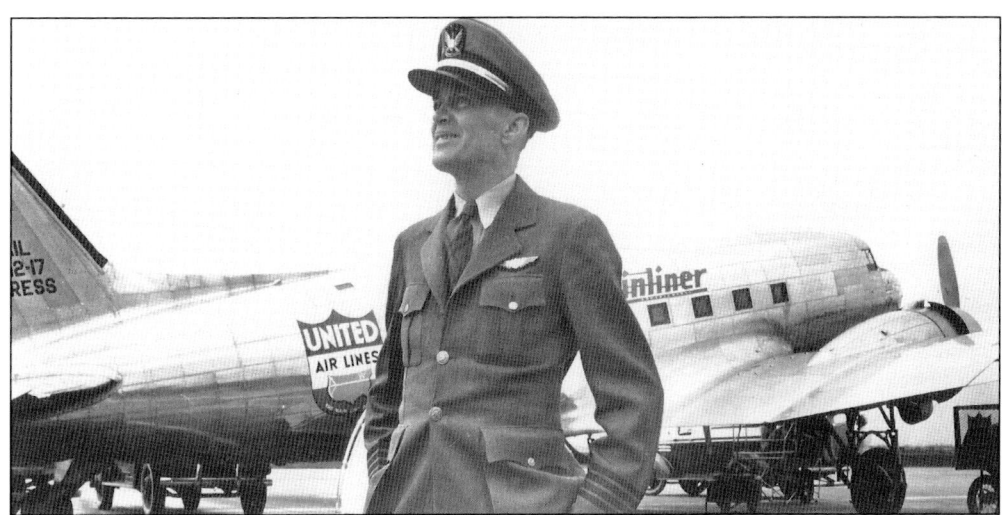

Many of the old barnstormers and airmail pilots—those who were still alive—found good employment flying for major airlines. Here, United Airlines captain Jack Knight, a former US Mail Service pilot, surveys the airfield where he once landed during his airmail flying days. (Courtesy of the Buchanan, Michigan, Historical Society.)

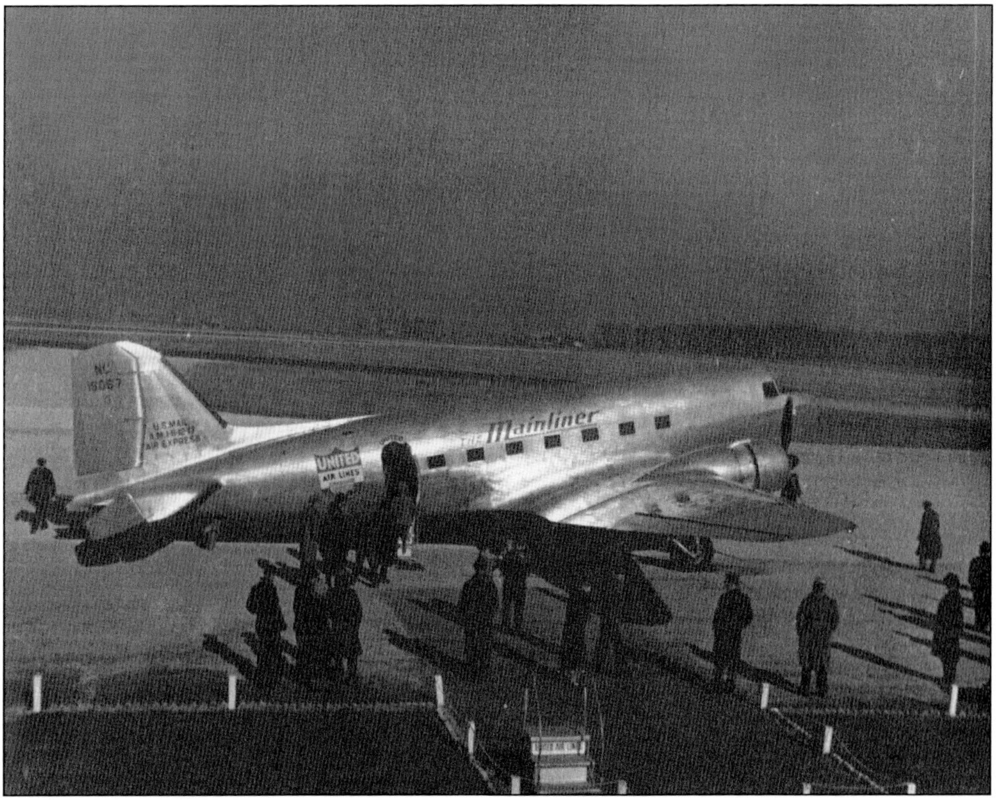

Major carriers were flying even larger airplanes like the Douglas DC-3, which United Airlines dubbed the "Mainliner." Far exceeding the load capacity and passenger comfort of the older Lockheed models, the DC-3 was soon pressed into military service in many roles as America prepared for war. (Courtesy of Irv Lindner.)

Five

WORLD WAR II AND THE POSTWAR YEARS
1940 TO 1950

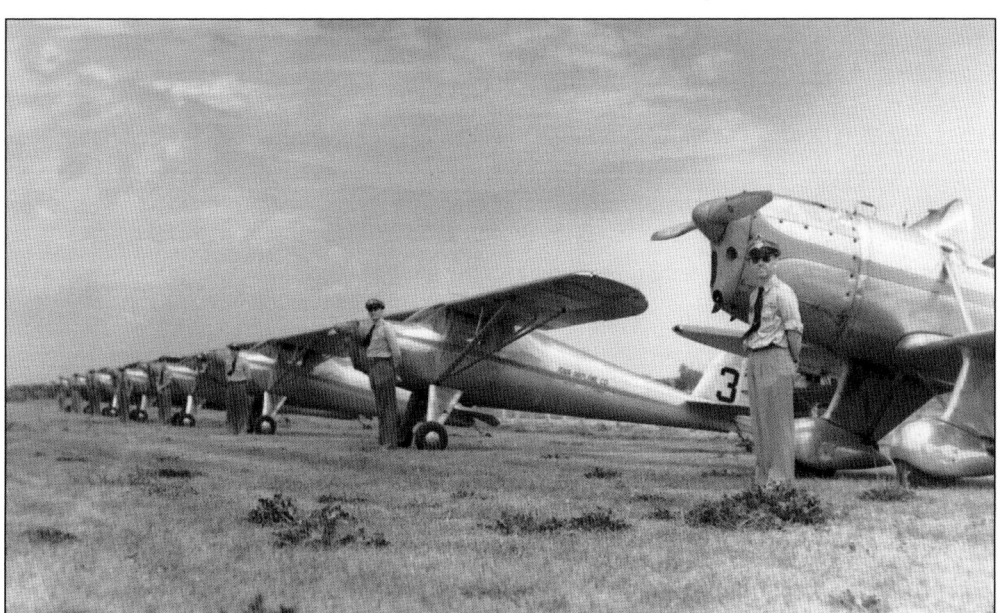

As the 1940s began, America was drawn closer to war. Envisioning a need for trained pilots, military and civilian aviation officials created training programs that prepared young male and female recruits in the basics of flying and navigation. Businesses like the Iowa Airplane Company provided facilities and fleets of aircraft like the single-engine training aircraft and instructors seen here. At the far right is F.C. Anderson with Leo Brennan just to the left of Anderson. (Courtesy of the State of Iowa Historical Society at Iowa City.)

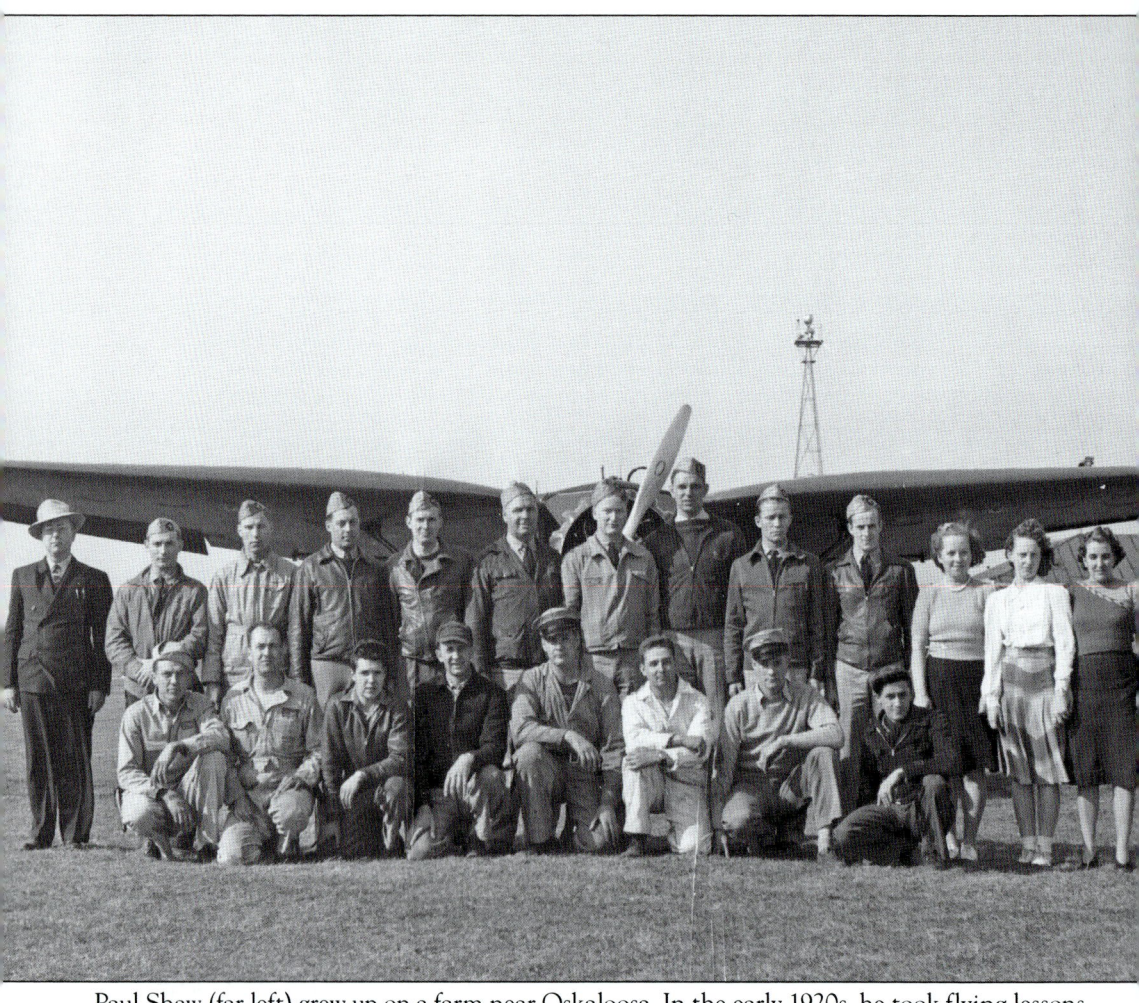

Paul Shaw (far left) grew up on a farm near Oskaloosa. In the early 1920s, he took flying lessons from Dan Hunter in Cedar Rapids before joining the air circus exhibition circuit in 1924 flying mostly Jennys. After operating a flying service out of Cedar Rapids, in 1928 he moved the business to Iowa City, teaching many local citizens to fly and promoting aviation throughout the area. As World War II approached, Shaw became one of the most active people in Iowa in coordinating military flight training, which was supported by his Shaw Aircraft Company staff. Staff members pictured are, from left to right, (first row) mechanics Robert Jehle, Wilson Putnum, Robert Kircher, John DeHoogh, William Boshart, William Everett, Dale Brower, and Everett Taylor; (second row, not including Shaw) flight instructors Clifford J. Leutholt, Lambert Fechter, Henry Vande Kerk, Jack Hamilton, Leonard Woeppel, Harold Rowe, Paul Hansmire, Wilton Hodges, and Homer Hagins, secretaries Gretchen Doerres and Juanita Rice, and accountant Betty Jean Cochran. (Courtesy the State of Iowa Historical Society at Iowa City.)

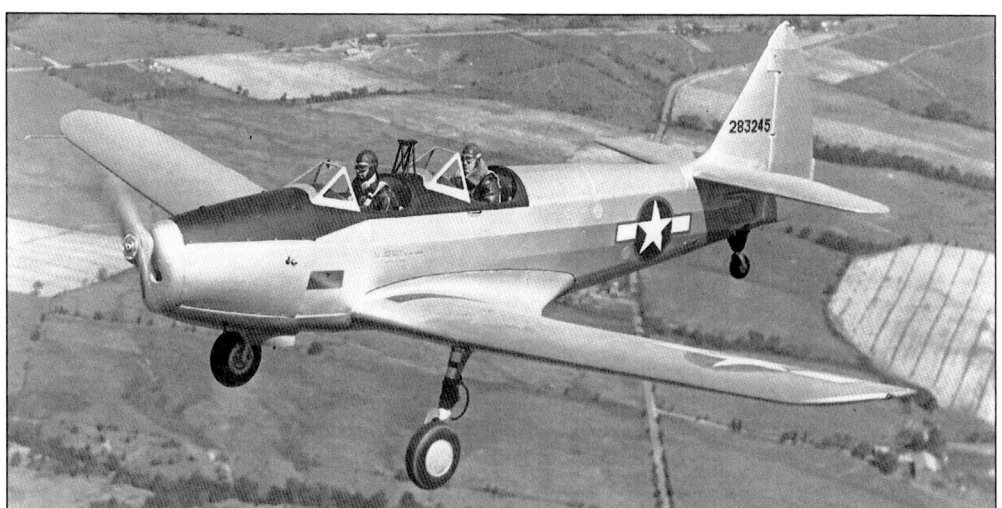

The Civilian Pilot Training Program (CPTP) was enacted by Congress in 1939 "to provide for the training of civil aircraft pilots, and for other purposes" (like national defense). Ten applications from Iowa institutions were received by the Civil Aeronautics Administration for approval. Of those, Iowa State College, Coe College, St. Ambrose College, and Drake University were selected as initial sites. Ground school coursework was taught at the college campuses and at the airfields, with students, including women, required to take 72 hours of classroom instruction. Students were given between 35 and 50 hours of flight instruction at nearby airfields, flying aircraft like this Fairchild PT-19 and Taylorcraft airplanes for primary training. (Courtesy of the Antique Airplane Association.)

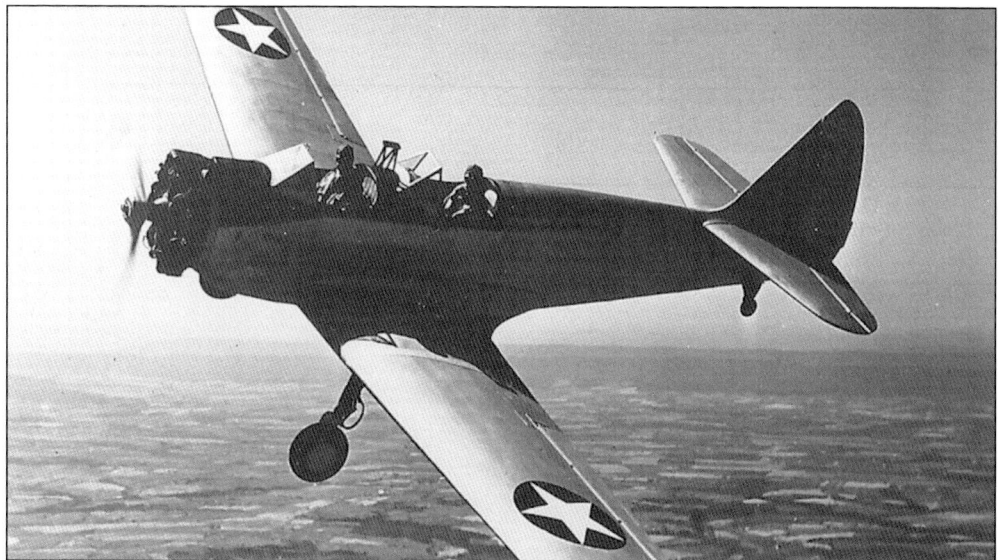

After the attack in Pearl Harbor, the CPTP was replaced by the War Training Service (WTS). More colleges and universities were added to the list of those who had been involved in the old CPTP with students required to enlist in either the Army or Navy Reserves. Receiving no pay, but room and board and travel expenses, these students trained full-time at dozens of Iowa locations for 24 to 40 weeks, using aircraft such as this Fairchild PT-23, Taylorcraft, and Meyers OTWs in preparation for active duty as liaison pilots, service pilots, glider pilots, or flight instructors. (Courtesy of the Antique Airplane Association.)

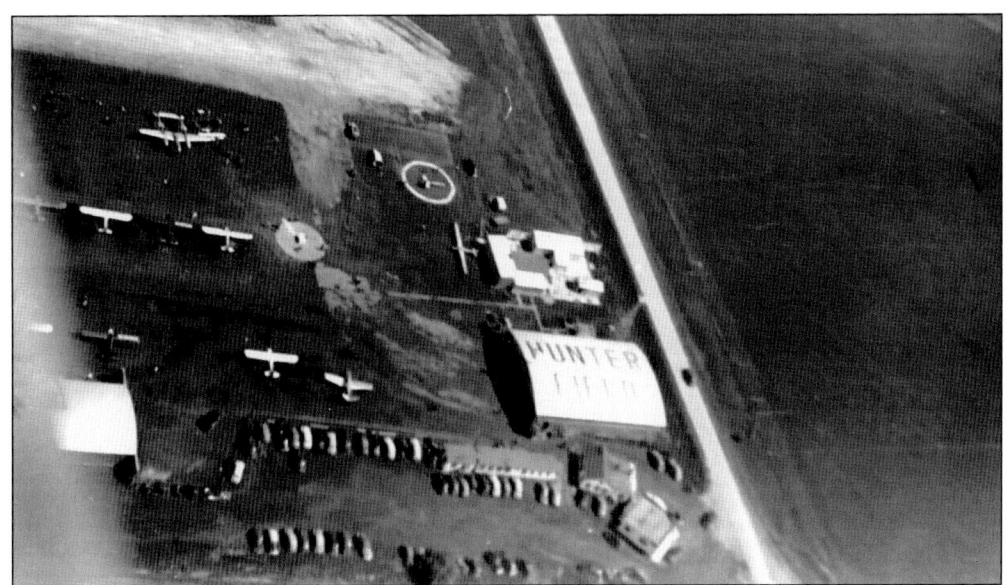

Dan Hunter, a World War I–veteran pilot, operated Hunter Field in Cedar Rapids, which was named one of three Iowa locations for CPTP Advanced Training Centers providing cross-country and flight-instructor training. Hunter also commanded Iowa's wing of the Civil Air Patrol. This photograph was taken of Hunter Field sometime during World War II. A Lockheed P-38 Lightning is visible in the upper left-hand corner. (Courtesy of the Carl and Mary Koehler History Center, Linn County Historical Society.)

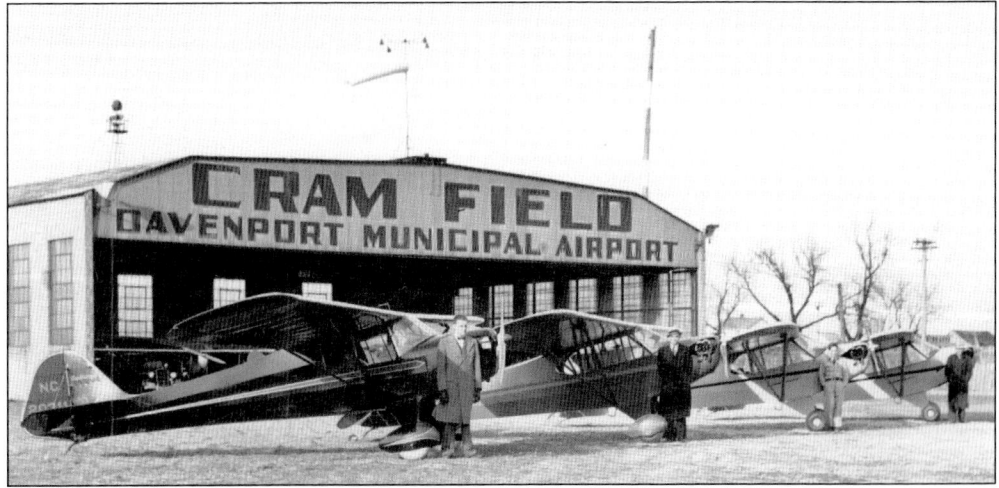

In Davenport, Cram Field was a large CPTP training facility, partnering with St. Ambrose College. Fr. Raymond James Kinnavey was appointed the program's director. The staff included Leon T. Bauer, who taught ground school and later took over as program director. O. Ray Hansen, the airport manager and president of Davenport Airways, was the chief flight instructor and was assisted by George Dixon. Chester Loose served as the chief mechanic for the fleet of 25 airplanes. Margaret Yates, the only Iowa woman who was a certified ground instructor (and one of only three in the country) taught meteorology, navigation, theory of flight, air-traffic rules, commerce regulations, and instruments, in addition to being in charge of the ground-instruction program. More than 90 students were served at any one time, with about 300 annually. (Courtesy of the Putnum Museum at Davenport.)

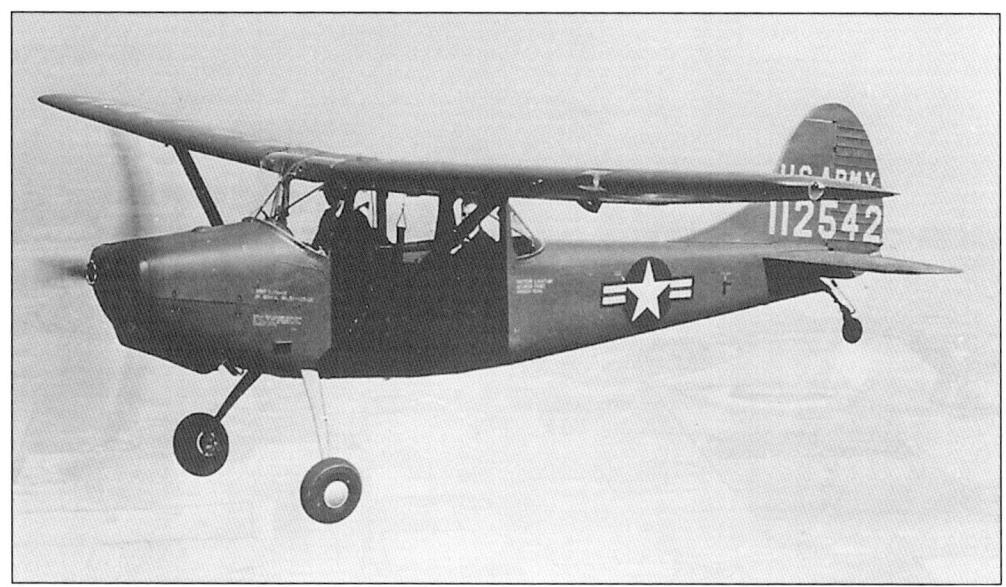

As World War II continued, more and more colleges and universities became part of the military flight-training programs. Because of the high failure rate, new cadets were required to take courses in science, math, and English to supplement their aviation coursework. In addition to the State University of Iowa, St. Ambrose College, Coe College, and the Iowa State Teachers College, other eastern Iowa schools involved in the program were Burlington Junior College, Cornell College, Grinnell College, Loras College, Luther College, Parsons College, University of Dubuque, and Washington Junior College. Civilian aircraft used for training and liaison flying were given military designations such as the Taylorcraft (designated L-2s), Aeroncas (L-3s), Piper Cubs (L-4s), Stinsons (L-5s), and, pictured here, Cessnas (L-19s). (Courtesy of the Antique Airplane Association.)

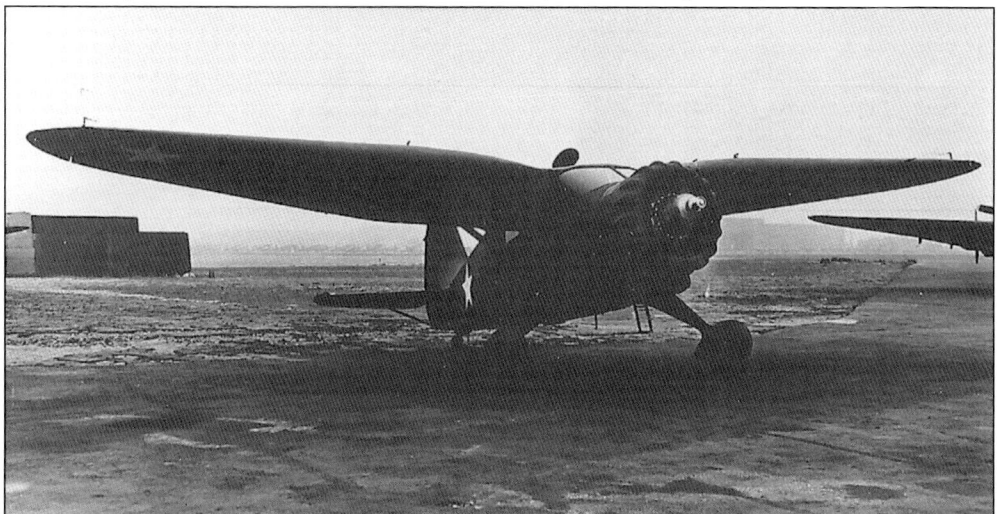

At Chapman Field, John and Bite Livingston formed a CPTP partnership with Waterloo's East High School and Iowa State Teachers College in Cedar Falls. In 1943, the Livingston brothers sold out to the Miller-Cavalier Flying Service, which continued the training program using Taylorcraft Cubs and Stinson C-81s (seen here) for advanced students. More than 3,000 students went through the Waterloo-based program with one casualty when flight instructor Homer Hansen was killed in a crash. (Courtesy of the Antique Airplane Association.)

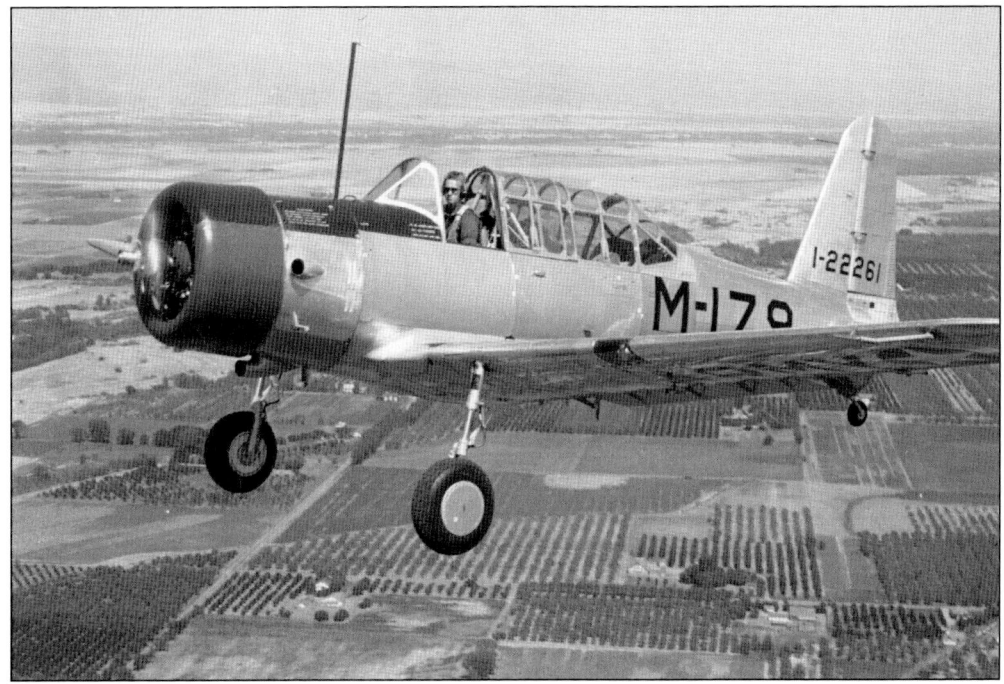

Many cadets "washed out" during basic flight-school training and were either encouraged to transfer to other service branches or simply sent home. Students who passed the basic ground-instruction courses and perfected their flying skills in small aircraft graduated to more challenging trainers like the North American AT-6s and Vultee BT-13s (pictured here). These full military trainers had more powerful radial engines of 450 horsepower and were the final phase of preparing student pilots for training in actual combat aircraft. (Courtesy of Bob O'Hara.)

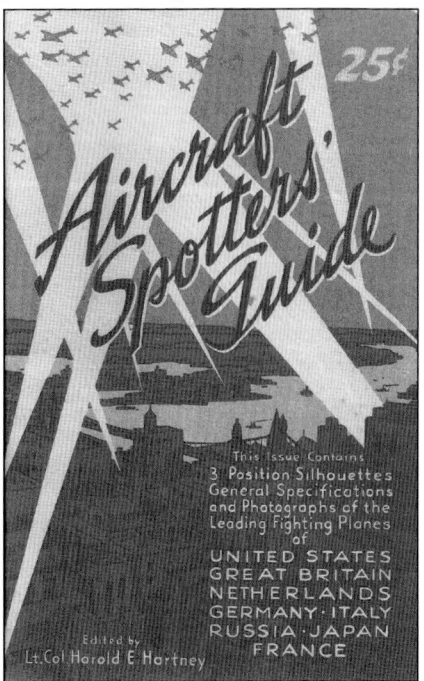

Iowa citizens unable to serve in the active military because of age or health restrictions could join other organizations. The Civil Air Patrol was the civilian auxiliary of the US Army Air Corps. Eastern Iowa squadrons were located in Dubuque, Burlington, Cedar Rapids, Davenport, Iowa City, Marion, Muscatine, Ottumwa, and Waterloo. Training included search and rescue, first aid, and aircraft-spotting classes to determine if an aircraft was "friend or foe." Every community had volunteer "civil defense officers" who, in addition to enforcing blackout and rationing requirements for homes and businesses, were trained in aircraft spotting. (Author's collection.)

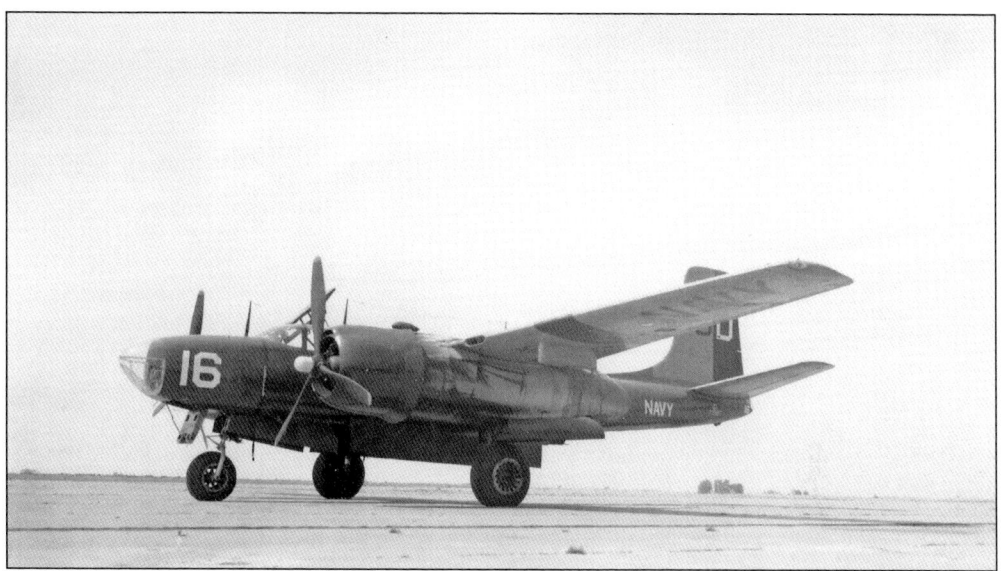

Ottumwa Airport was designated a US Naval Air Station for the duration of the war and was one of the largest in the Midwest. It was common for many different types of military aircraft to be seen there, like this Navy Douglas A-26 attack bomber. The planes were typically involved in training, liaison work, or were simply refueling. (Courtesy of the Antique Airplane Association.)

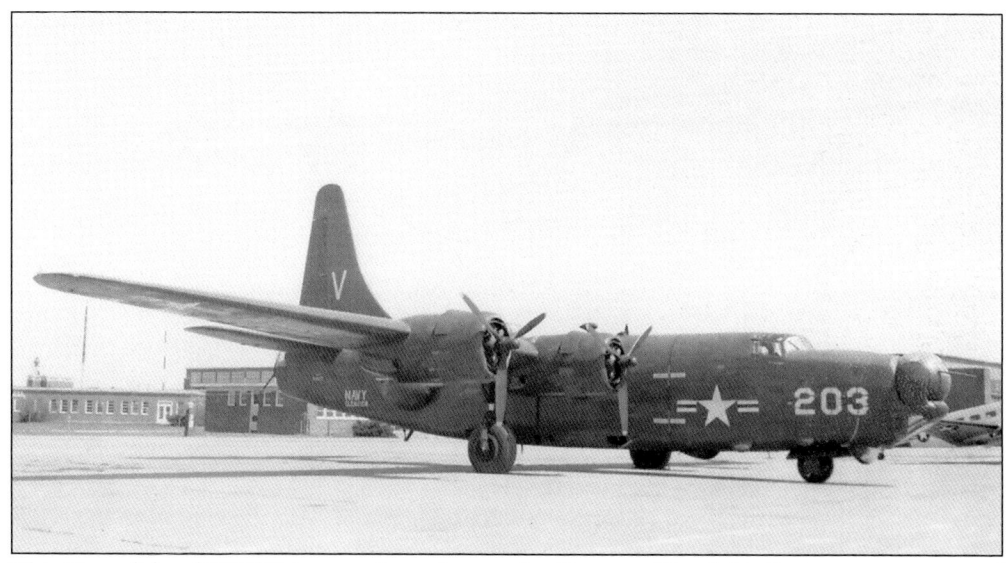

This Consolidated PB4Y Privateer, shown here at the Ottumwa Naval Air Station, was an unusual aircraft used by the US Navy for flight and navigational training, transport, and, on the coasts, antisubmarine patrols. (Courtesy of the Antique Airplane Association.)

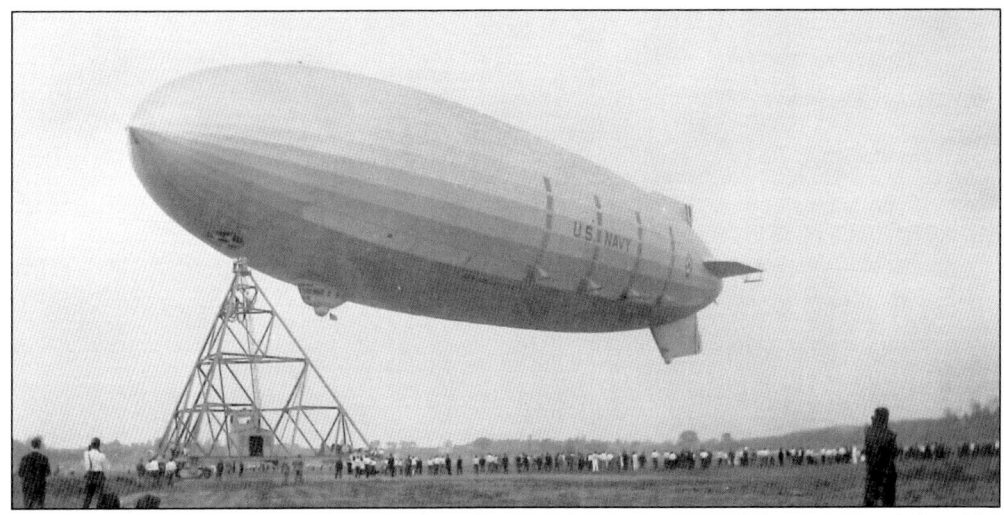

Because of its designation as a US Naval Air Station, Ottumwa moored the occasional dirigible. These "LTAs" (Lighter Than Air) or "blimps" were filled with helium using twin Pratt & Whitney engines that could move up to 70 knots with a crew of 10 on board and dozens of handlers on the ground to launch and recover the airship. (Courtesy of the Cedar Falls Historical Society.)

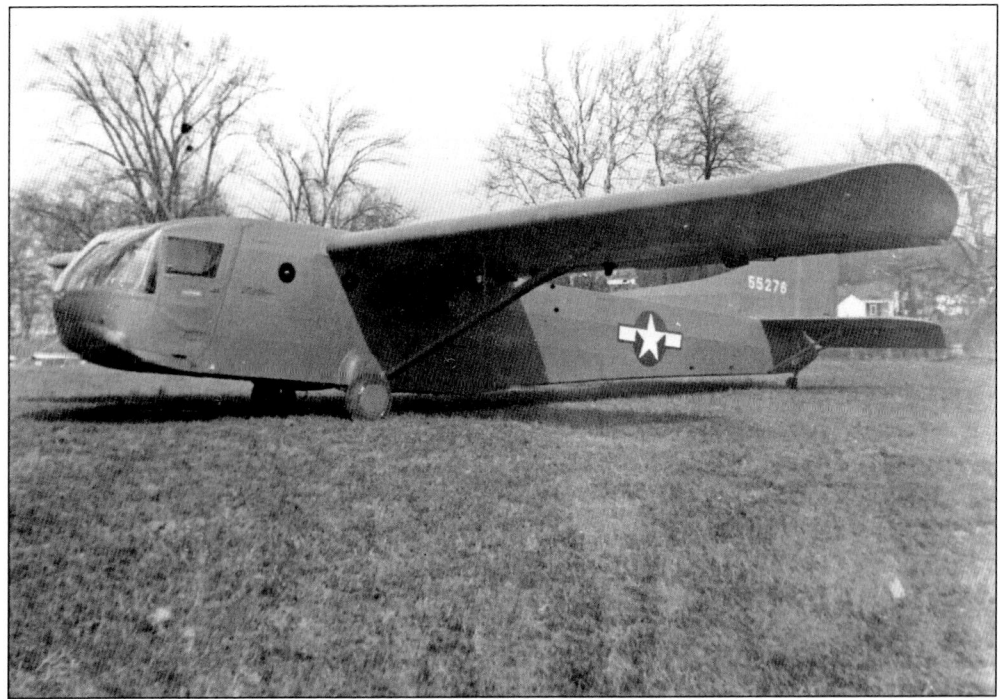

Dan Hunter, in addition to his Cedar Rapids–based flying service and training program, was contracted to provide civilian pilots, mechanics, ground-school instructors, guards, secretaries, and cooks for the Spencer-based glider training school—one of 29 in the nation. Glider pilots were volunteers, some of whom had experience from being in the civilian flight-training programs. After learning basic skills in smaller gliders, most glider pilots eventually flew this Waco CG-4A, which was made of wood and fabric and towed behind C-47 (DC-3) transports into combat. (Courtesy of the Antique Airplane Association.)

The US Army Air Corps established the Women Auxiliary Service Pilots (WASP) program, which trained women to test fly and ferry aircraft, freeing up more male pilots for combat assignments. Irene Gregory (later Lindner) was among the first to join the service, along with Iowa natives Marie Mountain, Madelon Hill, Dorothy Henry, and Jean Sidwell. (Courtesy of Irv Lindner.)

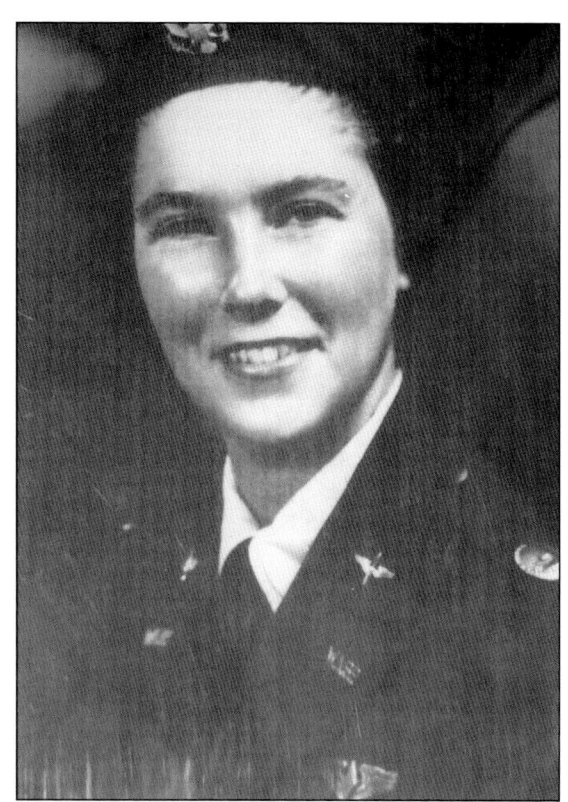

WASP cadets received primary training at Avenger Field in Sweetwater, Texas, before being sent to other training sites for the different aircraft types they would fly. Irene Gregory, fourth from the right in the front row, met her future husband, Irv Lindner, at pursuit aircraft school in Brownsville, Texas, where they had the same instructor and studied together. (Courtesy of Irv Lindner.)

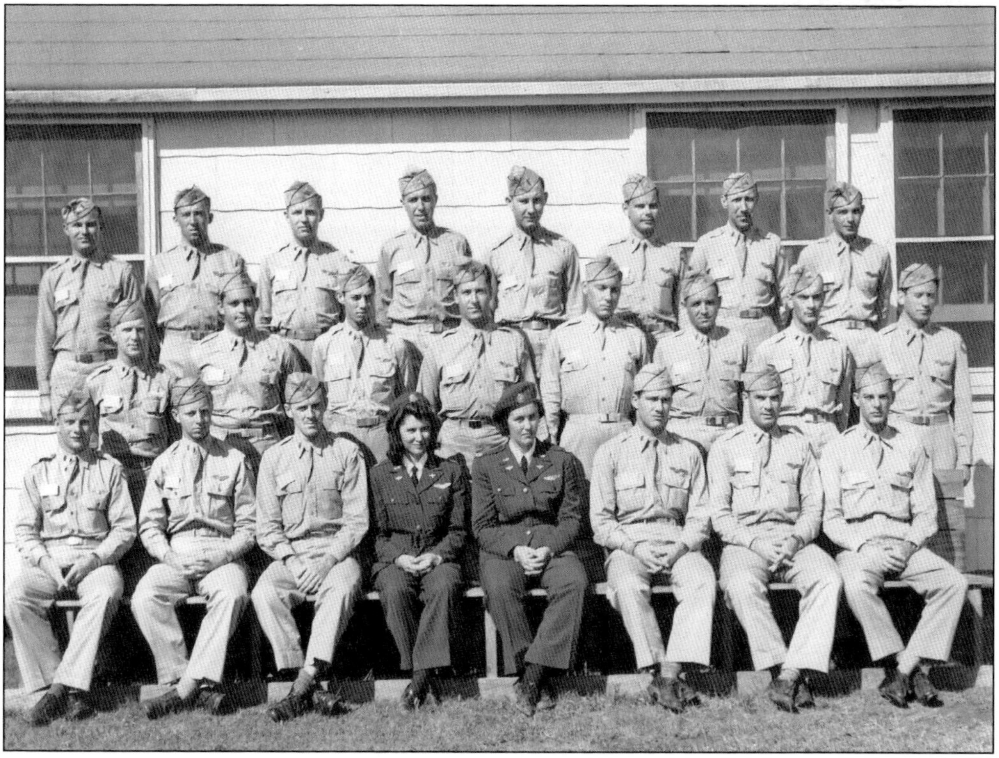

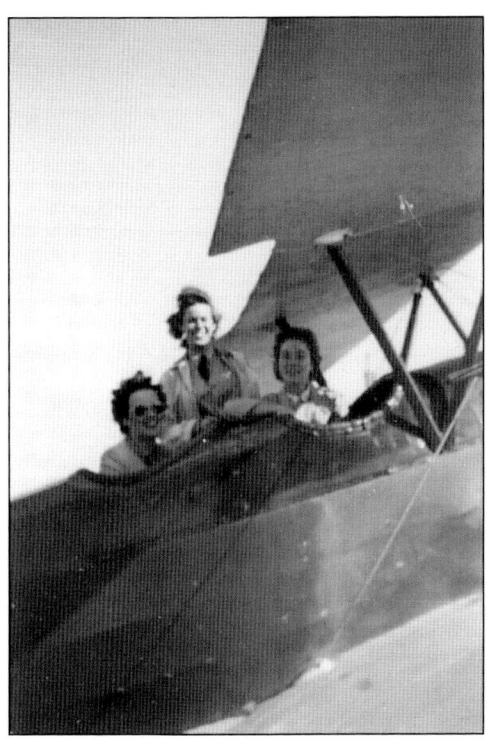

Women pilots trained alongside men and proved they could achieve the critical flying and navigation skills as quickly as male students. Some of the women had previous flying experience since they had been allowed to join the CPTP program before the war. Women flew everything from Cubs to B-17s. Irene Gregory is at the far right in a Stearman trainer with two WASP comrades. (Courtesy of Irv Lindner.)

More than a thousand women flew in the WASP program. Other Iowans who served in various WASP assignments were Jean Livingston, June Braun, Ann Darr, Martha Mace (Boshart), Marilyn Myers (Peyton), Merridee Newell (Schneberger), Dorothy Norris, Margaret Phelan (Taylor), Ursala Wald (Coventry), and Lavina Lippincott. Two Iowans, Gleanna Roberts and Beverly Moses, were killed in the line of duty. (Courtesy of Irv Lindner.)

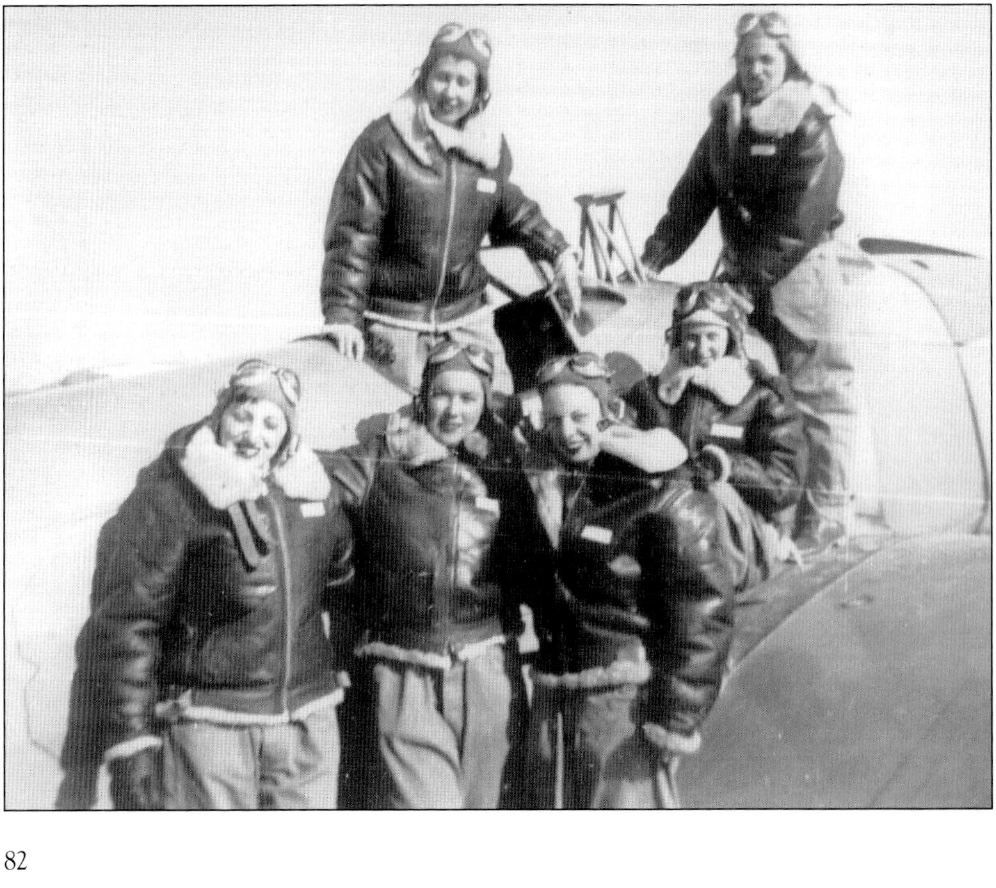

Irv Lindner of Keokuk was one of thousands of Iowa men who volunteered to serve during World War II. He learned to fly before the war and received his commercial and instructor ratings from Paul Shaw in Iowa City as part of the CPTP program. He was sent to Texas, where he flew PT-19s at Kelly Field in San Antonio and Houston. He later flew AT-6 Texans at pursuit school and then at Brownsville, where he and his future wife, Irene, first met. (Courtesy of Irv Lindner.)

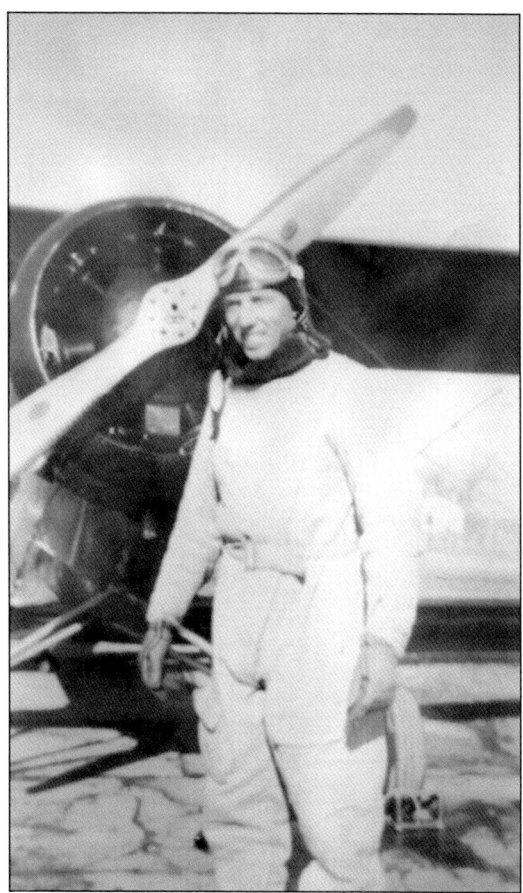

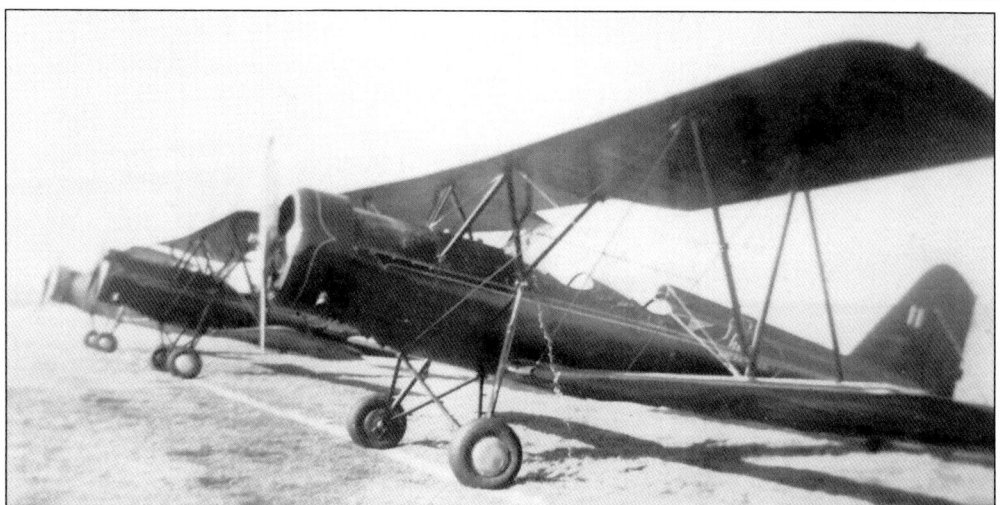

Starting out in Meyers OTWs (pictured) for his initial training, then Fairchild PT-19s, Irv Lindner trained the first classes of WASP pilots in basic flight characteristics and navigation techniques. He recalls, "We had no radios, so all the landing instructions were done with lights. It was one fine mess. The women were good pilots. In fact, one of them had more flying time than I did." (Courtesy of Irv Lindner.)

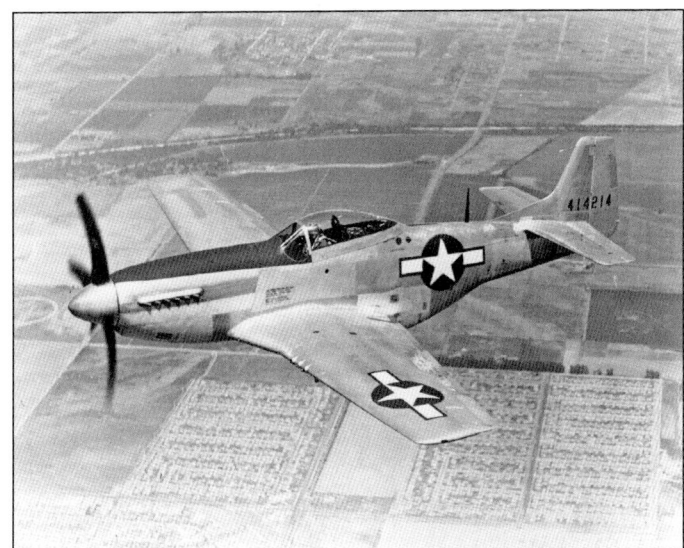

The one aircraft that both Irv and Irene Lindner agreed was the most fun to fly was the North American P-51 Mustang. "Now *that* was an airplane," Irv recalled. "A real hot rod; they ran as good upside down as right side up. Irene thought so too. She enjoyed ferrying those Mustangs all over the country." (Courtesy of Irv Lindner.)

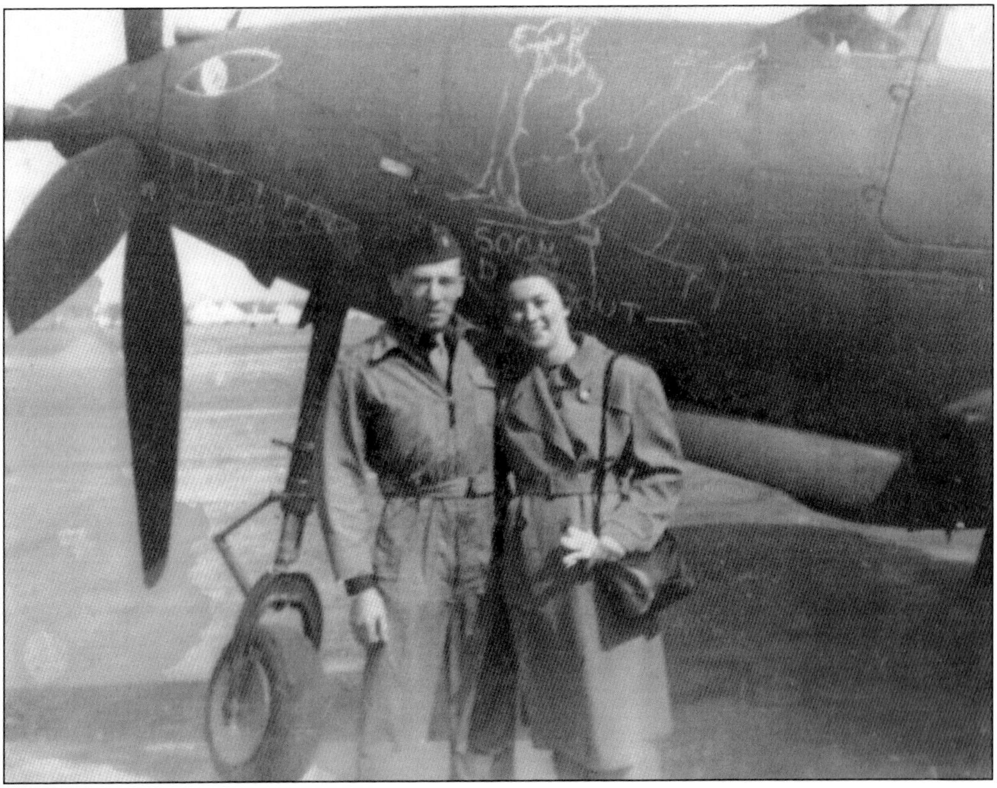

Irv and Irene crossed paths during the war as they ferried airplanes of all types to air bases all over the world. On the day that the WASP program was disbanded at the end of the war, the women were told they were no longer needed, with no consideration for any travel expenses they might need to return home. Irene had to call her parents in Philadelphia to ask them to wire her bus fare from California, where she had been preparing to fly a P-51 Mustang from the factory to an air base. Irv recalled, "We decided to get married and start our own flight operation." (Courtesy of Irv Lindner.)

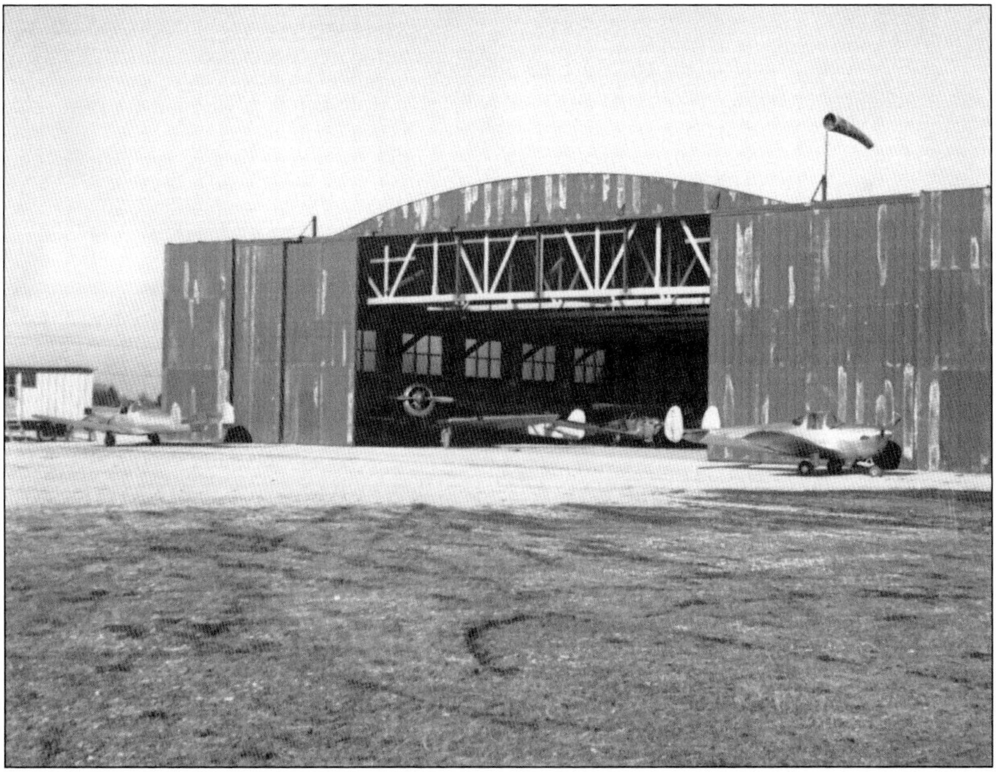

Irene and Irv Lindner, like many returning postwar veterans, decided to start their own business, taking advantage of the new GI Bill for financing, and settled in Keokuk. "It was just the two of us," Irv recalled. "There were three sod runways and an old house with a pump inside, with bees and skunks, and a cow shed we converted into a hangar." It was the beginning of Lindner Flying Service. (Courtesy of Irv Lindner.)

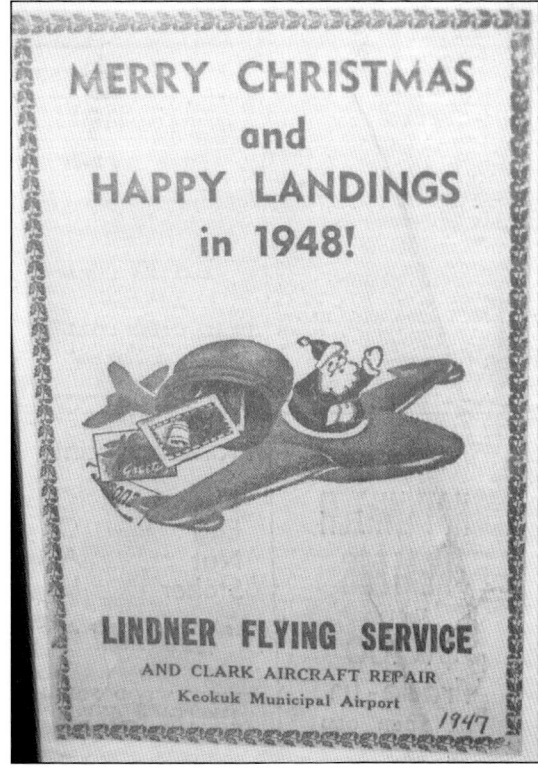

The Lindners built a reputation for excellent customer service at the Keokuk Municipal Airport. Irv recalled, "We bought a Taylorcraft for $1,500 and an old Aeronca Champ and we had students. We hired three instructors and each had 10 students. The smartest thing we did was to go to the FAA in Kansas City and told them we needed all the help we could get." (Courtesy of Irv Lindner.)

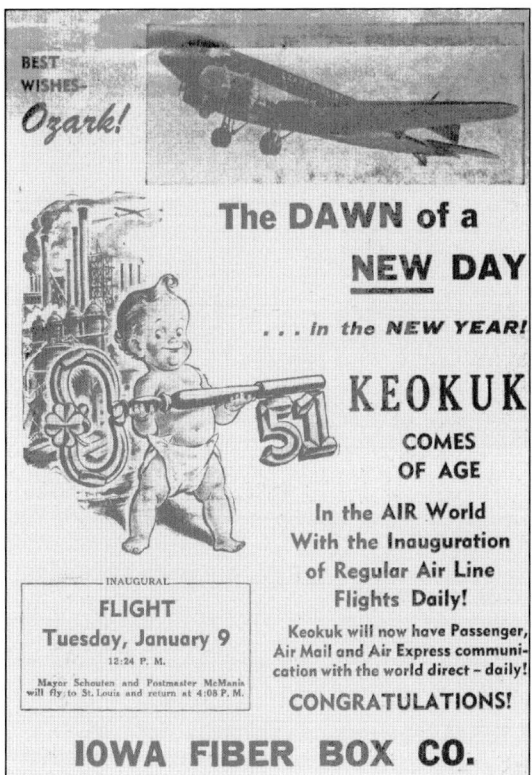

As the Lindners' business grew, they invested in more modern aircraft. Irv recalled, "We decided on all metal airplanes, and Cessna was the only one at the time, so we got 120s, 140s, and 180s." They promoted aviation all over the region, trying to encourage larger air carriers of freight and passengers to create stops in Keokuk. (Courtesy of Irv Lindner.)

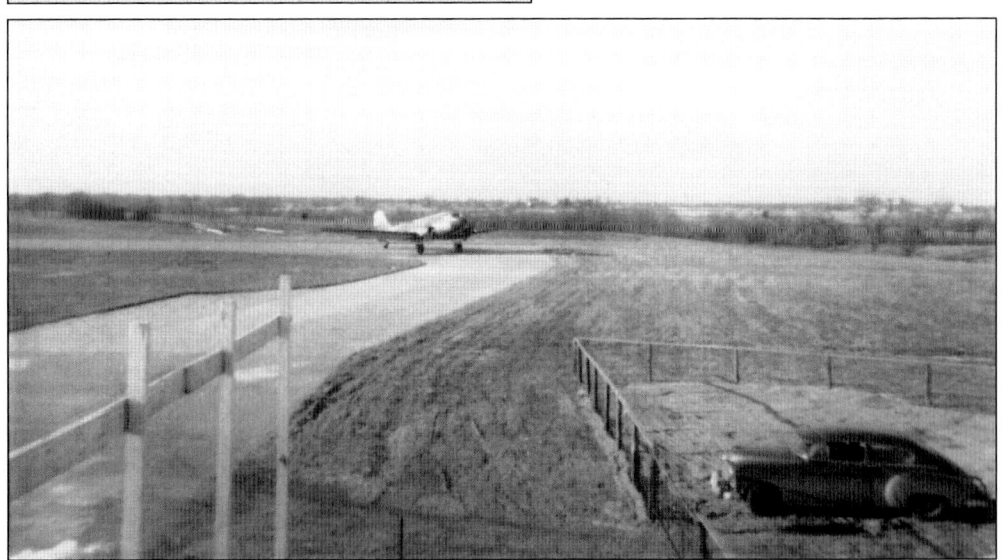

It took several years, but before long Keokuk leaders convinced Ozark Airlines that it would be profitable for them to establish regularly scheduled service to eastern Iowa's southernmost airport. Meanwhile, Irv Lindner offered flight instruction, hauled freight and passengers, and even did some crop dusting. "I flew a Cub with a big engine," Irv recalled. One day Irene happened to see him making what she considered dangerous maneuvers required to get the job done. "When I landed she said, 'I'd just as soon you quit spraying,' so that was the end of the crop dusting," Irv recalled. (Courtesy of Irv Lindner.)

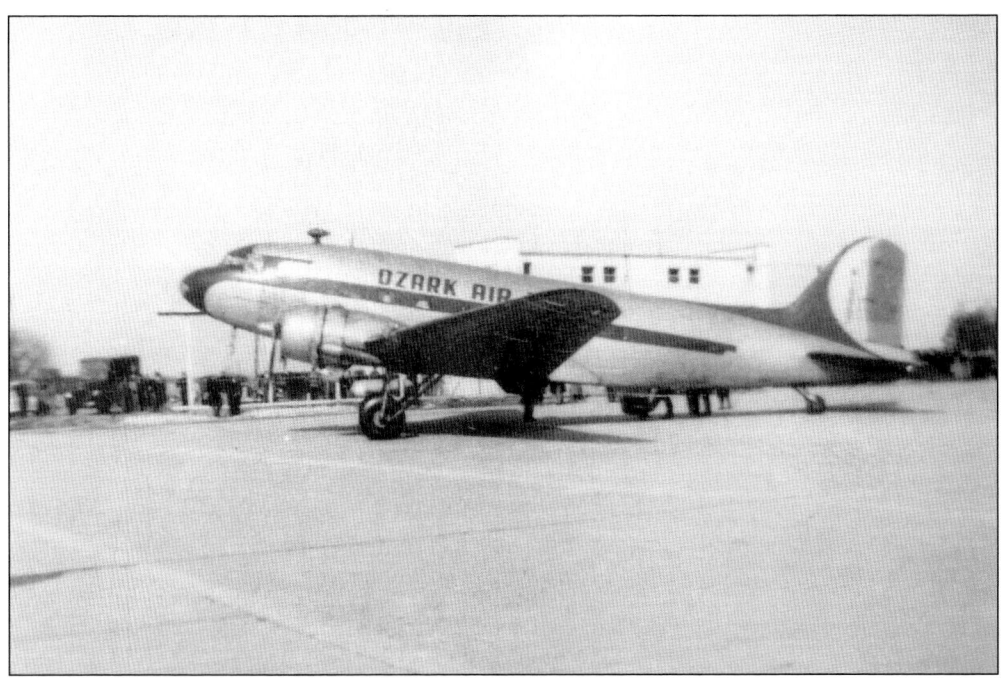

Improvements were made in the Keokuk runways and taxiways to accommodate Ozark Airlines' Douglas DC-3s. Irv and Irene kept promoting aviation, at one point running the Keokuk Airport while also managing facilities in Fort Madison and Quincy in Illinois and in Hannibal, Missouri. It was their philosophy, as Irv explained, to "observe the turtle; he never advances until he sticks his neck out." (Courtesy of Irv Lindner.)

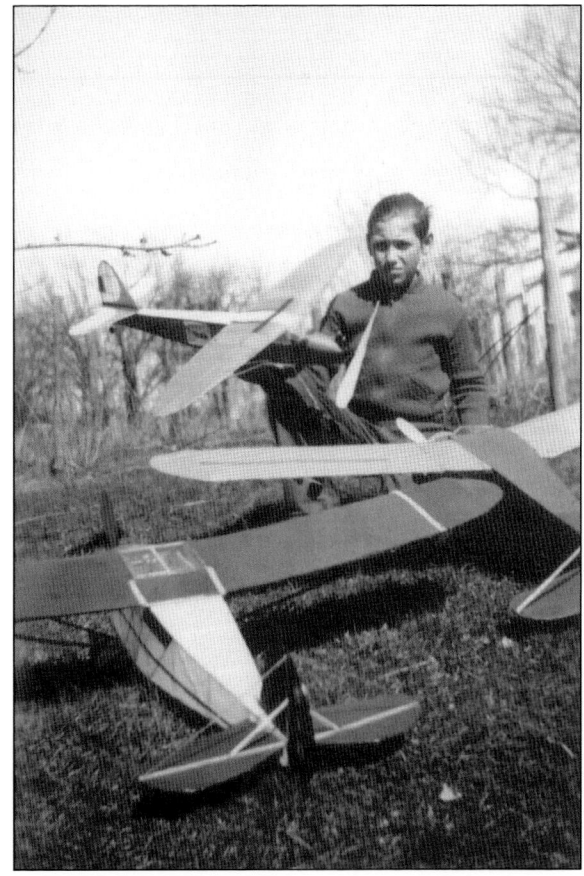

Sid Yahn of Ottumwa was always an aviation enthusiast. He built prize-winning model airplanes when he was nine years old. Like many eastern Iowa aviators who learned to fly during the war years, Yahn did not participate in the World War II air arena. In 1943, when still a junior in high school, he volunteered for the Army Air Force Cadet Program. The war began winding down, the cadet program was terminated, and Yahn was discharged. (Courtesy of Sid Yahn.)

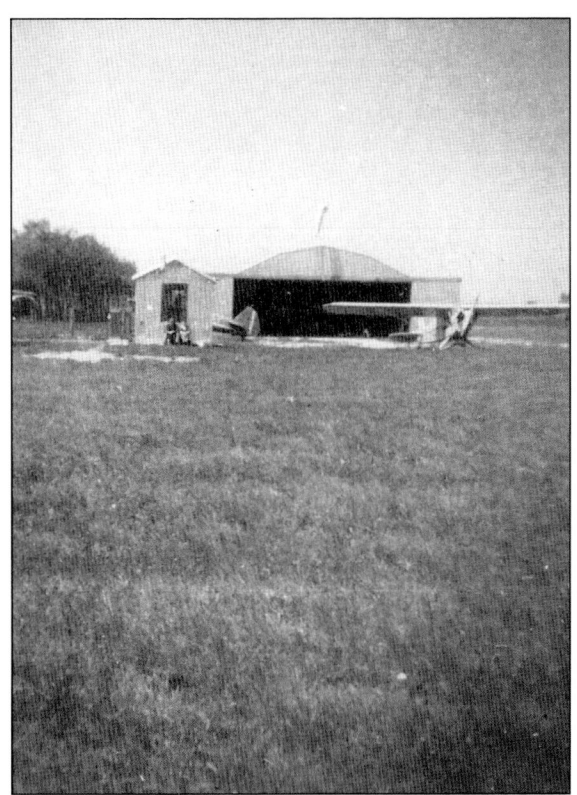

Sid Yahn owned several aircraft and kept them at Venture Field in Ottumwa, which was managed by Clifton "Ole" Oleson, who Yahn described as "a true aviation pioneer." There were hundreds of "Venture Fields" all over the Midwest. As shown here, they were quiet, rural airfields with maybe a building or two, where pilots could visit with each other between flights or give rides to enthusiasts. (Courtesy of Sid Yahn.)

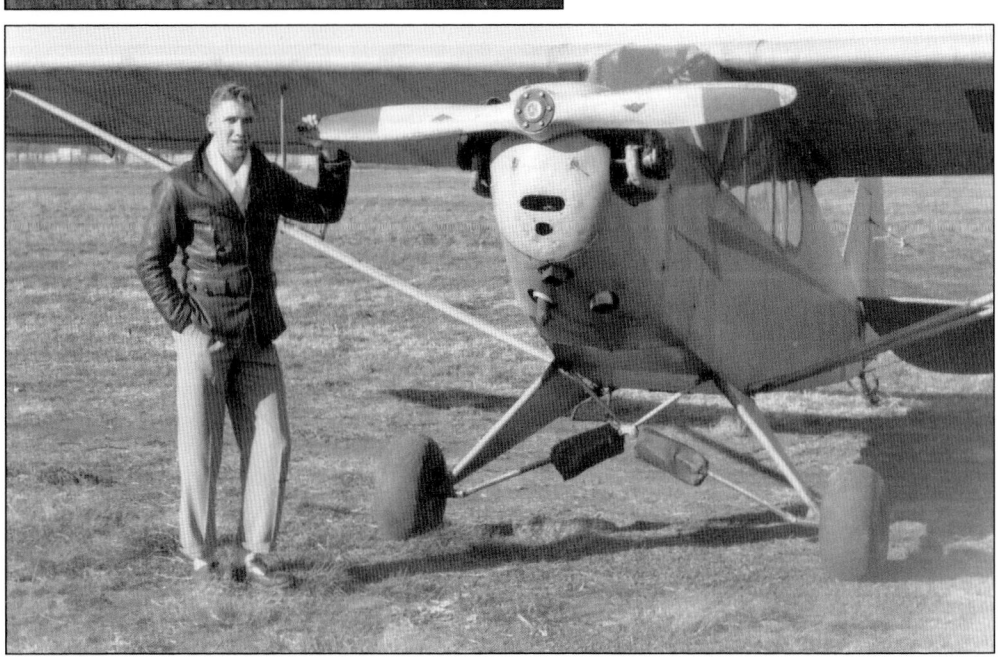

Like many new pilots of the day, Sid Yahn logged many hours flying his Piper J-3 Cub over southeastern Iowa farmland. In 1945, he sold the Cub to Clifton "Ole" Oleson. The 1943 Ottumwa chapter of the National Aeronautic Association listed 43 Ottumwans (including Sid Yahn) as members. (Courtesy of Sid Yahn.)

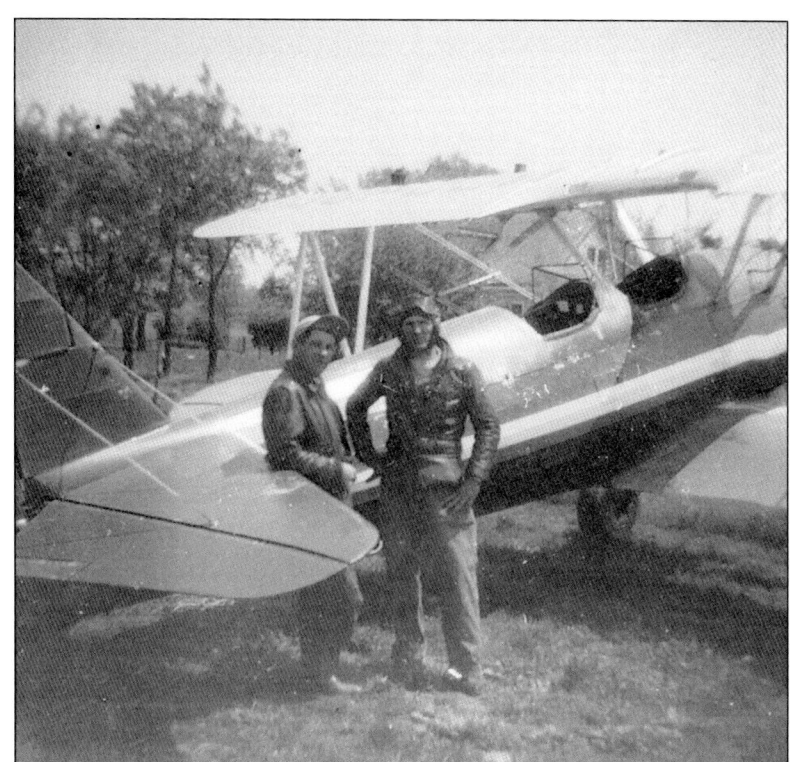

This 1946 photograph shows Clifton "Ole" Oleson (left) and Sid Yahn critiquing the PT-17 flight they just completed. Yahn asked Ole to demonstrate how a PT-17 should be flown. Yahn recalled, "No question, Ole was an amazing pilot." Years before, in the 1930s, Ole took Yahn for a ride in a Curtiss Robin, so their friendship went back a long way. (Courtesy of Sid Yahn.)

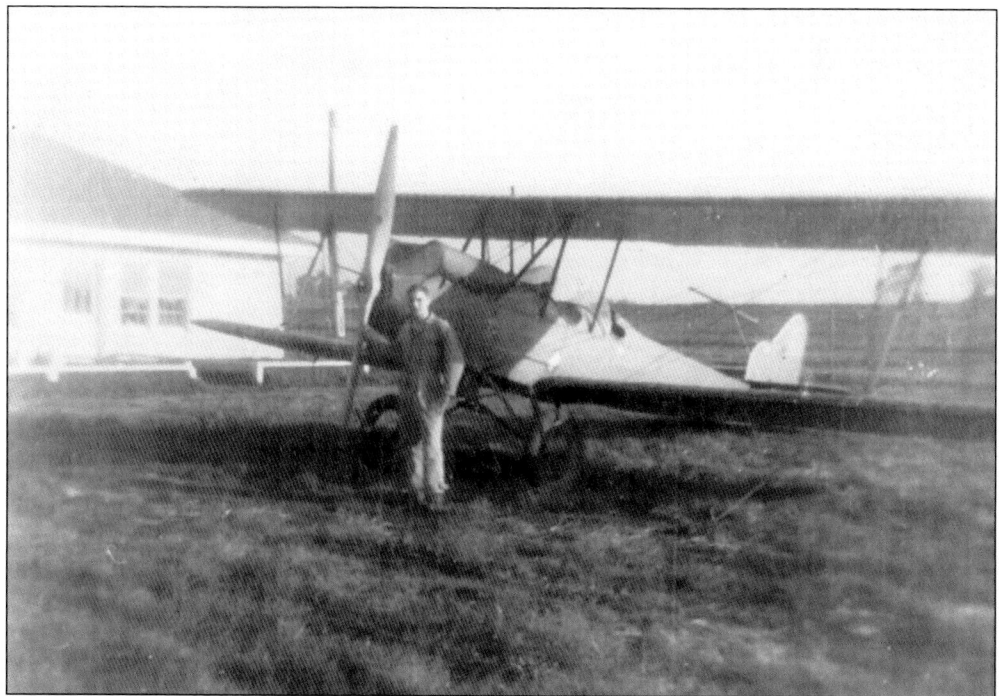

Sid Yahn flew many of the old prewar biplanes while building flight time, including this 1929 Lincoln Page biplane powered by a Curtiss OX-5 liquid-cooled V-8 engine. "It was the oldest airplane I ever flew," he recalled. (Courtesy of Sid Yahn.)

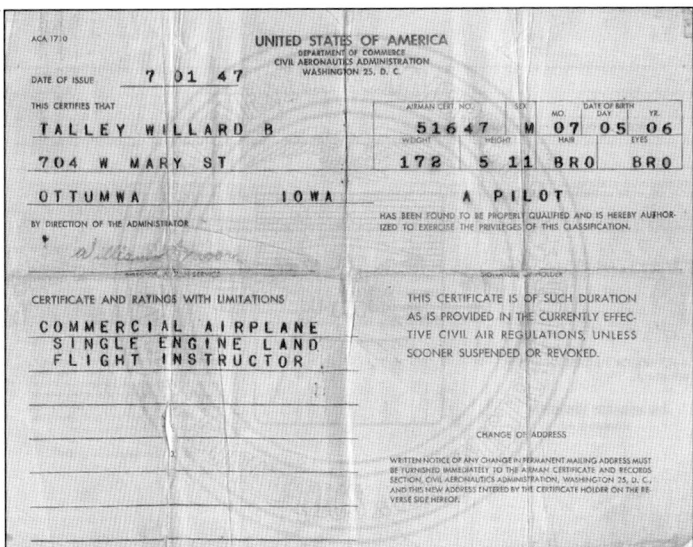

Some of the early barnstormers who had been WTS and CPTP instructors during the war, like Willard Talley, came home to eastern Iowa and renewed their civilian aviation careers. Talley worked at the Ottumwa and Fairfield Airports, performing restorations on older aircraft and becoming interested in helicopter design. (Courtesy of the Antique Airplane Association.)

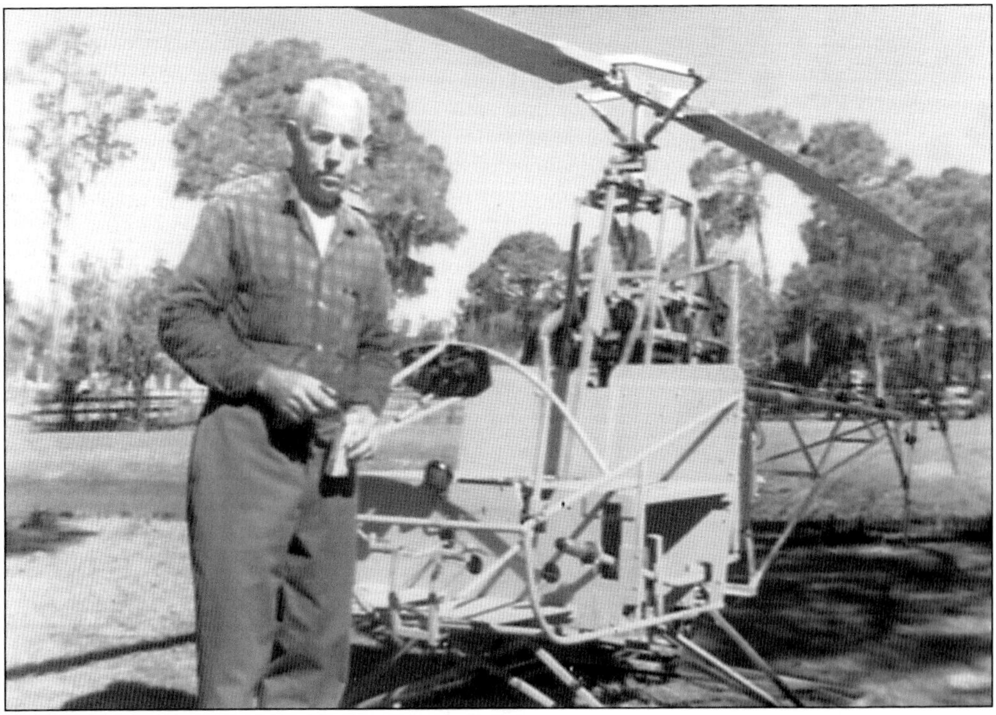

After moving to Florida for a few years, Willard Talley and his wife, Effie, returned to Iowa, retiring in Perry, where he continued to work on restorations, including Andersons, Travel Airs, and OX-5 engines. He also continued work on his helicopter designs, which were powered by everything from 40-horsepower outboard motors to 260-horsepower automobile engines. (Courtesy of the Antique Airplane Association.)

Six

INTO THE JET AGE
1950 TO THE PRESENT

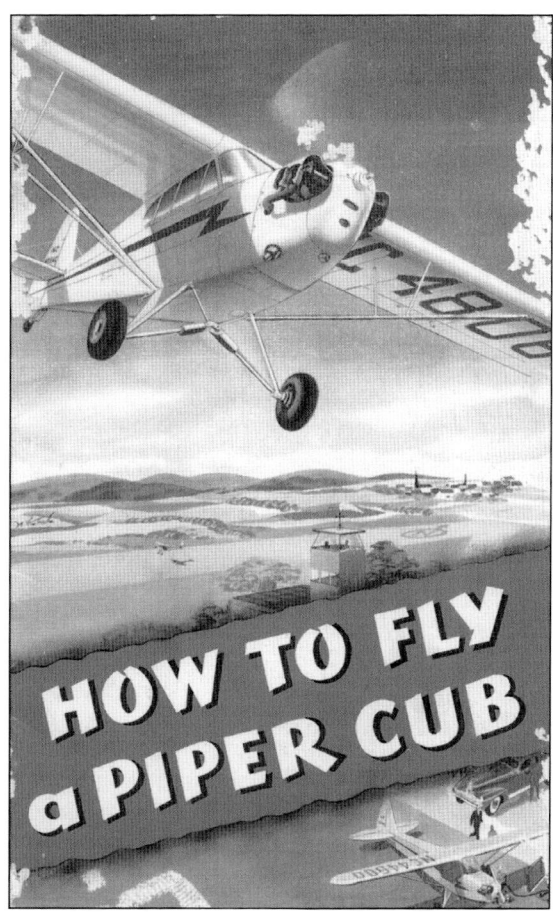

The 1950s began the modern era in which aviation technology, much of it learned during the war years, exploded onto the eastern Iowa scene. Leaders of the aviation industry, as a whole, were optimistic that thousands of young men who had served as military pilots and mechanics would return home and continue their affiliation with flying, using the GI Bill to obtain civilian pilot ratings and then purchase small, single-engine airplanes for their own use. Piper, one of the largest builders of small airplanes, including its popular Cub, advertised how easy it was to learn to fly one and how economical it was to own one. (Courtesy of the Antique Airplane Association.)

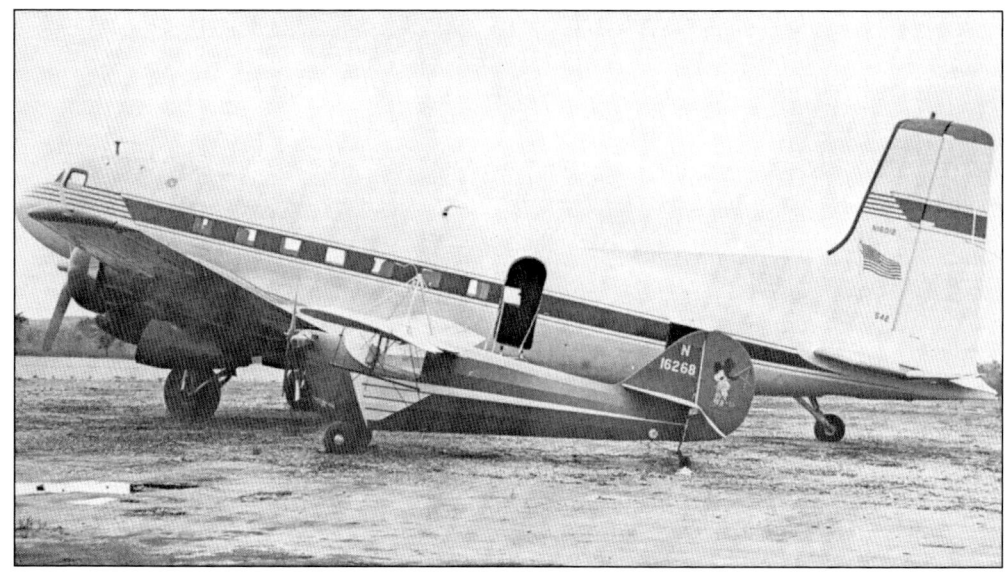

On any given day, a visitor to a local airport, like Cedar Rapids, could see a large, modern airliner, like this Douglas DC-3, sharing runways with airplanes from years earlier, like this Aeronca C-3. Air travel finally was commonplace, but the dreamers were still busy finding new ways for aviation to enhance the lives of Iowa's citizens. (Courtesy of the Antique Airplane Association.)

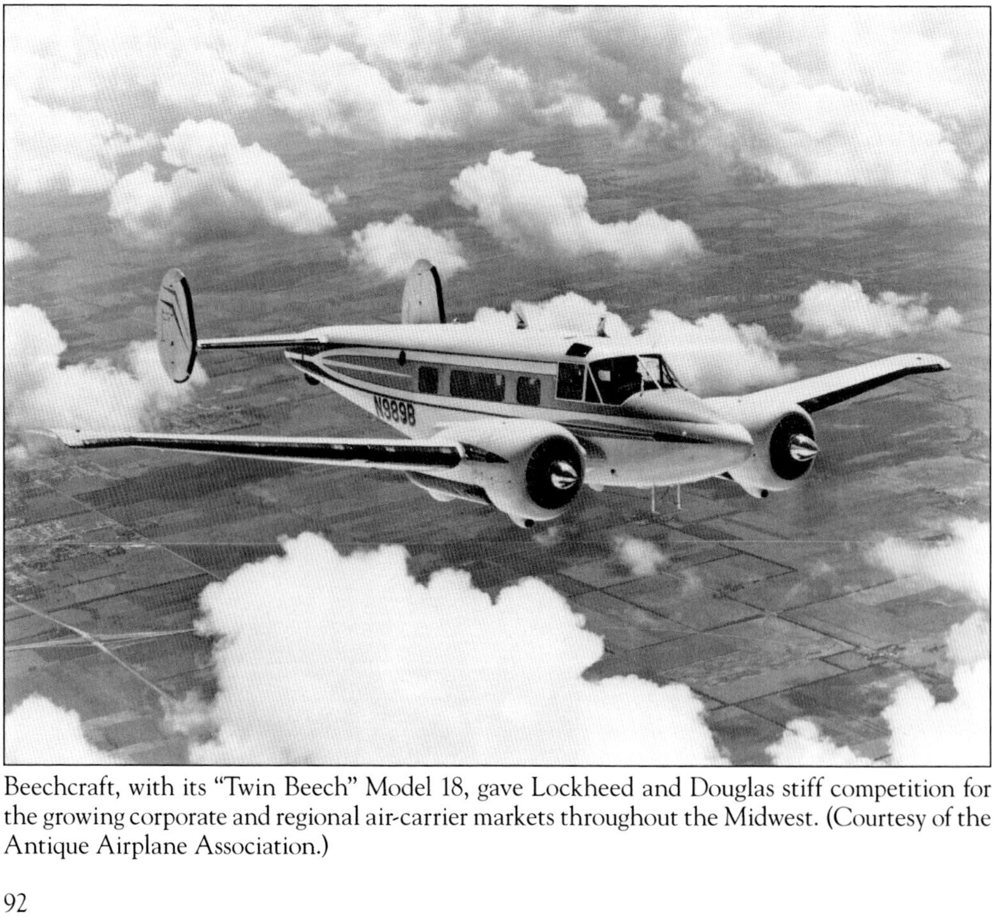

Beechcraft, with its "Twin Beech" Model 18, gave Lockheed and Douglas stiff competition for the growing corporate and regional air-carrier markets throughout the Midwest. (Courtesy of the Antique Airplane Association.)

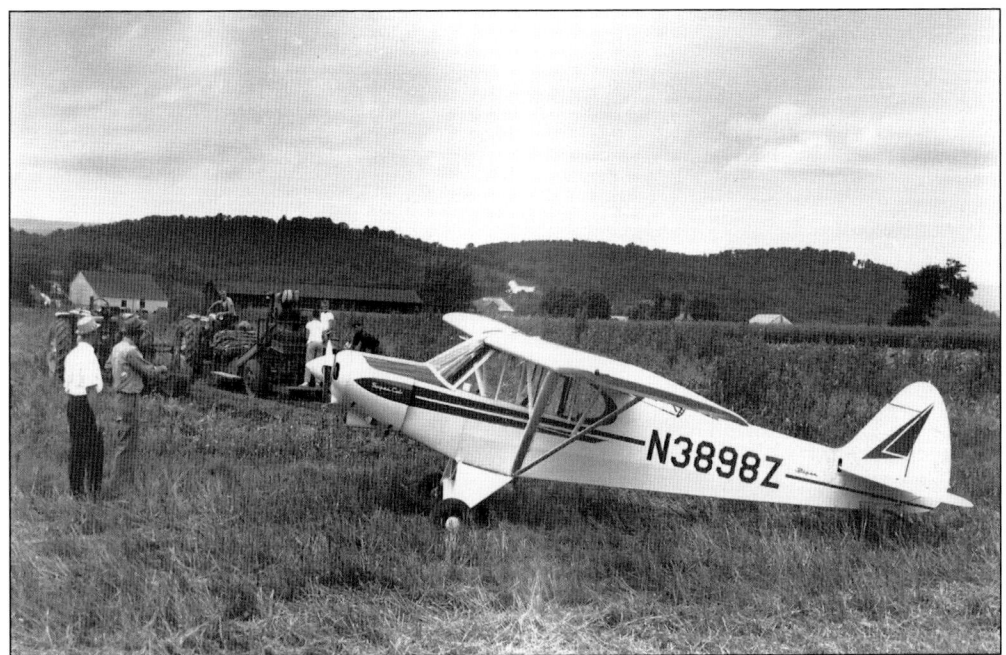

Even though Glen Phelps had called on his insurance clients in his Monoprep 20 years earlier, it was still considered a novelty for a claims adjuster or salesperson to show up in an airplane, like this Farm Bureau agent's Piper Super Cub in an Iowa field. Clubs of aviation enthusiasts formed organizations like the Flying Farmers. (Courtesy of the Antique Airplane Association.)

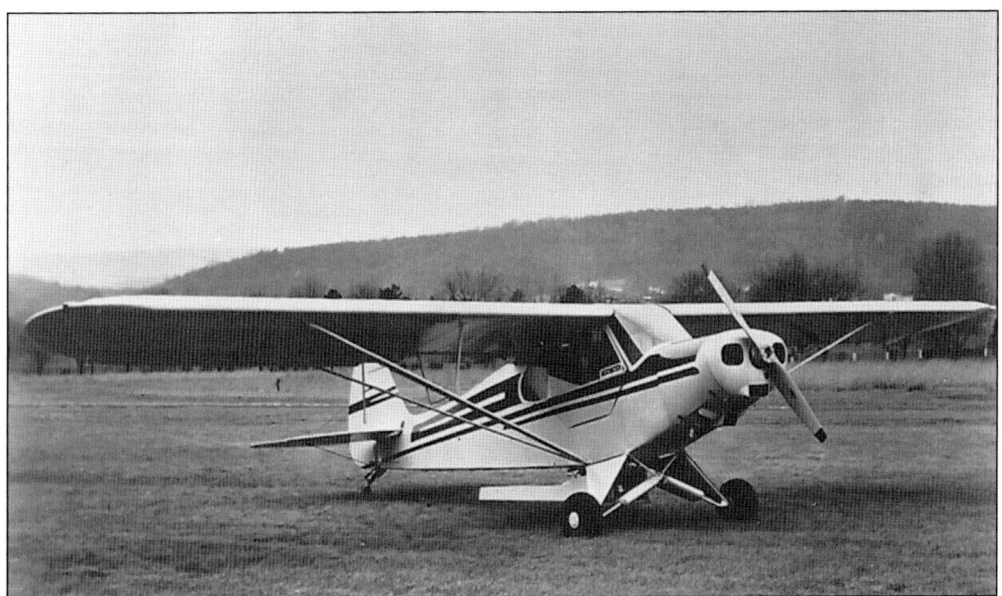

Dusting crops with airplanes was nothing new, but now there were more sophisticated systems that could be ordered ready to install on the aircraft right from the factory. The Piper PA-18 Duster (a Super Cub with spray equipment) was economical and easy to maintain, which was appealing to a new generation of agricultural businesses. (Courtesy of the Antique Airplane Association.)

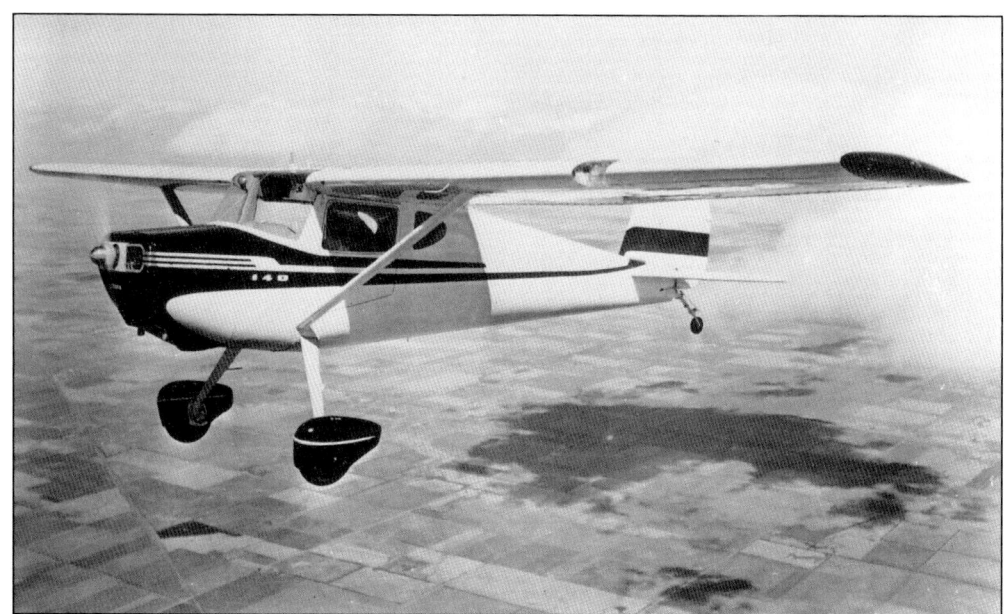

As World War II was ending, small airplane manufacturers hurried to grab the predicted trend of "a plane in every garage." Cessna Aircraft, in order to compete with Piper's Cubs and Super Cubs, designed the 120 and 140 models. They had all-metal fuselages, though the early models had fabric wings. Boasting maximum speeds of 120 miles per hour and ceilings of more than 15,000 feet, the basic versions sold for $3,245. Options included soundproofing, an electrical system including a starter, and deluxe seating. They became very popular for flight training and as entry-level airplanes at an affordable price. (Courtesy of the Antique Airplane Association.)

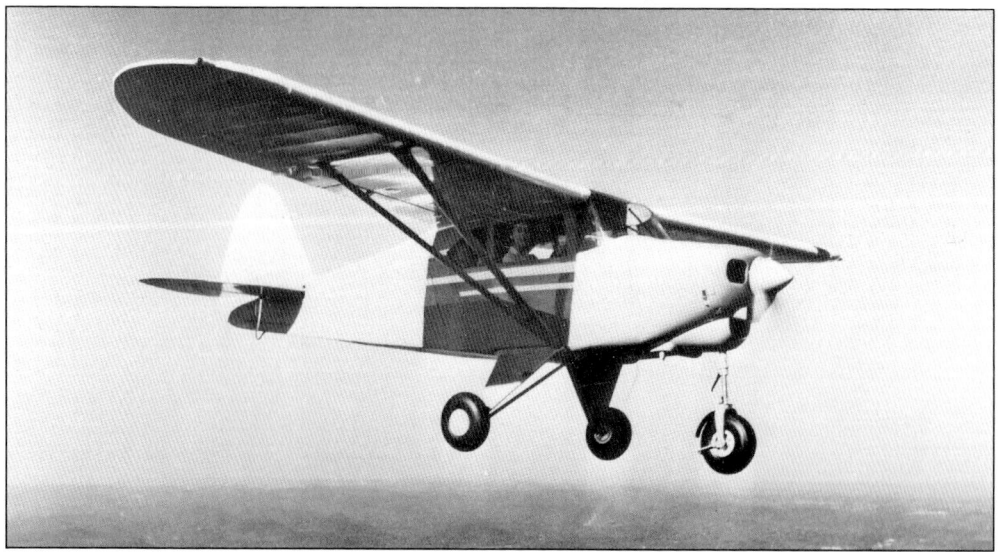

Meanwhile, Piper developed its own new Tri-Pacer and Colt models that sported tricycle-style landing gear. This design was easier for passengers to enter and exit the airplane, while providing pilots with better visibility on the ground and more positive control during landings, especially in crosswind conditions. These became the next level of private single aircraft for businessmen, sportsmen, and families who needed more space and power than the Cub models. (Courtesy of the Antique Airplane Association.)

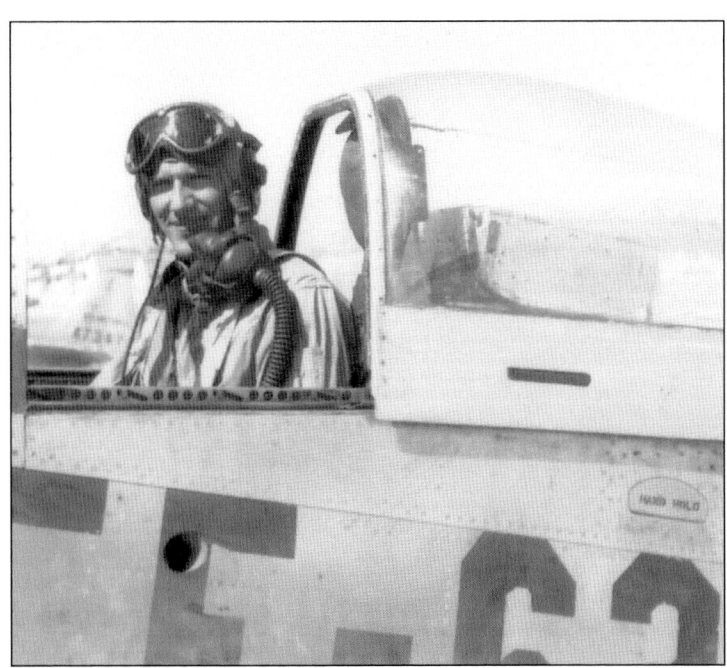

There were still wars being waged, and those who had "missed out" on World War II got their chance to serve in Korea. While assigned to Nellis Air Force Base in Nevada, Sid Yahn flew F-51s (shown here). On one occasion, his aircraft's engine quit during a formation takeoff. During another flight, Yahn was forced to bail out when his engine caught fire. In 1951, his base received a request for one volunteer for Korea. Yahn quickly said, "I'll take it." (Courtesy of Sid Yahn.)

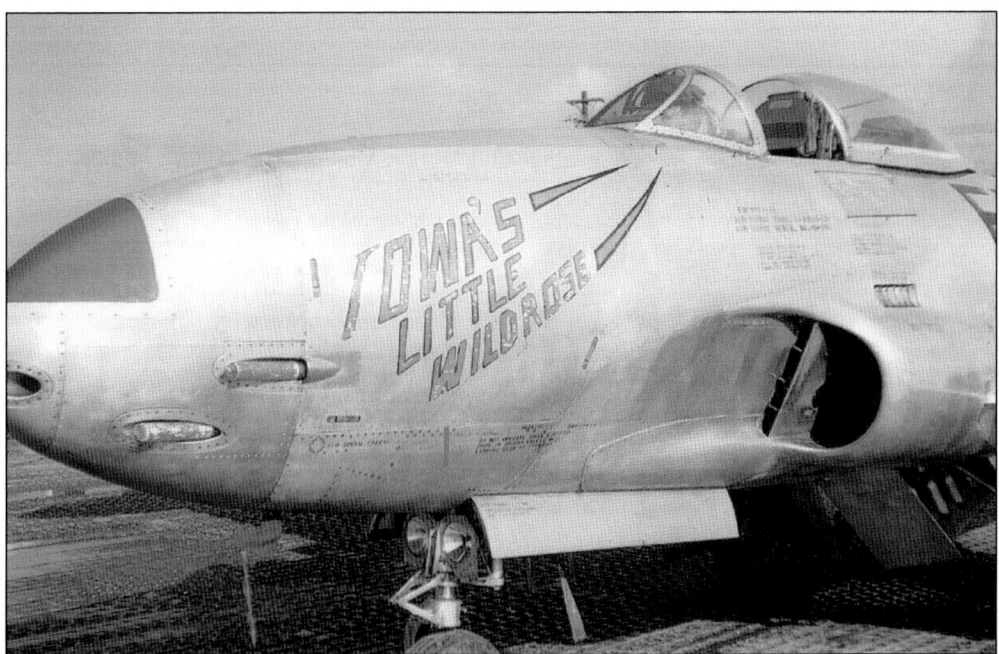

In 1952, Sid Yahn was assigned to the 80th Fighter-Bomber Squadron, known as the "Headhunters," at Suwan Air Base (K-13) in Korea. He flew 126 combat missions in F-80s. Both Sid and his crew chief were from Iowa, thus their aircraft was named *Iowa's Little Wild Rose* after the state flower. Yahn led a number of combat missions in this aircraft. When Maj. Charles J. Loring Jr. was assigned to the 80th, Yahn checked him out and flew flight lead during his first combat mission. Later, Loring was posthumously awarded the Medal of Honor—one of only four Air Force personnel to be so honored during the Korean War. (Courtesy of Sid Yahn.)

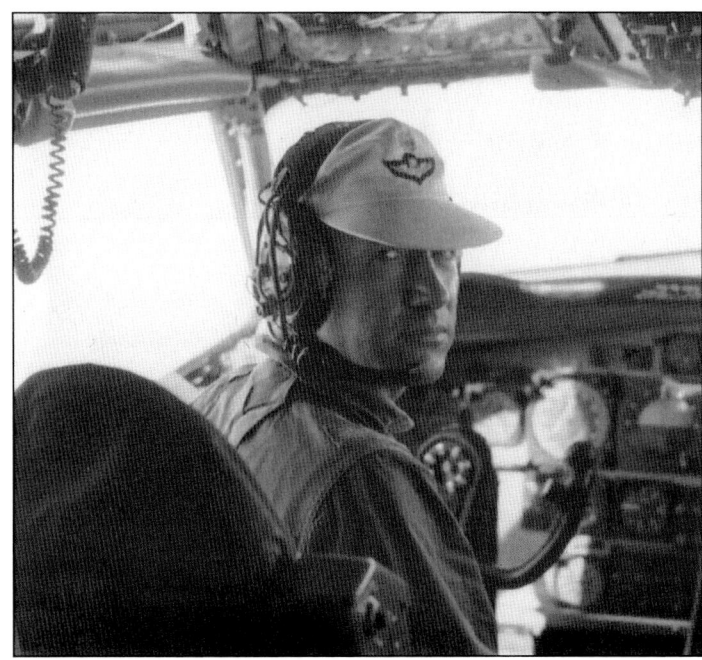

After Korea, Sid Yahn worked as operations advisor to the First Fighter Wing, Chinese Air Force (CAF) in Taiwan. During this period, he flew F-84s, F-86s, and F-5s with the Chinese. He accumulated more flying hours in Chinese fighters than any foreign national. During Vietnam, Yahn, then a lieutenant colonel in the Strategic Air Command, flew many types of aircraft. This photograph shows him flying a KC-135 tanker during one of his 111 Vietnam combat missions. (Courtesy of Sid Yahn.)

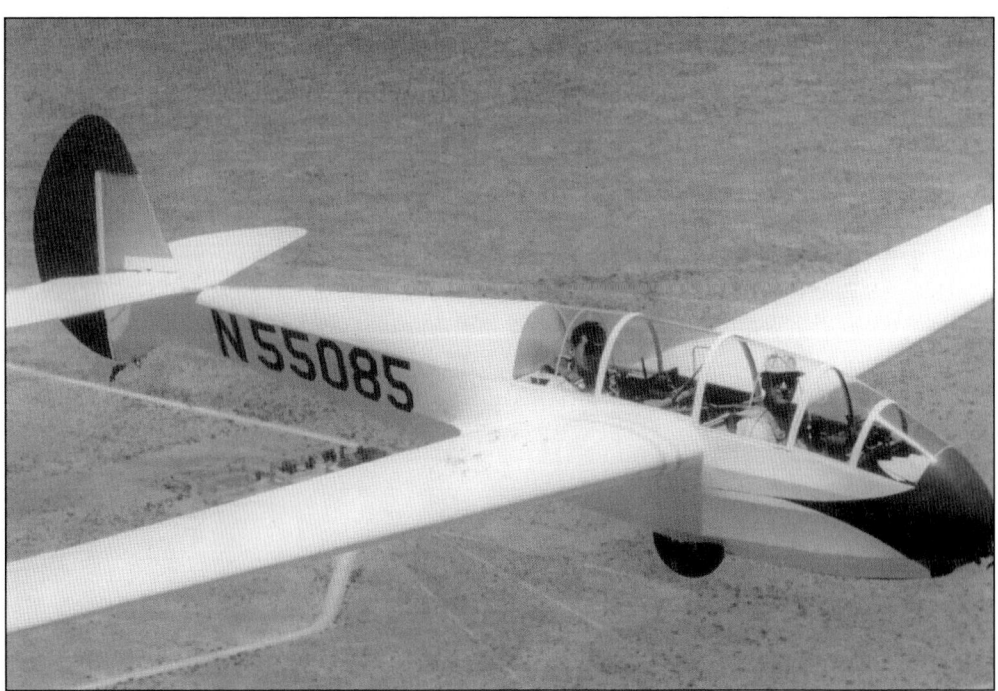

Prior to Sid Yahn's retirement from the military in 1974, he established a commercial glider operation. His plans changed, however, when Northrup Corporation offered him a position as a worldwide marketing representative. So he gave up soaring and entered the industrial aerospace community. Eventually, he returned to Taiwan as Northrup's resident director, a position he held for many years. (Courtesy of Sid Yahn.)

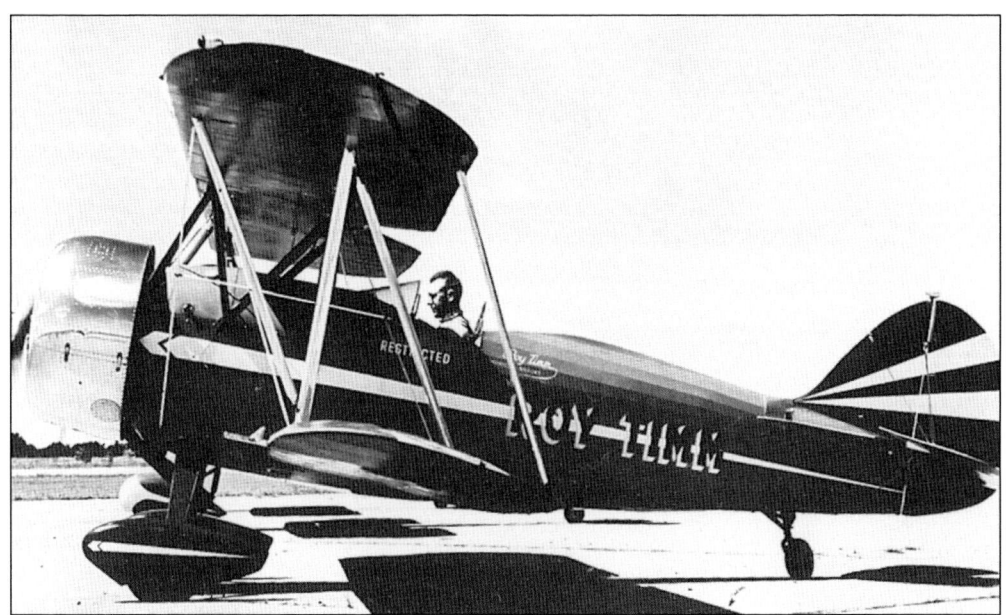

During the early 1950s, there were many pilots who upheld the tradition of the "air show," travelling around the country barnstorming in old military trainers just as the old-timers had done after World War I in old Jennys and Standards. The new generation of barnstormers used World War II surplus biplanes made by Stearman, Travel Air, and Wacos like the Special (pictured) flown by Roy Timm. (Courtesy of the Antique Airplane Association.)

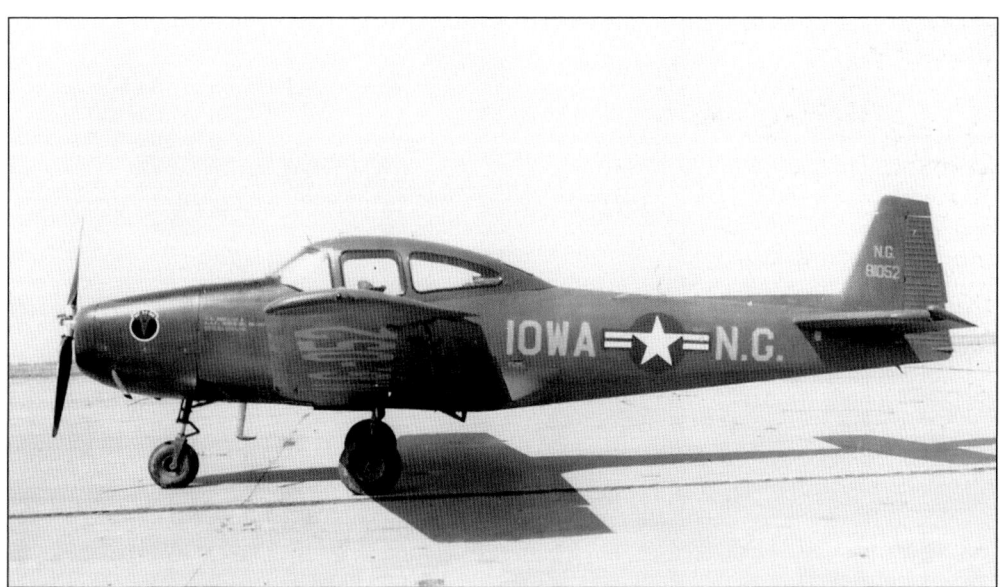

After World War II, many of the regional airports that had served as military training bases returned to exclusively civilian aircraft service. Some, however, like Ottumwa, maintained a relationship with the military, providing service for Iowa Air National Guard airplanes like this Navion. (Courtesy of the Antique Airplane Association.)

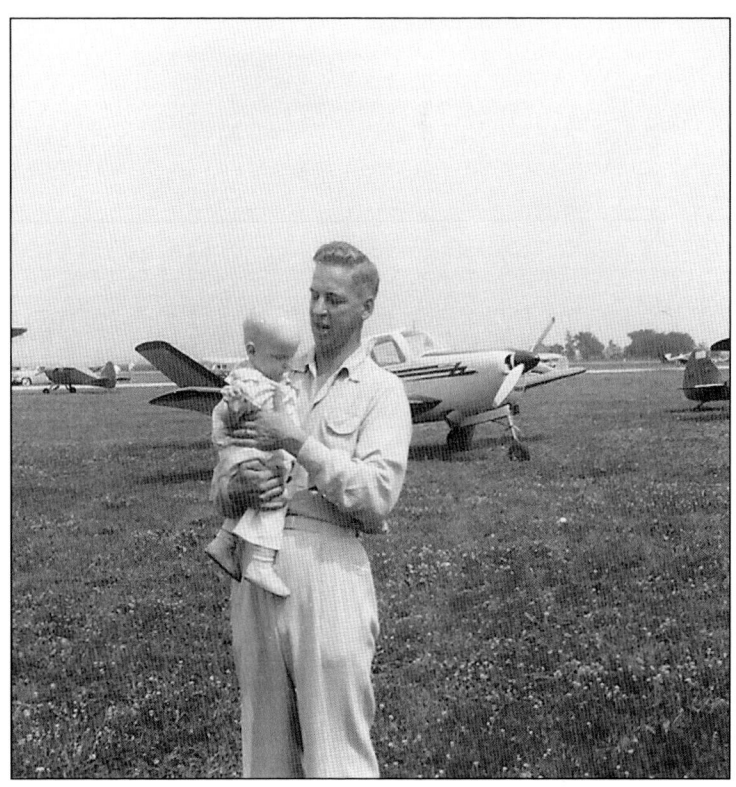

Typical of the thousands of Iowa military veterans who came home after flying World War II combat missions was Alvin "Jack" Cline, who flew B-17s in Europe. Like many veterans, he remained active in the US Air Force Reserve and was influential in promoting aviation to young people through his work with the Davenport wing of the Civil Air Patrol. He is shown here holding his son Jack in front of a new Beechcraft Bonanza. (Courtesy of the Cline family.)

Often entire families accompanied Dad to local air shows and Civil Air Patrol events. Opportunities for women in aviation were becoming more achievable, so it was just as likely that a young girl was influenced to pursue a future in aviation as much as a young boy. Here, the rest of the Cline family poses in front of a Beechcraft biplane at a Davenport aviation event. Mavis Cline holds young Jack, and from left to right are Janet, Cynthia, and Joyce Cline. (Courtesy of the Cline family.)

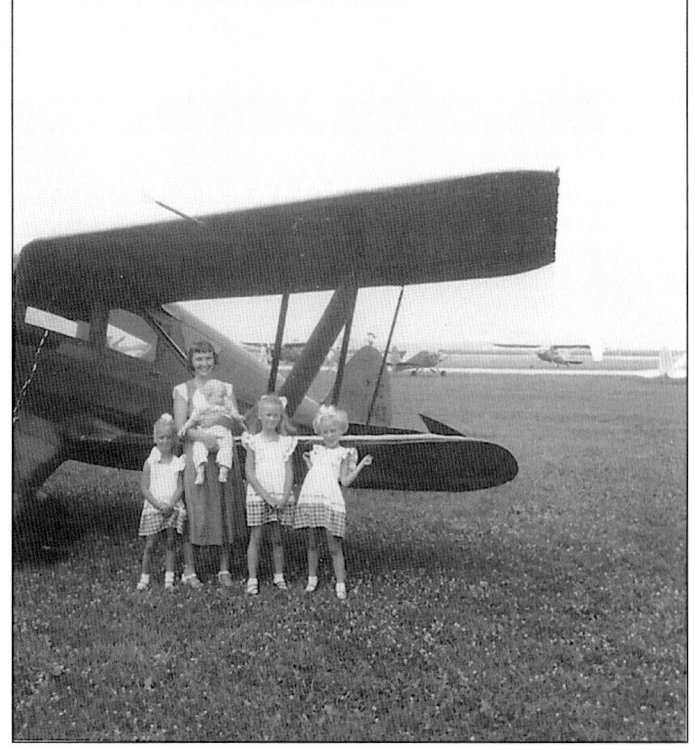

Willard F. Bridgeman was born in Ottumwa and had his first airplane ride in 1919 when a barnstormer performed nearby in a Canuck. Bridgeman took a few hours of flight instruction and then purchased his own Canuck—still in the crate. From 1919 to 1925, he barnstormed throughout Iowa, hauled passengers, and gave flight instruction. (Courtesy of the Antique Airplane Association.)

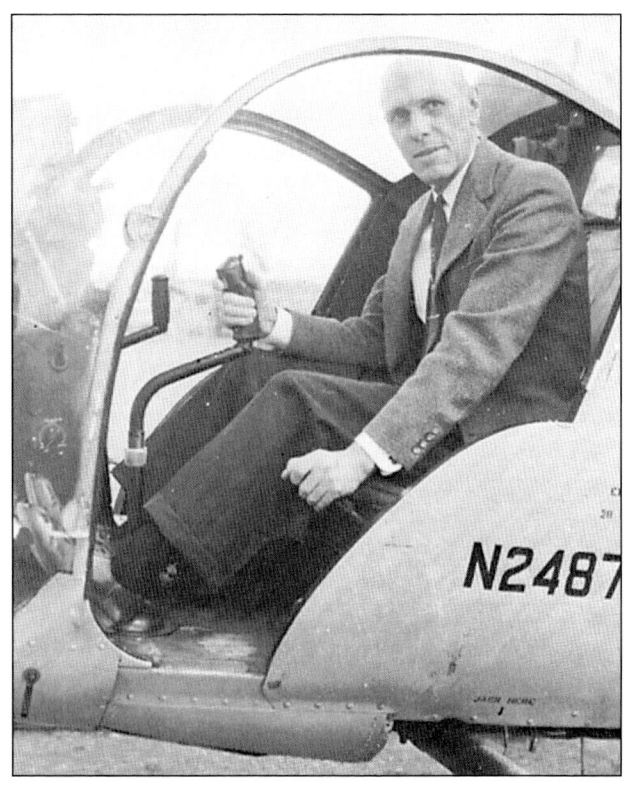

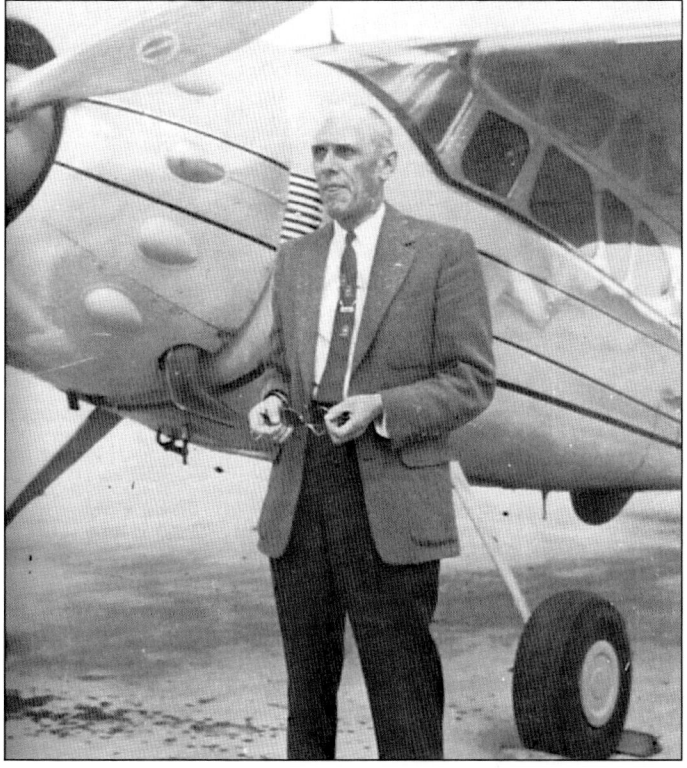

In 1926, Bridgeman purchased a Waco 9, powered by an OX-5 engine from John Livingston. A year later, he purchased a Chevrolet dealership in Ottumwa and started the city's first airport using OX-5 American Eagles. He later flew for the airlines and became an air safety inspector for the Civil Aeronautics Board. His son Bill was born in Ottumwa and, after service as a pilot in World War II, became a test pilot for Douglas Aircraft Company. (Courtesy of the Antique Airplane Association.)

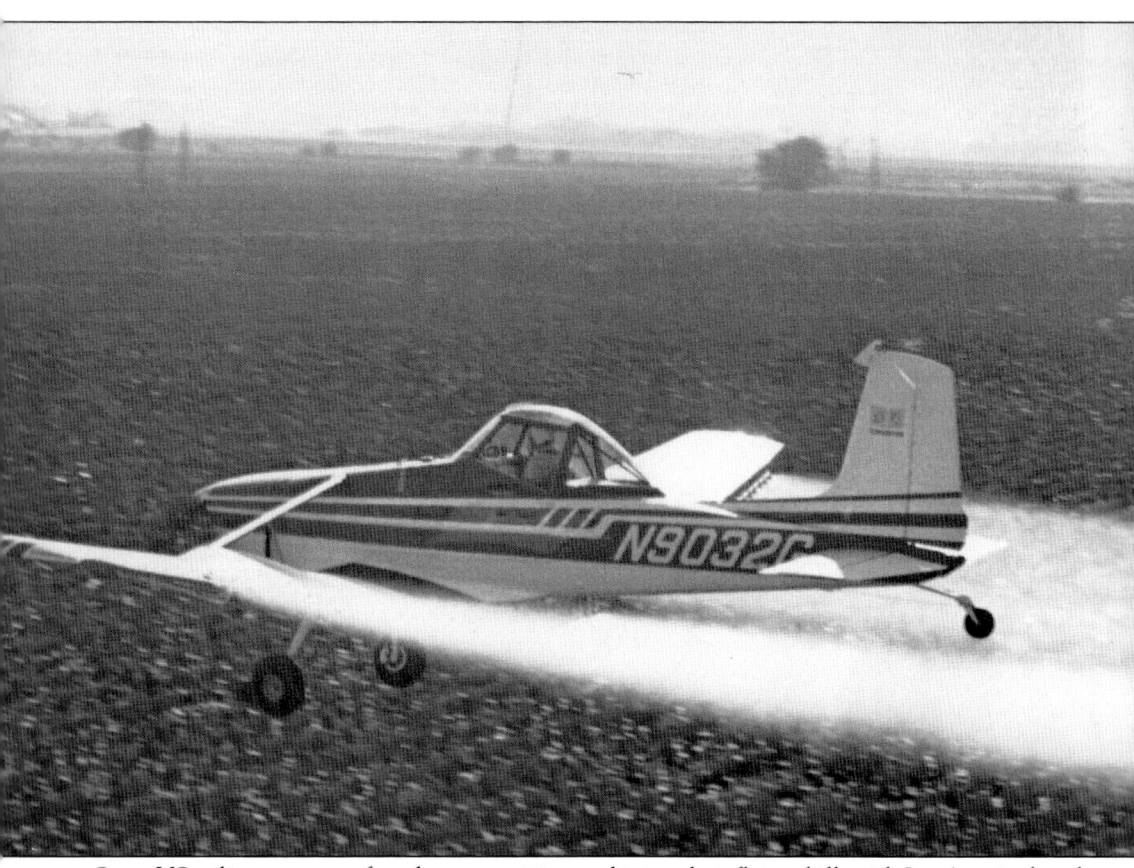

Some US military veterans found opportunities combining their flying skills with Iowa's agricultural needs. At first, farmers were skeptical of using airplanes to apply insecticides, herbicides, and fertilizers, but new methods and equipment, like this Cessna AGwagon, made them believers. Promoters of airborne application methods pointed out that the cost per acre was about the same as by conventional methods, but the airplane was much faster and there was no soil compaction caused by truck and tractor tires. The main consideration each pilot faced was the drift of chemicals onto adjoining fields, so, even today, spraying is usually done only when wind speed is below 10 miles per hour. (Courtesy of the Antique Airplane Association.)

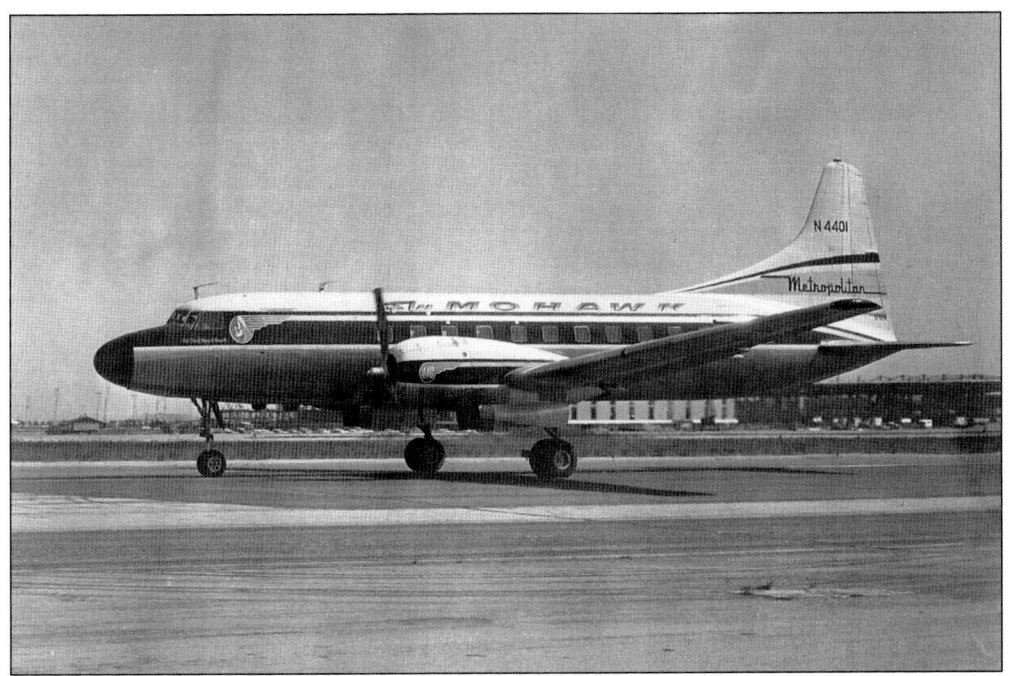

Shown here is a Consolidated Convair 440 airliner from Mohawk Airlines. (Courtesy of the Antique Airplane Association.)

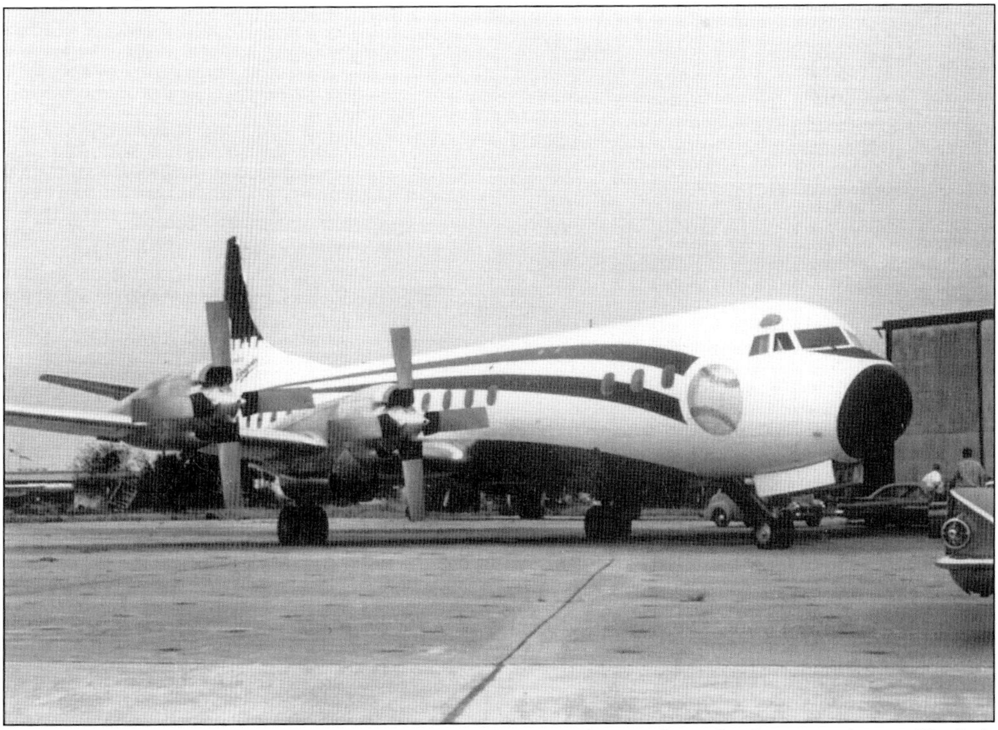

This Los Angeles Dodgers corporate Lockheed Electra turboprop brought the minor-league Keokuk Dodgers baseball team home from 1962 spring training in Vero Beach, Florida, landing at the Burlington Airport. (Courtesy of Shane Etter via Rudy Matulka and Steve Smith.)

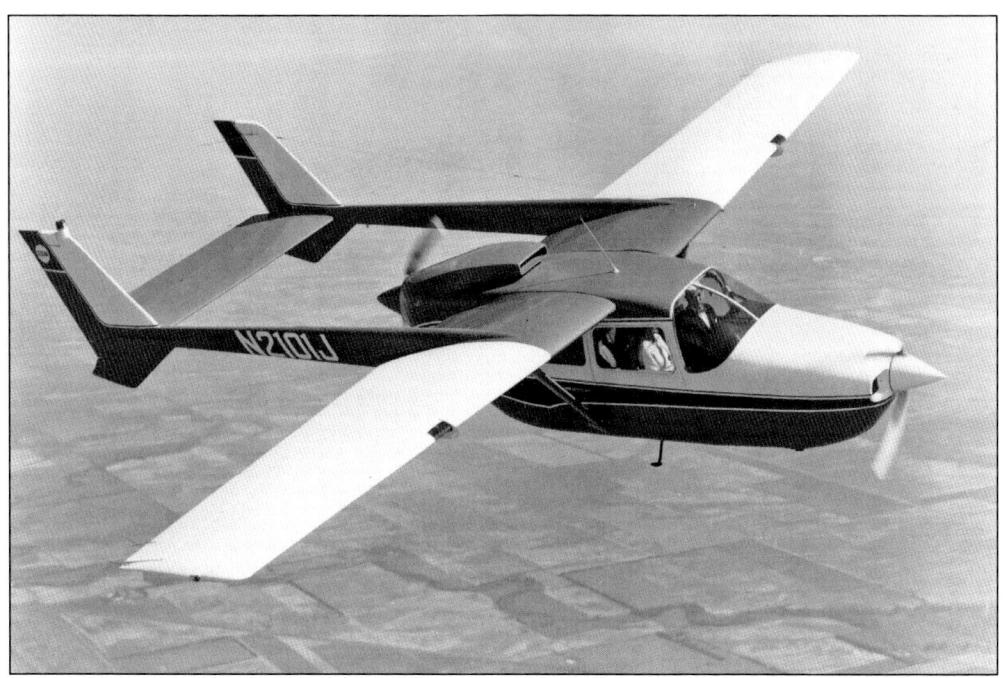

New aircraft designs were appearing all over Iowa as manufacturers competed for the growing small twin aircraft market. Cessna Skymasters like this one could be seen at many Iowa Cessna dealerships and used an unusual tandem twin-engine design. Irv Lindner sold these and used them to transport passengers and freight commercially from his dealership in Keokuk. (Courtesy of Irv Lindner.)

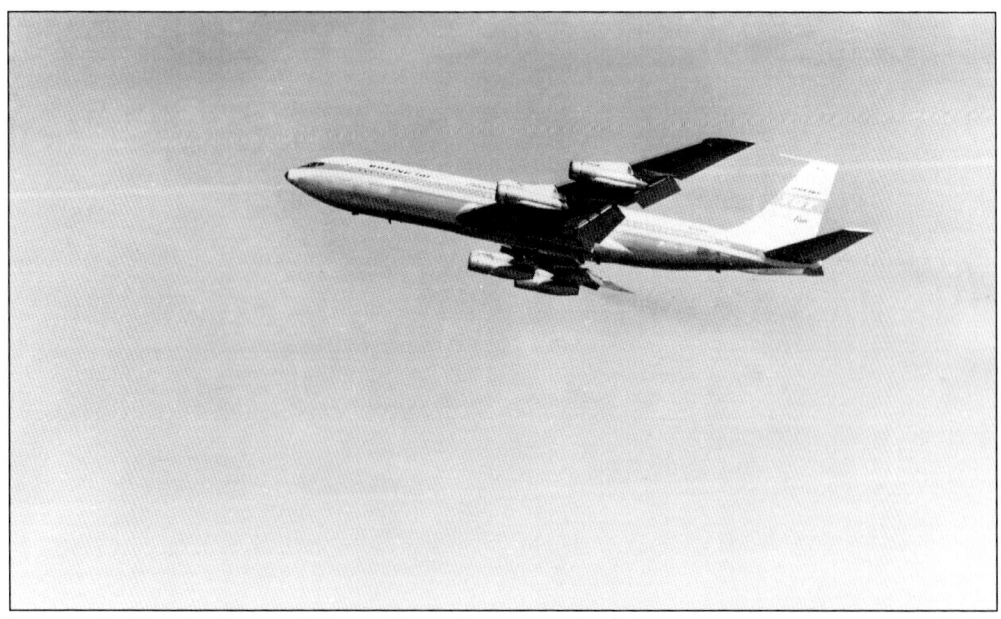

Jet aircraft, like this Boeing 707, quickly took over much of the passenger service to major hubs. They are still seen in the skies over Iowa, decades later, flying for the Air Force and Air National Guard units as aerial refueling tankers. (Courtesy of the Antique Airplane Association.)

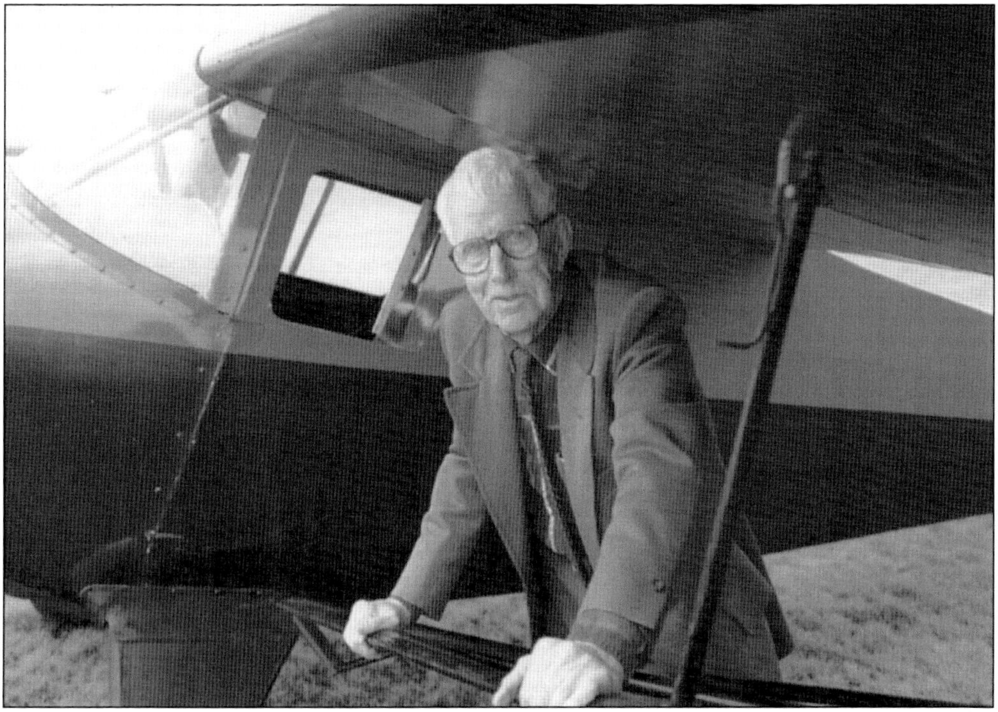

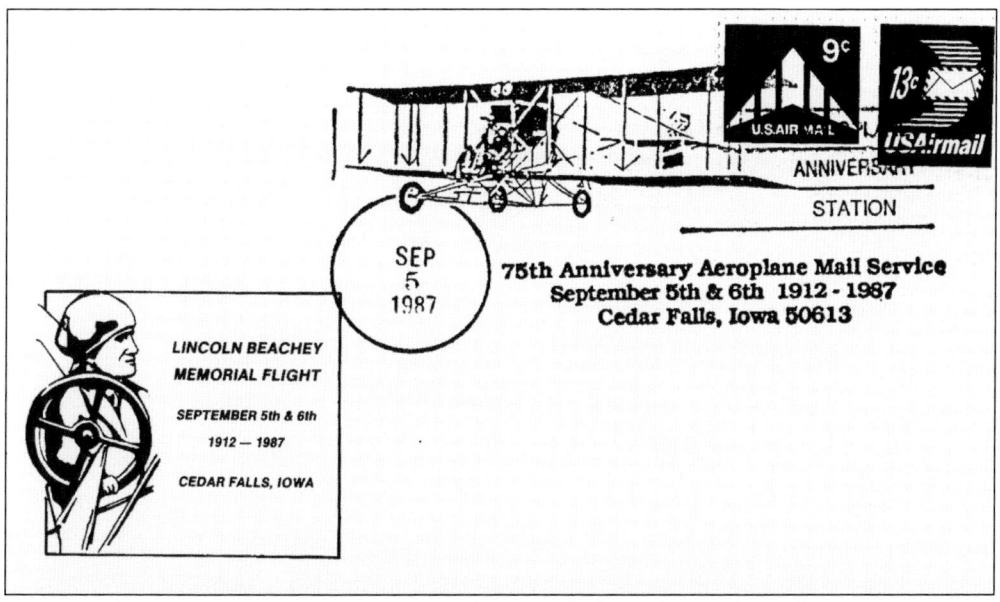

Bite Livingston was still flying in the late 1980s as Iowa's oldest active pilot. Flying a restored 1946 Taylorcraft Cub from Isley Field, a small grass strip east of Cedar Falls, he raised money for many community activities while promoting aviation. (Courtesy of the Cedar Falls Historical Society.)

In September 1987, Bite Livingston made a historic flight in his Taylorcraft, commemorating Lincoln Beachey's 1912 airmail flight in Cedar Falls. Covers were issued to record the 75th anniversary of the event that Livingston had witnessed as a nine-year-old boy. He passed away in 1995 at the age of 92. (Courtesy of the Cedar Falls Historical Society.)

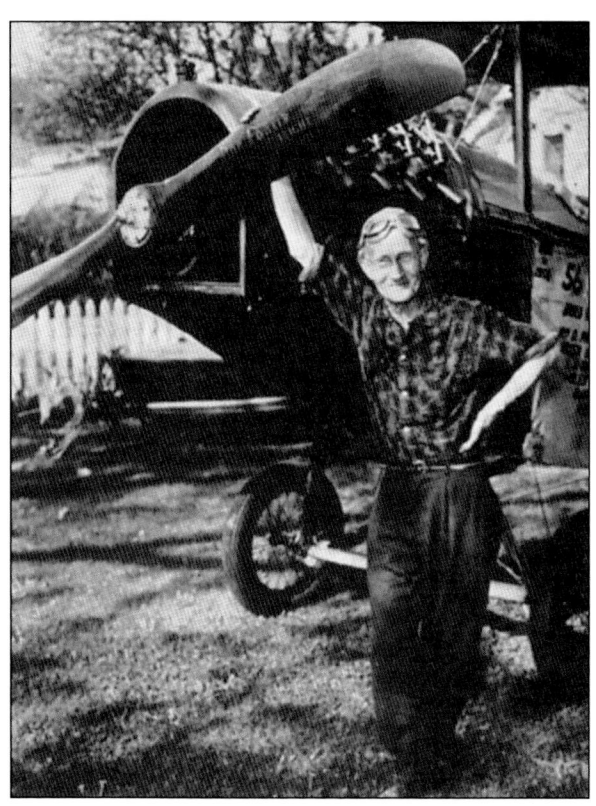

Art J. Hartman, Burlington's "Mr. Aviation," continued restoring old airplanes at his shop well into the 1960s, even though he had retired a decade earlier. The replica of his 1910 monoplane hangs in the Pioneer Museum in Minden, Nebraska. (Courtesy of the Des Moines County Historical Society at Burlington.)

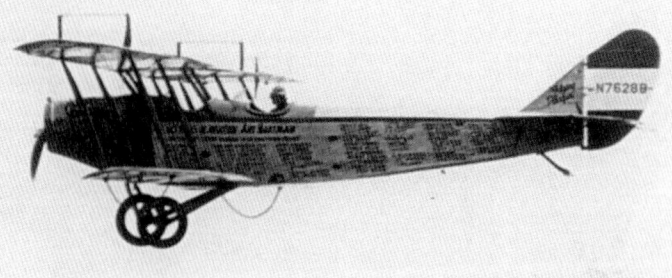

LAST FLIGHT. Art Hartman flies his Memory Jenny at Burlington Air Show August 25, 1963. Show sponsored by Junior and Senior Chambers of Commerce. Hartman, celebrating his 60th anniversary in aviation, said he would retire Memory but would not hang up his helmet and goggles.

Art J. Hartman restored a Curtiss Jenny that he named *Memory*, which he described as a "Flying Plaque" dedicated to all of his early flying friends. More than 200 names, with the dates of their first solo flights, were hand painted on the aircraft. Here Hartman flies *Memory* at the Burlington Air Show in 1963. Hartman passed away in 1970. (Courtesy of Sid Yahn.)

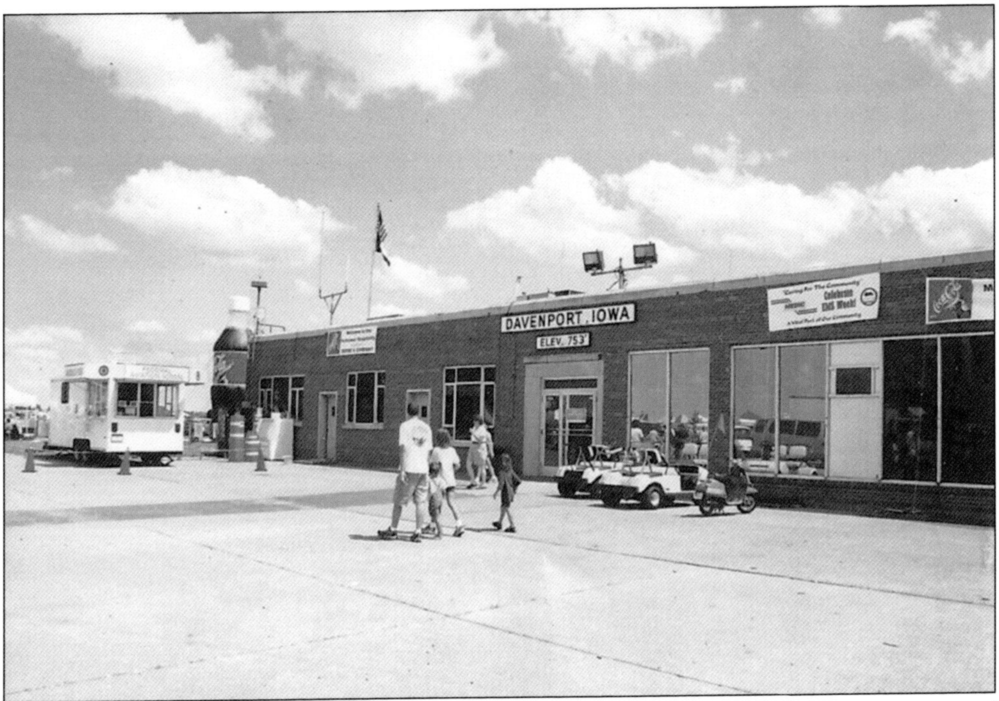

Air shows continue their popularity all over eastern Iowa, inspiring a whole new generation of aviation dreamers. This show held at the Davenport Airport, now located at Mount Joy north of the city, is a popular annual early summer event. (Photograph by the author.)

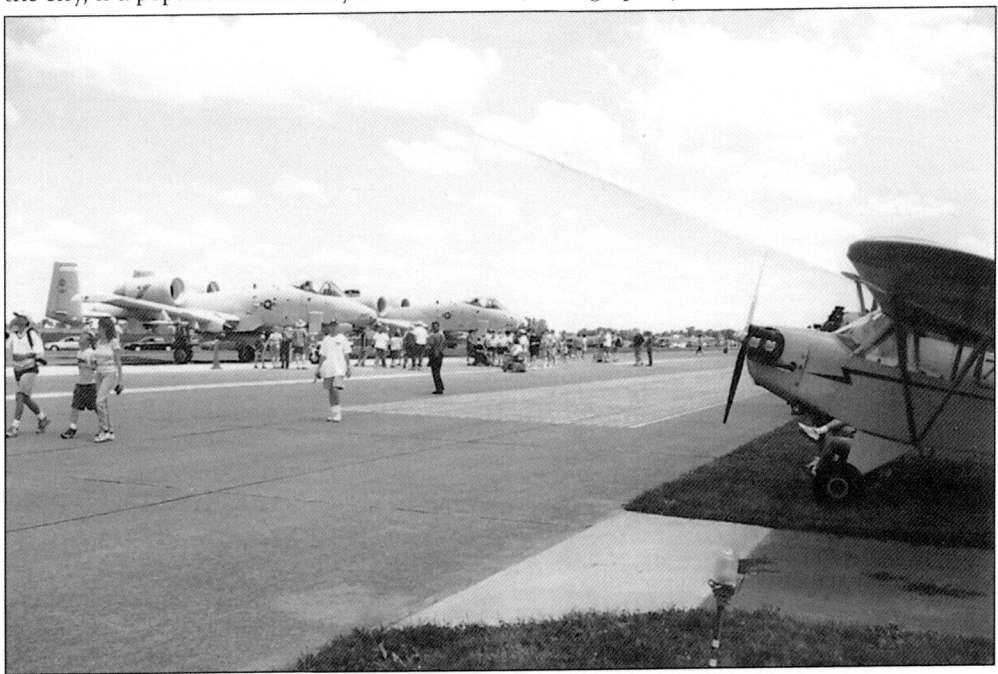

Along with the homebuilt and antique airplanes, visitors to modern air shows are treated to static displays of modern jets as well as exhibition flights by precision teams and aerobatic stunt pilots. (Photograph by the author.)

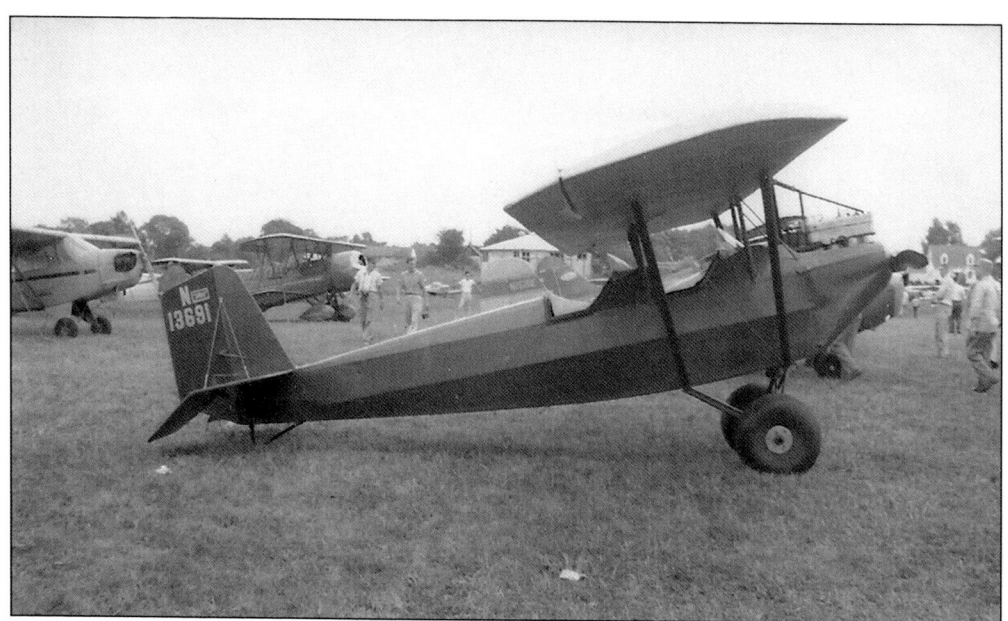

For many years, homebuilt airplanes were banned in most states in America, but they were eventually reinstated after World War II and are now a familiar sight at air shows. One popular model is this Pietenpol Air Camper, designed by Bernard Pietenpol in the 1930s. He furnished plans for his airplanes to people who could construct the entire airplane with average woodworking skills and materials found at any hardware store. He sold plans to builders all over the world. (Courtesy of Pietenpol family.)

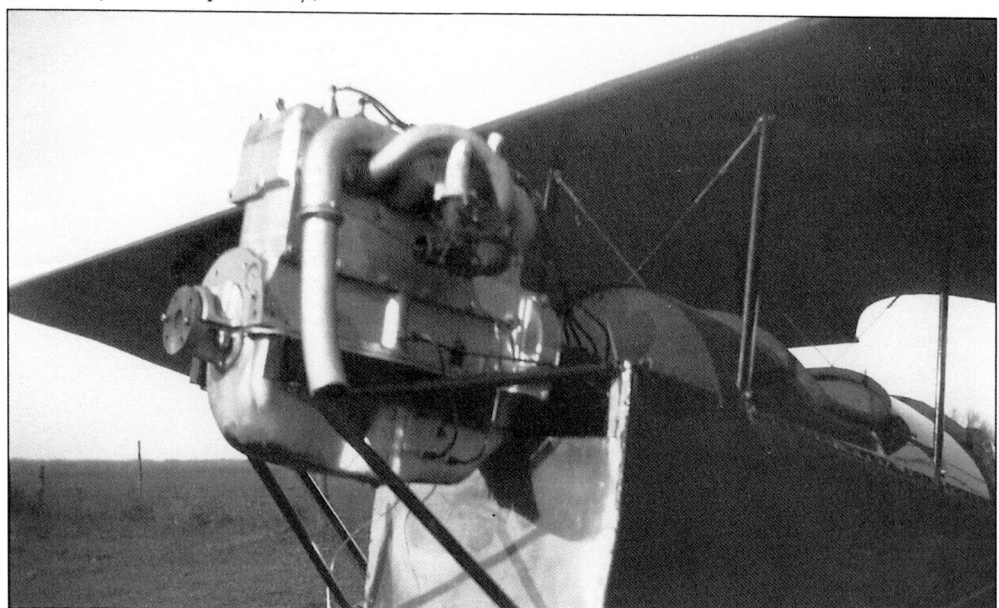

Like most homebuilt airplanes, the Pietenpol models use a variety of engines, but most "purists" prefer the original Ford Model "A" four-cylinder engine shown here. Today, Bernard's son and grandson continue to provide the original plans to buyers. Visitors to air shows are sure to see a row of homebuilt airplanes, and there is usually a Pietenpol or two in the mix. (Courtesy of the Pietenpol family.)

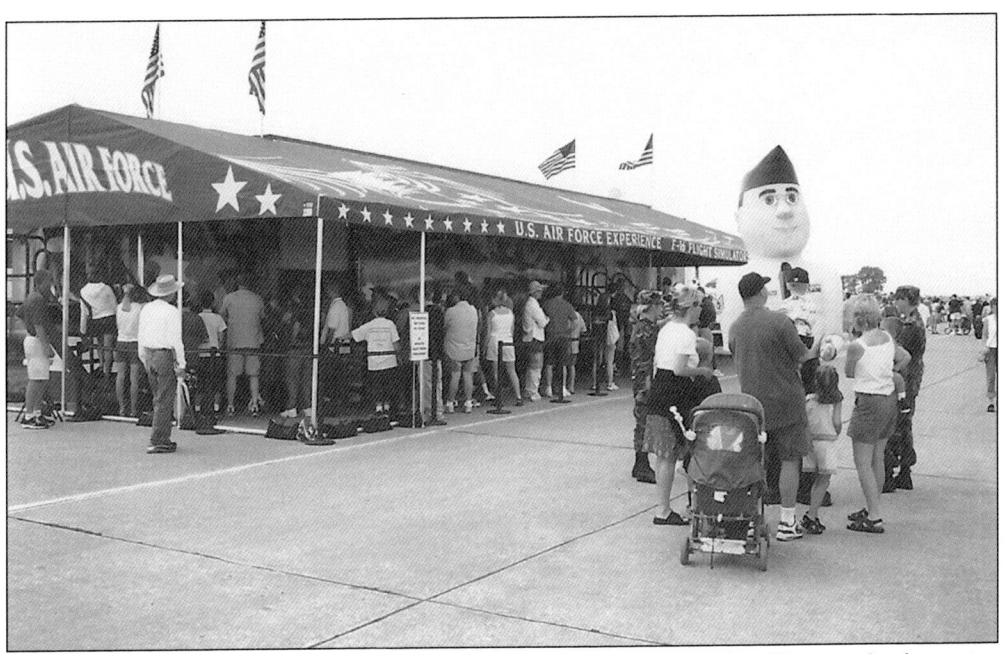

Besides airplanes and static displays, today's air show provides educational and historical information honoring America's military men and women. (Photograph by the author.)

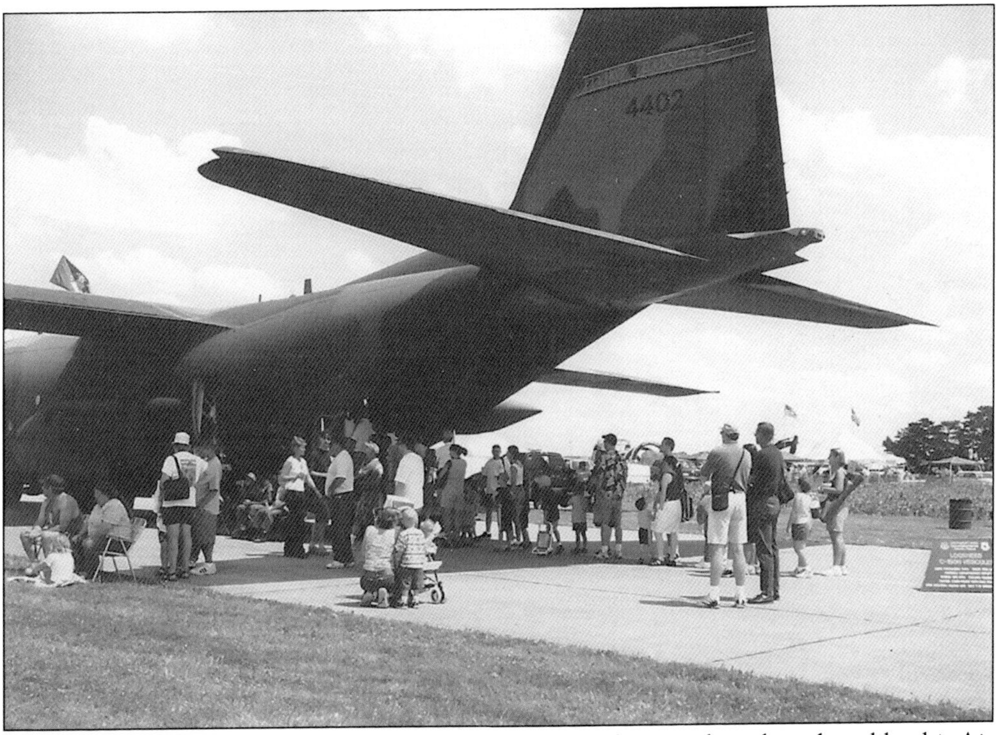

Military aircraft are big favorites, especially those that can be toured inside and out like this Air National Guard C-130. (Photograph by the author.)

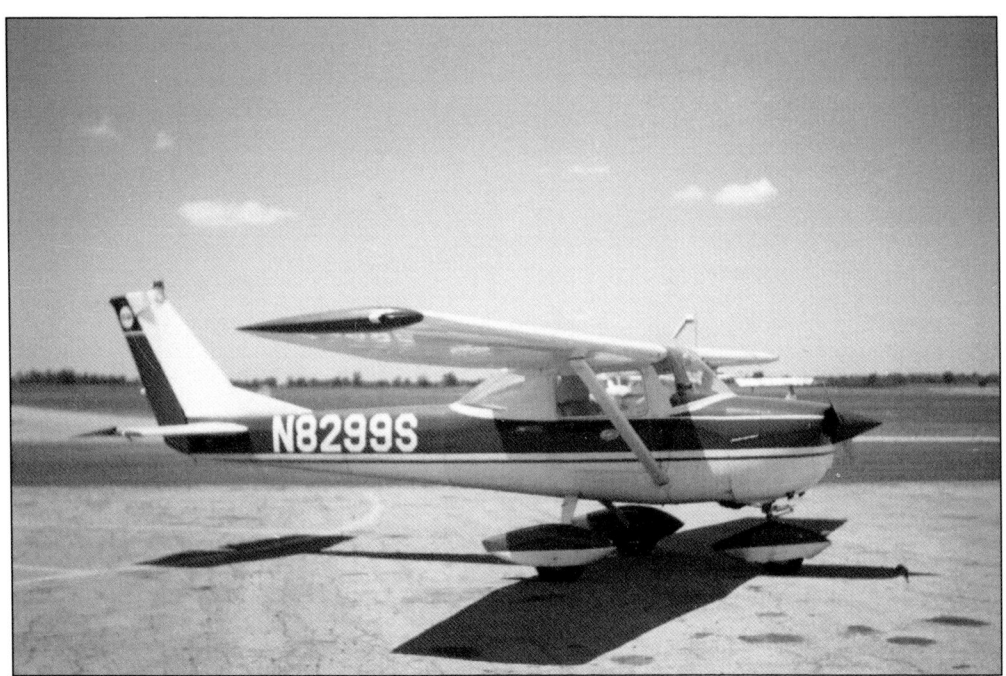

Flight instruction evolved during the 1960s and 1970s, moving away from the old "tail-draggers" to tricycle-style landing gear. Many of today's pilots got their start in Cessna's 150 two-seater Commuter and 172 four-seat Skyhawk. (Photograph by the author.)

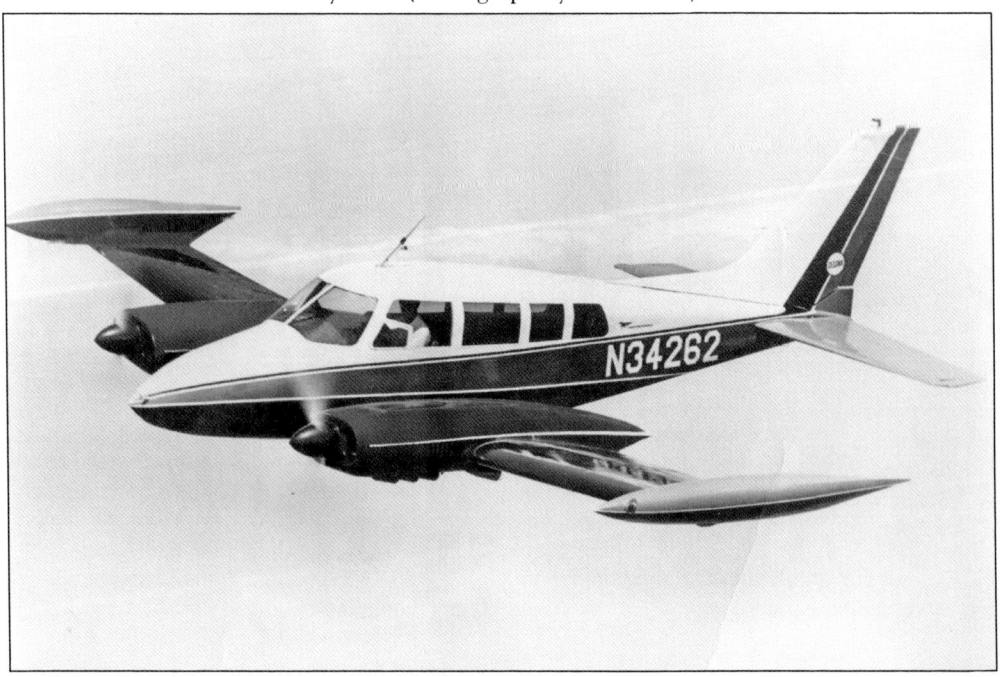

Like the training aircraft, small twin-engine airplanes like this Cessna 310 became familiar sights at Iowa airports. They were used by businesses, government agencies, flying clubs, and young pilots building hours in preparation for careers in civil and military aviation. (Courtesy of the Antique Airplane Association.)

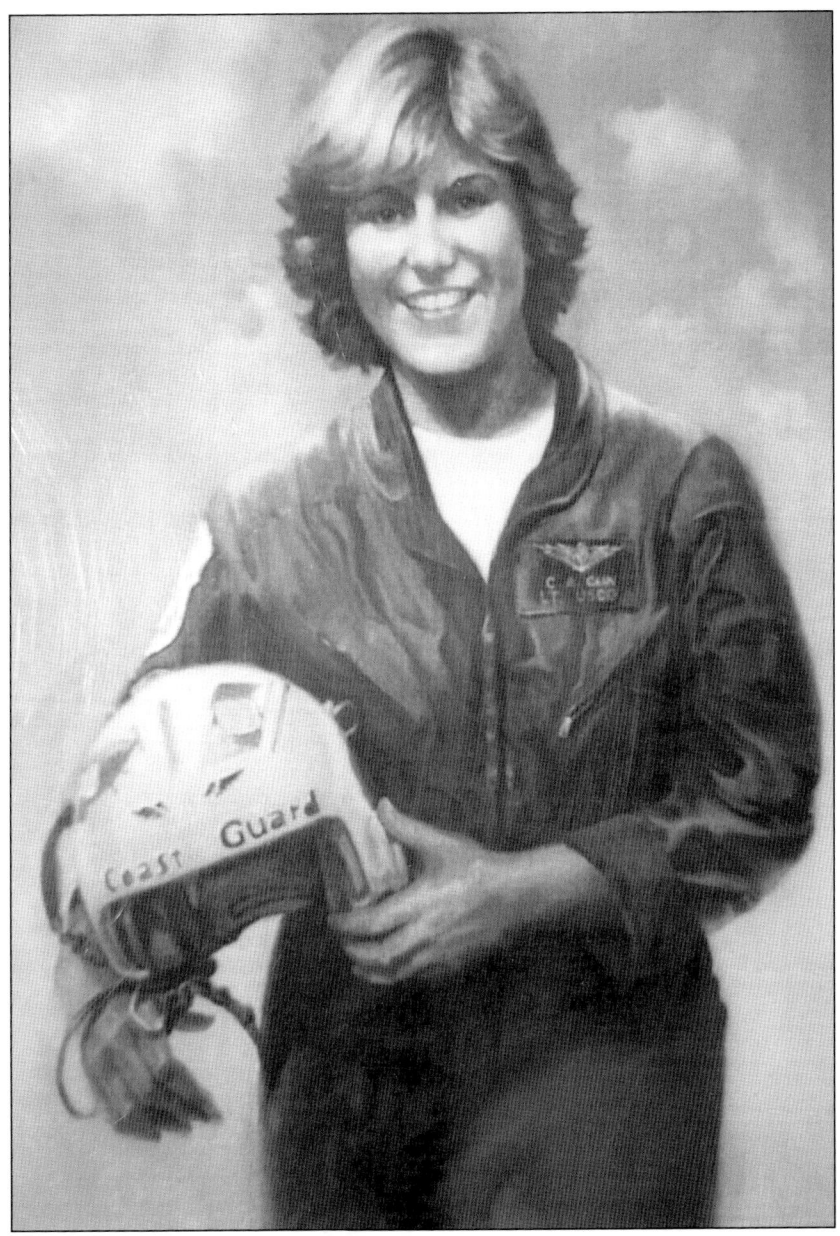

One eastern Iowa military pilot was Lt. Colleen Cain. After graduating from Burlington Community High School, Cain went on to college before joining the US Coast Guard. While enrolled in Officer Candidate School, she took flying lessons on her own to qualify for Coast Guard flight training. In 1979, she earned her pilot wings and began flying Coast Guard rescue helicopters—the first woman to do so. When Cain's mother heard about another Coast Guard helicopter pilot who had been killed while on duty, Cain told her, "Remember, I love my job. I'm sure he loved his." On January 7, 1982, Cain's helicopter, which she was copiloting, responded to a distress call from a ship carrying seven fishermen off the coast of Hawaii. The weather was bad, and the helicopter crashed into a mountainside, killing the entire crew. Faulty air-control equipment was later blamed as contributing to the accident. Cain was 29 years old. (Courtesy of the Southeast Iowa Regional Airport.)

The Iowa State Patrol Airwing continues to serve citizens of Iowa, from spotting lost children to chasing down fugitives. On June 30, 1989, the Cass County Sheriff's Department contacted the patrol requesting help in locating an elderly man who had wandered away from his nursing home during the late afternoon. Trooper and pilot Lance G. Dietsch, a Waterloo native, prepared the patrol's Maule aircraft for the search, hoping to get into the air before it became too dark to see. (Courtesy of the Iowa State Patrol.)

Trooper Stanley E. Gerling volunteered to ride along with Dietsch to help with the spotting. It was about 5:45 p.m., and light was beginning to fade as the Maule crisscrossed the search area, aided by officers on the ground. They were just about to leave the area when they spotted the man in a field. Circling at an altitude of about 200 feet, they were leading the ground team to the man's location. Suddenly the nose of the aircraft dropped sharply and crashed into the ground. Both troopers died in the crash, the first officers killed in a patrol aircraft since the airwing had started in 1957. (Courtesy of the Iowa State Patrol.)

Iowa State Patrol trooper and pilot Allen Nieland was an experienced pilot with more than 1,500 hours of flight time and six years of flying experience in the patrol airwing. On October 14, 1990, a Sunday morning, he took off in his patrol Cessna 172 to help in the pursuit of a robbery suspect driving a stolen pickup truck. Nieland spotted the suspect's vehicle near Highway 151, south of Little Amana about 20 miles from Iowa City. (Courtesy of the Iowa State Patrol.)

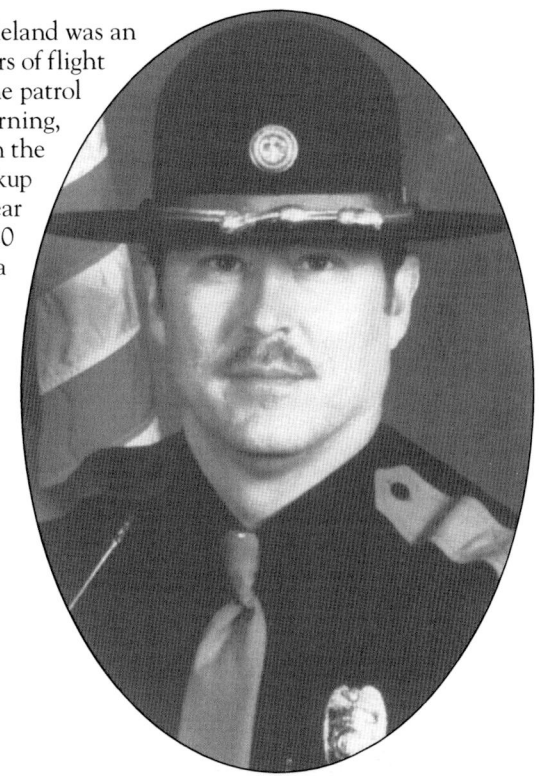

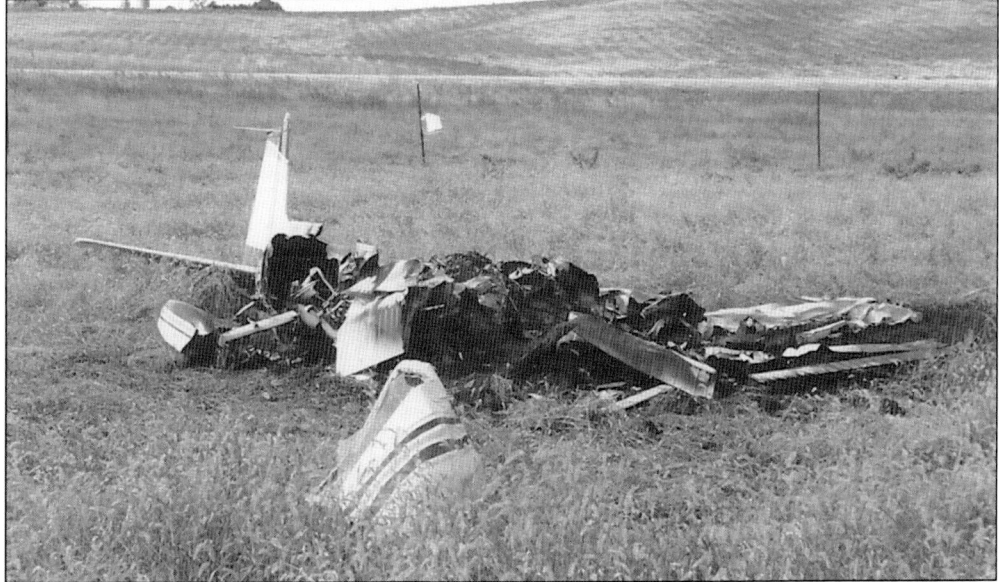

Nieland was circling the suspect's truck as troopers on the ground converged on the area when the aircraft nose-dived into the ground in a field. The severity of the impact killed Nieland instantly. A witness to the crash said, "I knew when he hit the ground it was all over. The impact was terrible. I don't think the poor man would have survived even if the plane hadn't exploded." The suspect was charged with vehicular homicide. Nieland left behind a wife and four children. (Courtesy of the Iowa State Patrol.)

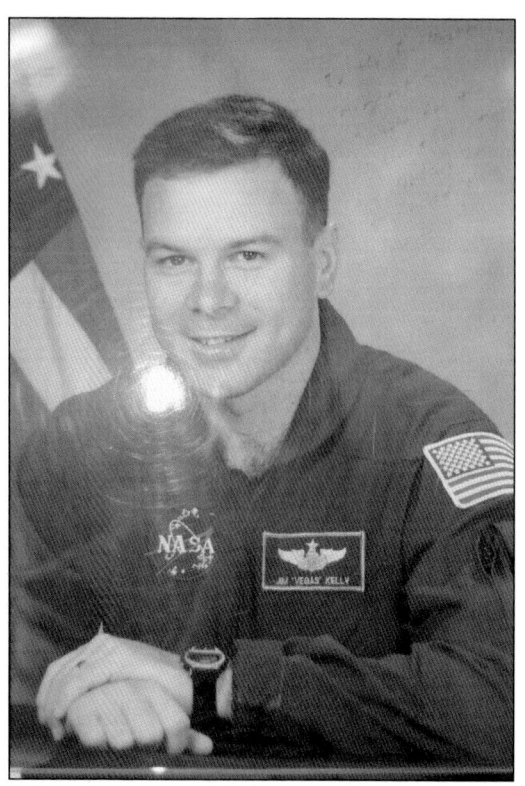

NASA astronaut Col. James M. Kelly graduated from Burlington Community High School in 1982. He went on to the US Air Force Academy, where he received a bachelor of science degree in astronautical engineering before earning a master of science degree in aerospace engineering from the University of Alabama. After tours of active duty flying F-15s, he was an instructor and test pilot before being selected for the astronaut program in 1996. (Courtesy of the Southeast Iowa Regional Airport.)

Kelly had many responsibilities at NASA, including two space shuttle missions, STS-102 and STS-114, during which he logged more than 641 hours in space. Both shuttle missions docked at the International Space Station: one to deliver a new crew to the station and the other to test and evaluate procedures for shuttle flight safety and repair techniques. (Courtesy of the Southeast Iowa Regional Airport.)

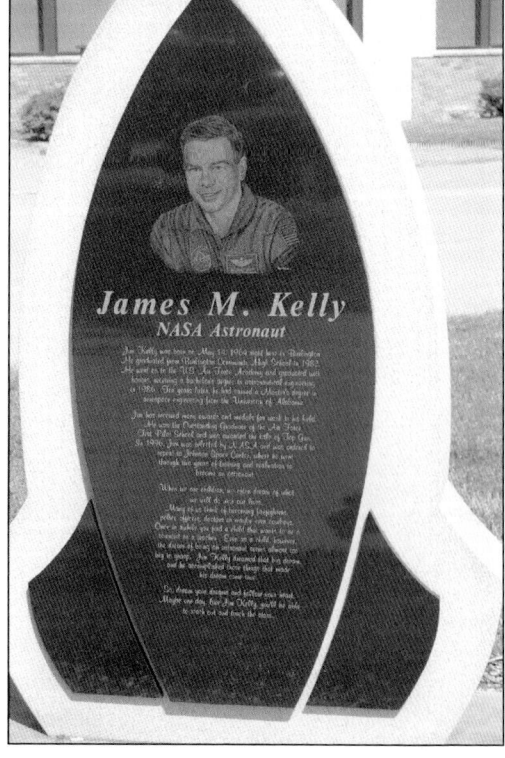

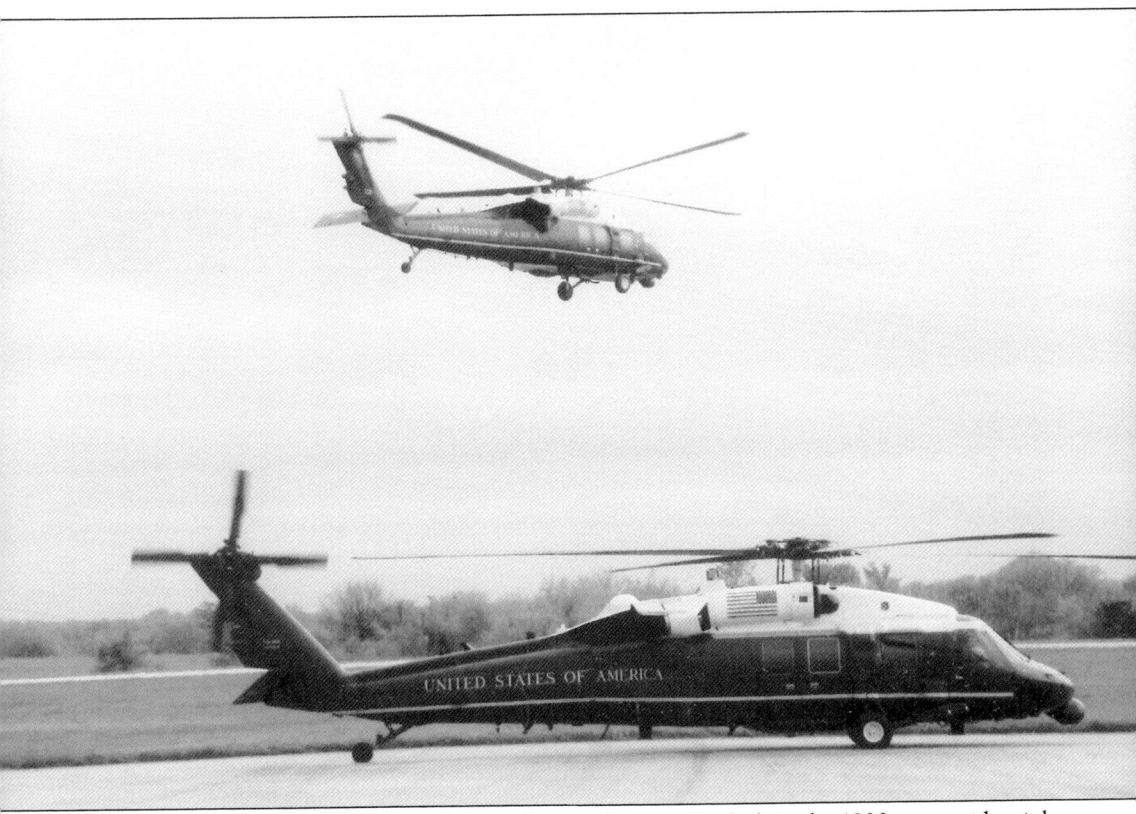

From the first balloon flights ascending from the riverfront in Keokuk in the 1800s to presidential helicopters landing at Lindner Field in 2010, eastern Iowa's aviation heritage has come a long way and continues to move into the future. Today's dreamers perpetuate the vision of the early Iowa aviation pioneers. (Courtesy of Irv Lindner.)

www.arcadiapublishing.com

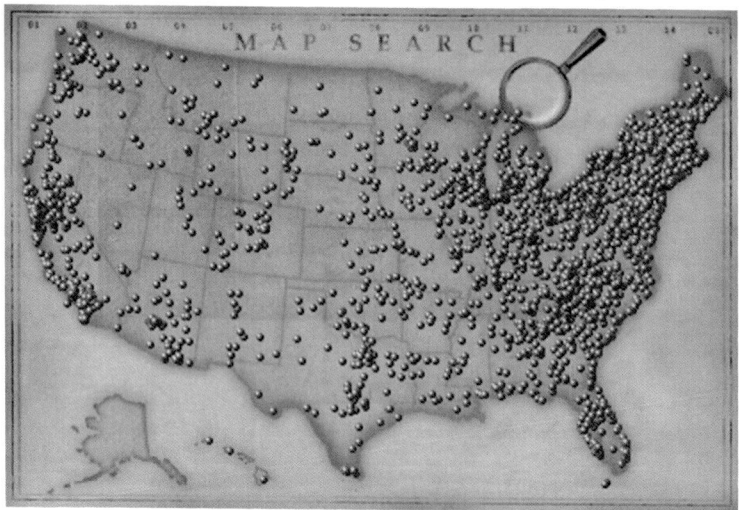

Discover books about the town where you grew up, the cities where your friends and families live, the town where your parents met, or even that retirement spot you've been dreaming about. Our Web site provides history lovers with exclusive deals, advanced notification about new titles, e-mail alerts of author events, and much more.

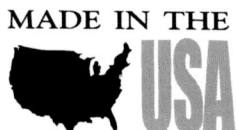

Arcadia Publishing, the leading local history publisher in the United States, is committed to making history accessible and meaningful through publishing books that celebrate and preserve the heritage of America's people and places. Consistent with our mission to preserve history on a local level, this book was printed in South Carolina on American-made paper and manufactured entirely in the United States.

This book carries the accredited Forest Stewardship Council (FSC) label and is printed on 100 percent FSC-certified paper. Products carrying the FSC label are independently certified to assure consumers that they come from forests that are managed to meet the social, economic, and ecological needs of present and future generations.

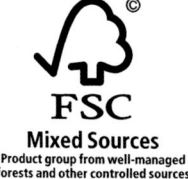

Mixed Sources
Product group from well-managed forests and other controlled sources

Cert no. SW-COC-001530
www.fsc.org
© 1996 Forest Stewardship Council

Find Your Place in History.